The UNVEILING TRUTHS of The END TIMES

The UNVEILING TRUTHS of The END TIMES

Vera Forbes

XULON ELITE

Xulon Press Elite
2301 Lucien Way #415
Maitland, FL 32751
407.339.4217
www.xulonpress.com

© 2017 by Vera Forbes

All rights reserved solely by the author. The author guarantees all contents are original and do not infringe upon the legal rights of any other person or work. No part of this book may be reproduced in any form without the permission of the author. The views expressed in this book are not necessarily those of the publisher.

Unless otherwise indicated,Scripture quotations taken from the King James Version (KJV)–public domain.

Printed in the United States of America.
"Edited by Xulon Press.

ISBN: 9781545604823

TABLE OF CONTENTS

Preface ix
Introduction xiii

PART 1: PRESENTATION OF THE UNVIELING

One	The Revelation of Jesus Christ	1
Two	Symbols Relating to the Unveiling	7
Three	The Old Testament Kingdoms and the Kingdom of Heaven	16
Four	The Fate of the Kingdom of Heaven	24
Five	An Overview of the Book of Revalation	34

PART 2: THE RULE OF THE SEVEN CHURCHES

Six	The Government of the Church	37
Seven	The Golden Age of the Church	47
Eight	The Silver Age of the Church	53
Nine	The Brass Age of the Church	60
Ten	The Iron Age of the Church	65
Eleven	The Church of the Two Witnesses	71
Twelve	The Last Church Age	77

PART 3: THE FATE OF THE CHURCH

Thirteen	Unveiling of Revelation Chapters Four and Five	85
Fourteen	The Fall and Decline of the Church Age	94
Fifteen	Doctrines Responsible for the Decline	103
Sixteen	Judgement in the Sardis Church Age	109

PART 4: THE UNVEILING OF REVELATION CHAPTERS SIX TO TWENTY-TWO

Seventeen	Unveiling of Revalation Chapters Six and Seven	117
Eighteen	The Great Tribulation and the Day of the Wrath of God	124
Nineteen	Unveiling of Revelation Chapters Eight and Ten	129
Twenty	Unveiling of Revelation Chapter Eleven	132
Twenty-one	Unveiling of Revelation Chapter Twelve	145
Twenty-two	Unveiling of Revelation Chapters Thirteen and Fourteen	149
Twenty-three	Unveiling of Revelation Chapters Fifteen to Eighteen	157
Twenty-four	Unveiling of Revelation Chapters Nineteen to Twenty-Two	169

PART 5: OTHER BOOKS OF THE BIBLE SUPPORTING THE MYSTERIES OF REVELATION

Twenty-five   Books Supporting the Unveiling.............................. 177

                  Jonah Chapters 1 and 2.

                  Ezekiel Chapter 19

                  Daniel Chapter 8

                  Job Chapters 1 and 2

Notes 189
Symbols and Phrases used in Interpreting the Book of Revelation 193

PREFACE

*A*nyone with spiritual insight, or who views the Bible from a historical, prophetic, or doctrinal perspective, can discern that the end of this Age and the second coming of Christ are near. Consequently, the hidden truths and mysteries preserved in prophecies concerning the end times are being revealed through a greater understanding of the parables of our Lord Jesus Christ, and through the symbols contained in the Bible from Genesis to Revelation. This book captures and explains with consistency and relevance the parables and symbols that throw greater light on these truths.

Humanity constantly has needs for which solutions are required. The message of the Kingdom is God's solution to humanity's needs, especially the need for salvation, which the doctrine of Christ teaches. Sin is a real and active enemy, but God undoubtedly has a purpose for him (*Gen. 4:7*) to be operative in this world; therefore, everyone should be reminded of this need in order to see one's hopelessness without God. There must also be a presentation of the solution to give hope and ensure the right decision is made, which is to serve God in holiness.

The Bible speaks of a time when people will fall into a sleep of security because much of the truth that should substantiate their hopes seems to have lost its virtue. However, God's limitless knowledge and perfect wisdom enable him to work beyond the bounds of human reasoning; hence, he has written biblical truths in symbols and parables to bring about a reawakening in the minds of those who may walk in depravity or sleep in the security of their own folly. These truths can come as fresh knowledge that confirms the love of God for humanity or as a reminder of the purpose of God for mankind; they can also bring about a reawakening of minds to the perilous times in which we live and are yet to experience. The book of Revelation has in it hidden truths which when unveiled will help the reader understand the need for salvation and holy living as God's solution to overcome sin that blocks the way to victorious and prosperous living, because Christ has paid the price for man's redemption.

Every purpose has a time frame for fulfilment and there is no doubt that the world is already living in such a time. God's new creation will be finally rid of sin forever. The Bible confirms in *Isaiah 21:27–31* that: *"Zion shall be redeemed with judgements and the unfruitful ones will be punished with those who do wickedly."* The Christian is called to spiritual fruitfulness as *"trees of righteousness"* God has planted in the world to fulfil his mandate to Adam. It is, therefore, understandable that many Christians, like the rest of mankind, will be judged for their failure to fulfil the mandate of dominion over sin and the sinfulness in the world. John the Baptist in admonishing the Pharisees and Sadducees confirmed that *(Matt. 3:10–12)*: *"The axe is already laid at the root of the trees"* of righteousness which the person in Christ has become *(Isa. 61:3, Isa. 41:19–20)*. Evidently, even in this dispensation, there are trees which will bear no fruit and will be hewn down and cast into the eternal fire of the wrath of God. God's people must look to him for revelations that will re-affirm his plan so that those who understand will find their security in him. The Book of Genesis contains the foundation upon which rests many of the cardinal doctrines of our Christian faith. These doctrines make the fulfilment of purpose possible and hold much of the secrets that can unlock the prophetic books to help the people of God, read the end time clock.

Many people today question whether there will be an actual second coming, and if so, when. In the past, people have cried "wolf" in their attempt to predict the time of the second coming. The revelations contained in this book will show that no one need speculate on when the end will come because the events leading up to that time will be explicit. God created man, and he knows that lack of knowledge causes complacency and neglect; therefore, it cannot be his will to hide the truth from the generation upon whom the end of the Age will come. However, what is important for any true Christian to do at this time is to heed the advice given by our Lord Jesus Christ in the book of Matthew and *"stand in a holy place."* This means that each person should seek to live a Christ-like and godly life with patience, long-suffering, and a desire to make the truth known to as many people as possible. The need for this resolve is crucial, especially in this third millennium since the death of Christ, bearing in mind that everything that pre-figures his return or associated with his earthly ministry is often linked to the morning of the third day.

The Bible is, first and foremost, a spiritual book, and the parables and symbols have been applied with apt consistency that brings to life the events of the end time in an amazing way. The events of the book of Revelation revolve around the activities of seven churches which are revealed when the seven seals are opened; and it shows how they cope with the world of sinfulness. The judgements of God are eternal and from time to time the sinfulness of humanity is judged. The weapon God uses to execute his judgements is people's response to one another. God said of the Babylonian King and his Empire: *"Thou art my battle axe and weapons of war: for with thee will I break in pieces the nations, and with thee will I destroy kingdoms. . . And I will render unto Babylon and to all the inhabitants of Chaldea all their evil that they have done in Zion in your sight, saith the LORD"* (*Jer. 51:20–24*). Evidently, because sin is in the heart of every unregenerate soul, even the weapons God uses will be judged for their sinfulness and arrogance.

Preface

    This book will not delve into history to single out any nation or people, or identify any particular sect that was or will be used to execute God's judgement other than that which is necessary to bring understanding to the mysteries of Revelation. Spiritually, there are two forces in the world: good and evil, and both have the capacity to influence people's behaviour through words and spirit. To depart from the word of God that has the power to equip for the fulfilment of God's mandate is to lose the help of the Spirit of God and succumb to evil and its attendant woes. John begins Revelation by showing readers the glorious end of human history as the Church is gathered around the throne of God in heaven and seal after seal is opened to reveal the journey of the Church through time, and God's judgement on sin and the nations of the world. The events are consistently revealed as things past, things present, and things to come; each aspect is clearly explained, and its relevance corroborated in a conclusive way.

INTRODUCTION

"Through desire a man having separated himself seeketh and intermeddleth with the source of all wisdom"
Provers 18:1

The mysteries of the truths of the end time events, which are also heralding the unfolding calendar for the coming of the Lord Jesus Christ, are carefully concealed in the book of Revelation. All who read the book are mystified by its contents and many have written variant views on its hidden truths. Fascinated and challenged to bring to life the mysteries, and on the strength of *Proverbs 18:1*, I began to study the book more closely and this book is the result of my studies. The book of Genesis begins by revealing truths concerning the beginning of creation and the book of Revelation reveals the truth of the end of life on earth as we know it. Whichever way one sees these books, they both hold series of mysteries concerning the coming of Christ and the unveiling of the Church made up of all races and generations of people as God's holy nation. I pray that it will serve as a study guide that will encourage many to seek to know Christ and not only live for him, but by him, because he is coming back soon.

In the first century, after the death of Christ, John was exiled on the Isle of Patmos as a punishment because he was an apostle of our Lord Jesus Christ. Little did his persecutors know, that they were setting him up to bring to the Church the greatest revelation of things to come in the Church Age. Many times the kingdom of darkness, ruled by the devil through evil wisdom of the world, fallen angels, and sinful human beings, conspire to perpetuate evil against the children of God; but even such circumstances are sometimes used by God to further his purpose on earth. Whilst even now I feel John's pain as he was exiled on this island by evil hands, I rejoice and thank God for giving him the spirit of endurance and for his testimony. Had he not been there, we would not have these glorious revelations of the kingdom of heaven and the second coming of Christ to strengthen the Church and give hope that the end will certainly come.

In the revelation of Jesus Christ John saw what would transpire many centuries after his death. He saw far ahead into the future what would happen in the "fullness of time," when God will *"gather together in one all things in Christ, both which are in heaven and which are on earth."* His revelation was three fold: that which is, which was and which is to come. He wrote about promises of the Old Testament; things that were happening in the churches then and future events that would take place on earth prior to the return of Christ. While he was on earth, Christ said that no one knows the exact time when he will return, for God had not revealed this secret to him. However, he promised that whatever the Father told him, he would make known to his prophets, because it is his responsibility as the eternal word of God and the head of the body to do so. The book of Revelation is partial fulfilment of this promise. *"All things are delivered unto me of my Father: and no man knoweth the Son, but the Father, neither knoweth any man the Father, save the Son and he to whomsoever the Son will reveal him"* (Matt. 11:27). The pertinent *'things'* that are delivered to Christ are the souls of men that he should make alive and keep alive for eternity.

The above scripture may be considered in three parts. First, Christ reaffirms the relationship between him and his Father, stating that his Father had delivered all *souls* into his hands. We know this is true because it is confirmed by the scripture that *"all things will be gathered together in one"* under his headship. The revelation that "no man knows the Son but the Father" has implications for us, too, because God knows every one of us better than we know ourselves; he knows those who are his and we cannot pretend to be faithful to God when we are not. Secondly, as children of God we must seek to know him and be able to reveal him to others. This remains a challenge to the Church and it is because of her failure to retain the power that makes the mission possible, that she must go through the judgement of the great tribulation as the Sardis Church and the bruising of *Genesis 3:15* as the Philadelphia Church in order to be one with Christ.

Christ's disclosure to John was revealed in signs and symbols, therefore in this exposition they are to be understood in this way. The fact that they are signs means that there are some things we ought to be looking for in the natural world that will confirm that the end of all sinful *things* is drawing near. Some of these signs will not be seen until much nearer the end; but there are signs we will definitely see when the time is right. These disclosures are the revelations of Jesus Christ, which God gave to him, to show unto his servants about things, which must shortly come to pass. Since the term is **must** and not *might*, it is right that we should know them, and how to interpret them, because they are things which will affect every person that is born into the world: big or small, old or young, rich or poor. When reading this book of Revelation, we should have one thought at the back of our minds: how will this affect me and where will I spend eternity?

The Bible is *a compendium* of God's infallible words that give directions of life to man and contain, among other things, the story of creation. Like every other puzzling story, the plot is concealed at the beginning, but somewhere towards the end wisdom will be required to fathom what the conclusion might be. This book unveils the depth of knowledge that Jesus Christ gave to John to show to his servants the things to come.

Introduction

The plan of God for the world was completed before the foundations of the earth. That he does not reveal all he has in mind to anyone shows that he is the Sovereign God of the Universe; his plans are final; he does not have to consult with anyone because he is wiser than anyone he has created. He knows the best solution to any problem and needs no advice from anyone. God makes known the mysteries of his will which he purposed in himself, according to his good pleasure (*Eph. 1:9*). The timing of his revelations is within his personal remit and he chooses when to make them known.

There are at least four schools of thought for interpreting Revelation: the *preterists* believe that the book was meant mainly for the people of John's day and had its fulfilment then. The *historicists* believe that Revelation takes the whole period of history from John's day, to the present time. The *spiritualists* believe that the symbols portray spiritual realities. The *futurists* believe that the bulk of the book has to do with the future. A safe position as to the interpretation of Revelation may be the blending of a little of the historical theory with much of the spiritual and futurist's view. Thus this book is written from a spiritual perspective and links together a series of events relating to the Nation Israel, which have spiritual significance in the Church Age, and tries to put them in their proper order. Finis Jennings Dake, author of *the Dake Study Bible*, disagrees with the spiritualization of the Book. According to Dake: *"To spiritualize the book of Revelation is to deny what it professes to be."*[1] This conclusion seems rather odd, since the Bible is written to be understood by people who are spiritually discerning. Dake proffers that: *"If the passage does not admit a literal interpretation then we must look elsewhere for an explanation."*[2] There is no doubt that behind the entire Bible is one superintending mind, directing the thoughts of all who have written the Holy Scriptures, even to the intent that the principle of *"out of the mouth of two or three witnesses a thing is established"* can be found amongst the prophetic books. Therefore, one does not have to look too far to find words to refute Dake's statement. The Book of Daniel can be interpreted literally in places; yet the vision as sealed up for its spiritual relevance to be revealed much nearer the end of time. However, this version is not meant to challenge any other expositions on the topic, and relies mainly on the symbolic references as they appear through the Bible. Although most of the symbolic references may not be universally known, the context in which they appear does not make them objectionable because they are contextually well explained.

In unveiling the truths of Revelation, references will be made and support drawn from other prophetic books of the Bible as much as possible. According to Robert T. Boyd's comments on the *Book of Isaiah*, *"Prophecy is God's way of writing history in advance. For those who accept the Bible as the revealed Word of God, there is no question regarding prophecy. Fulfilled prophecy is one of the infallible proofs of the inspiration of Scripture. It assures the believer that unfulfilled prophecy will, in God's time come to pass."*[3] Each chapter of this book is well explained and some sections may be repeated because they appear in different times in history. At any point in time until the end comes, the revelations will always be about things past, present, and future.

PART 1
PRESENTATION OF THE UNVIELING

CHAPTER ONE

THE REVELATION OF JESUS CHRIST

Revelation 1:1 "The Revelation of Jesus Christ, which God gave unto him, to show unto his servants things which must shortly come to pass; and he sent and signified it by his angel unto his servant John."

The Bible begins this living story by telling us what was in the beginning. The book of Genesis contains God's record of creation. It summarises God's plan for man; and tells the story of the fall of man. It shows God's promise of redemption unto everlasting life; and reveals God's eternal judgement on sin and sinners in their generations. It testified of and confirmed the birth of Christ who was promised since the fall of man, as God's solution for sinfulness. Its secrets are meant to be understood by servants of God, who will benefit from them through the help of the indwelling Holy Ghost. Christ confirmed this to his disciples when he spoke to them in parables in *Matthew 13:11 "It is given unto you to know the mysteries of the kingdom of heaven."* The problem from the beginning is that man did not understand the plan. Sinfulness came into the world because one man listened to the words of the devil instead of to the words of God. This was made easy because evil knowledge fights against good knowledge to rule in human hearts. Therefore, in every dispensation God emphasises the need for mankind to keep his commandments that the soul may prosper in life.

Revelation tells us how humanity's final victory over the devil and his principalities and powers will end. Unfortunately, there will be many casualties from among the human race and those who will overcome the wiles of the devil, must ensure their safety by accepting the blood of Jesus Christ as the legitimate atoning sacrifice for sin and practice holiness in order to spend eternity with God and his Son Jesus Christ.

The work of the Holy Ghost in people's lives transforming them to the status of sons of God is evident from the beginning. His work is described in the New Testament; but in the Old he, like Christ, is hidden in symbols. We see from the book of Genesis how the knowledge of his work in the past can help us understand the book of Revelation.

The Bible affirms that God created all things and since he is the Almighty all are subject to him and his desire will be accomplished no matter how long it takes. Author Pink in his book *Gleaning in Genesis* agrees that: *"Man is not an independent creature, for he did not make himself. Having been created by God he owes a debt to his creator . . . and is subject to Divine government."*[1] It is this failure of man to submit to the divine government of the Word of God and the Spirit of God in him that must lead to human activities being judged. Judgement therefore is not primarily upon races, or empires, but upon the sinfulness of all mankind, whether Jews or Gentiles. To interpret and correctly respond to all that is revealed concerning the end time events, we must know what God desired of the people he created. God's plan from the days of Adam is that mankind should have dominion over all the works of his hands. This honour has been fulfilled in Christ as the first-born of the new creation; he is also head of the angels in heaven and spiritual and natural things on earth. See *Ephesians 1:20–21, "And set him on his own right hand in the heavenly places. Far above all principalities and power, and might, and dominion, and every name that is named, not only in this world, but also in that which is to come."*

It takes one spiritual being to dominate over another; and man of flesh must definitely be transformed to be able to dominate over spiritual beings. The new birth was, therefore in the plan of God from creation, as well as all the other things which must take place in the life of man before he can be glorified with Christ. God intends that people prevail over sin and vessels of sinfulness, through continued adherence to his words and ultimately through the aid of the fullness of his indwelling Holy Ghost, who would teach, instruct and counsel the righteous to sustain them in holiness and love that they might do his will on earth—*Ps. 32:8*.

When Adam sinned and his soul died in sin he needed restoration to life before he could fulfil God's mandate of dominion, for man can only truly dominate when God is with him and he is led by the LORD the Holy Ghost. Despite the various animal sacrifices made over time for the atonement of man's sinfulness, he could not dominate over sin, for sinfulness had become a part of his nature. For this reason Christ came as the second Adam and the lamb that was slain in the mind of God before the foundation of the earth to pay the price for human redemption so that through his death people's spirits would be quickened into life through the hearing and adhering to the word of God; as it is written:

"And you hath he quickened who were dead in trespasses and sins" (Eph. 2:1). "But we speak the wisdom of God in a mystery, even the hidden wisdom which God ordained before the foundation of the world to our glory: Which none of the princes of this world knew: for had they known it, they would not have crucified the Lord of glory"(1 Cor. 2:7-8). "But we preach Christ crucified, unto the Jews a stumbling

block, and unto the Greeks foolishness; But unto them which are called, both Jews and Greeks, Christ the power of God and the wisdom of God" (*1 Cor. 1:23–24*).

Christ has also restored humanity to the glorious presence of God from where we were driven (*Gen. 3:24*). His intercession in *John 17:5, "And now O Father glorify thou me with thine own self with the glory I had with thee before the world was"* was not for himself alone but for the benefit of all who would accept him as their Lord and Saviour. He prayed for man's restoration to the glorified position God intended for him, so that God could work with him and perfect his image and likeness in him; and through the renewed man as living creatures with life reach all the nations of the world with salvation (*Matt. 28:19–20*). Therefore, it is the failure of the new creation to fulfil the mandate that will result in the final judgement on the Church and the World.

The birth and death of Christ were important milestones in human history because they ushered in the era when God would indwell human beings by his Holy Spirit. In announcing the birth of Christ the angel said his name shall be called Emmanuel, which means "God with us." Christ was present with his people as the Mighty God, who heralded a change in the status of the man who repents. It also meant that the time had come and still is, when God indwells the new creation in accordance with his plan from the beginning. Christ confirms this status when he says that *"If any man loves me he will keep my words: and my Father will love him, and we will come unto him, and make our abode with him"*(*John 14:23*). The new creation has both the Word of God and the Spirit of God at work in them (*John 14:10–12*).

There are also many symbolic signs and references in the Bible to show how God interacts with people; for example, in the Tabernacle in the wilderness, God spoke with the High Priest from underneath the wings of the Cherubim. The Cherubim, is the name for a spirit being affected by sin and as we will come to understand later, is God's new name for the person who has repented of sin and is fully conformed to the image and likeness of God in Christ. According to *Vines Expository Dictionary*:

"Cherubim are regarded by some as the ideal representatives of redeemed animate creation. In the Tabernacle and Temple they were represented by the two golden figures of two-winged living creatures. They were in one piece with the golden lid of the Ark of the Covenant in the Holy of Holies, signifying that the prospect of redeemed and glorified creatures was bound up with the sacrifice of Christ. This in itself would indicate that they represent redeemed human beings in union with Christ, a union seen, figuratively, proceeding out of the mercy seat."[2]

God always provides a point of reference to which fallen humanity can return; in this case it is that we conform to his image that is in Christ. It is also in the revelation that the Cherubim are God's perfect species of human beings that makes it a position to be desired. The seven churches are also significant bench marks to the unveiling of the truths of the book of Revelation. They provide reference points for the Church Age to know exactly where we are at in time; and what must be done by those who *"have ears to hear"* what the Spirit is saying to the Church at every stage.

The kingdom of Israel united and divided, presents a model for the interpretation of Revelation; and reflects the mercy of God to those who understand their purpose.

God teaches us in all the ways he created man to learn: intellectually, by experience or hands-on. *"And when the people heard this, they were pricked in their heart, and said to Peter and the rest of the apostles men and brethren what shall we do?"(Acts 2:37)*. Richards and Bredfeldt writers of *Creative Bible Teaching*, relates this passage to Bloom's cognitive, affective and behavioural domains of learning. They note that Peter's teaching ministry affected each of these domains. First, Peter's teachings provided content that had to be mentally understood, processed, and considered by his audience. His listeners had to understand the message and change their thinking. They were "pricked in their heart." This refers to their readiness to change in attitudes and values.[3] Not only did Peter's teaching produce learning in the cognitive and affective domains, it also motivated a behavioural response. Affective learning may also include a demonstration, whilst behavioural learning requires hands-on performances. Really, Bloom may have discovered these domains through careful study, but the fact is, God created man to learn in this manner and he teaches man in all three ways. God uses the natural things that happened in the lives of the Jews to demonstrate to the Church Age the weakness of the flesh, the ways of God, and the pitfalls and problems of living in a sinful world. All so that we can know how the spiritual life we are called to live will be affected if we depart from the words of God and the counsel of the Holy Ghost. The Bible tells us that all scriptures are for learning, for reproof and for correction. Everyone will be reproved by the things he or she is emotionally convicted of, and the wise will make correction.

CHAPTER TWO

SYMBOLS RELATING TO THE UNVEILING

The Bible was written to be interpreted intellectually and prophetically through parables, as well as allegorically and symbolically. Christ confirmed in one of his discourses with his disciples in *Matthew 13:15* that he spoke to the people in parables so that by hearing they would hear and not understand, and by seeing they would see and not perceive. The reason he gave for this mystery, which holds true even in our times, is:

"For this people's heart is waxed gross, and their ears are dull of hearing, and their eyes they have closed; lest at any time they should see with their eyes, and hear with their ears, and should understand with their heart, and should be converted, and I should heal them."

Another reason could be that truths are progressively revealed therefore they are hidden in these various ways, to make them relevant to those who will need them at a particular time. A list of symbols relating to the end time prophecies is at the back of this book. Each is consistent in meaning throughout the Bible. One or more may refer to the same object: for example gold, the lion, and the river Pison refer to the righteous generation. One of the symbols of the Holy Spirit in Genesis is the River of Eden.

"And a river went out of Eden to water the garden: and from thence it was parted, and became into four heads. . . And the name of the third river is Hiddekel: that is it which goeth towards the east of Assyria. And the fourth river is Euphrates"(Gen. 2:10–14).

The name Eden is a symbol for *pleasure, paradise or kingdom life*.[1] Some theologians believe the name means *"the presence of the LORD."*[2] With God's idea of fruitfulness and multiplication in mind, it is not surprising that the exact location of the garden is obscured to human knowledge; because human beings would have typically turned it into an object of worship. It is easy, therefore, to conclude that anywhere the presence of the LORD is with his people is a place of pleasure and delight where also kingdom life is being manifested. Eden can, therefore, be everywhere God is present with his people. In the Garden of Eden there was one river. The word *river* is a known symbol of the Holy Ghost *(Ps. 36:8)*. The name of the river of Eden is not mentioned in the Bible, which would lend credence to its symbolism, for where the presence of the LORD is manifested only the Holy Ghost can be present. As the river went out from Eden it was divided into four heads. This exposition will treat the four heads as symbolic reference to the four generations of people whom God called into being:

"And God said, Let the earth bring forth the living creature after his kind, cattle and creeping thing, and beast of the earth after his kind: and it was so. And God made the beast of the earth after his kind, cattle after their kind, and everything that creepeth upon the earth after his kind: and God saw that it was good. And God said: Let us make man in our image, after our likeness: and let them have dominion over the fish of the sea, and over the fowl of the air, and over the cattle, and over all the earth, and over every creeping thing that creepeth upon the earth" (Gen. 1:24–26).

The spiritual things called forth at creation were to form part of the kingdom of light which would manifest with the coming of Christ, whereas their natural counterparts are of the Earth. There was a calling forth of the spiritual man as the living creature, the ungodly generation as cattle; the creeping thing as the wicked generation and the beast of the earth as the evil generation. God called these generations into being before he created man as a living soul. *"Who hath wrought and done it, calling the generations from the beginning? I the LORD, the first, and with the last; I am he"* (Isa. 41:4). The question may be asked why are these generations necessary? The answer proffered is derived from the knowledge that the body of Christ is one. Our natural bodies have avenues to dispose of waste. There must be similar means of purging the body of Christ of sinfulness, by providing a means whereby God can justly judge iniquities, transgression and sin uniformly by fashioning the hearts of the generation alike, according as each person is submitted to the rule of the Word of God and the Spirit of God over their lives. (See *Psalms 33:15*).

God also determined that the making of the spiritual man would be in stages, as he called them forth. *"And God said, Let the earth bring forth grass, the herb yielding seed, and the fruit tree yielding fruit after his kind, whose seed is in itself, upon the earth: and it was so"*(Gen. 1:11). Other scripture references:

Grass: Luke12:28; Isaiah 51:12; 1 Peter 1:24.

Seed: Hebrews 11:18; Galatians 3:29;

Trees: Isaiah 41:19–20; Luke 3:9.

God created man from dust and said of him: *"In the sweat of thy face shalt thou eat bread, till thou return unto the ground; for out of it wast thou taken: for dust thou art, and unto dust shalt thou return"* (Gen. 3:19). The formation of the spiritual man is, however, the work of the Word of God and the Spirit of God. (See *John 14:23*.). According to Pink:

"There is a wide difference between "creating" and "making": to create is to call into existence something out of nothing; to "make" is to form or fashion something out of materials already existing. A carpenter can "make" a chair out of wood, but he is quite unable to "create" the wood itself."[3]

Paul confirms that man's completion is in Christ. *"And ye are complete in him, which is the head of all principalities and power"* (*Col. 2:10*). The Bible reveals that the man of flesh is as grass. The fact that grass does not bear fruits, would confirm that man is being progressively formed.

"The voice said, Cry. And he said, What shall I cry? All flesh is grass, and all the goodliness thereof is as the flower of the field: The grass withereth, the flower fadeth: because the spirit of the LORD bloweth upon it: surely the people is grass. The grass withereth, the flower fadeth: but the word of God shall stand forever" (*Isa. 40:6*).

Genesis 3:15 "The seed of the woman shall bruise the head of the serpent."

Isaiah 61:3 "That we should be called trees of righteousness, the planting of the LORD that he may be glorified."

Creating may require constant improvement, but making means completion. The work of the making of man in the image and likeness of God will be completed when man become as the angels. God began with the natural but definitely had the spiritual man in mind when he gave the mandate of *Genesis 1:26–28*. There was a calling forth but the actual work to be done is still in progress. For the spiritual man to be formed, his will has to be submitted to the moulding hands of the Father, even as the clay is submitted to the hands of the potter. The lesson Jeremiah learnt when God sent him to the potter's house was one on submission (*Jer. 18:3–6*). The mind of the natural man provides the material for the making of the spiritual man. However consistently throughout the Bible, God judges sin by generations:

"Keeping mercy for thousands, forgiving iniquity and transgression and sin, and that will by no means clear the guilty; visiting the iniquity of the fathers upon the children, and upon the children's children, unto the third and to the fourth generation" (*Exod. 34:7*). We know that the LORD God created all things by his spoken word and that his word became flesh in the person of Christ Jesus. *"By the word of the LORD were the heavens made; and all the host of them by the breath of his mouth. The LORD looketh from heaven; he beholdeth all the sons of men. . . He fashioneth their hearts alike; he considereth all their works"* (*John 1:14; Ps. 33:6, 13–15*). Based on these scriptures it is reasonable to conclude that these words refer to the four generations of men belonging to the two spiritual kingdoms of the world.

By this knowledge it is easier to understand why the mandate God gave in *Genesis 1:26–28* first had to be fulfilled by Christ before it could be spiritually fulfilled by man—because sin destroys the soul and renders man incapable of a consummate relationship with God. (See *John 10:10, Genesis 1:24–26, and Psalms 8:4–8*.)

"What is man that thou are mindful of him? And the son of man, that thou visitest him? For thou hast made him a little lower than the angels, and hast crowned him with glory and honour. Thou madest him to have dominion over the works of

thy hands; thou hast put all things under his feet: All sheep and oxen, yea, and the beasts of the field; The fowl of the air, and the fish of the sea, and whatsoever passeth through the paths of the seas."

Christ received dominion over all the works of the hand of God for humanity. Through him, the new creation is well able to influence the spiritual as well as the natural. The four generations of people are of the two spiritual kingdoms of the world: the kingdom of light and the kingdom of darkness. There are two types of people in each kingdom, which is an indication of their transiency, and proves that God is working all things to a perfect end. Christ confirms that *"a kingdom divided against itself will not stand."* The generations and natural things over which the righteous should dominate are also symbolic of spiritual things, as the following list indicates:

Symbols	*Meaning*
Feet	The walk and ways of the believer; To put under feet symbolises total subjection:[4] *Romans 16:20; 1 Corinthians 15:27*
Sheep	The righteous generation; divine righteousness[5] Symbol of God's people Israel or the Church[5]
Oxen	Refers to labour and servanthood:[5] *Amos 6:12; Isaiah 1:3; Romans 14:4* The patience, strength and ability to labour for others[4]
Beasts of the field	Man acting in carnal energy and independence of God in the earth[4] The ungodly, wicked and evil generations: *Isaiah 60:5; Psalm 68:22*
The fowl of the air	The devil: *Matthew 13:9; Ephesians 2:2*
The fish of the sea	Sinful mankind: *Luke 5:10; Matthew 4:19* Scattered Jewish people in the last days:[4] *Ezekiel 29:4–5* Souls of men:[5] *Ezekiel 29:4–5; Matthew 13:47–48;*
The living creature	The righteous generation: *Genesis 1:24*
Creeping thing	The serpent: *Revelation 12:9*

Beasts of the earth	The ungodly, wicked and evil generations of the earth: *1 Corinthians 15:32*
Cattle	The ungodly generation: *Ezekiel 34:15–17; Matthew 25:3*
Over all the earth	Christ has been given dominion over all the earth so that the righteous generation may dominate over sin: *Colossians 1:15–18*
Thorns and thistles/ Thorns and berries	The wicked and evil generations: *Genesis 3:18 Ezekiel 2:6*

A generation of people may also be described as those who were born within a specific period, descendants from a specific ancestral lineage, or a set of people who are considered as sharing the same belief or attitudes. In the Old Testament we see the rule of the world of that time expressed in the image of a man, passing from one kingdom to another, declining in effectiveness according to the value of the symbols that describe them. These generations are referred to by their various symbolic representations in the dreams of Nebuchadnezzar and Daniel in the book of Daniel chapters two and seven: see *Figure one*. Therefore, a generation may be referred to as one type of people. See *Daniel 7:3 "the four great beasts."*

SYMBOLS

NT kingdom of Heaven	Parts of the Body	Generations Dan 7:1-8	Metal Dan 2:32-35	Animals Dan 7:4-8	Rivers Gen 2:11-14	OT Kingdoms Dan 2:31-45
1	The head	Righteous	Gold	Lion	Pison	Babylonian
2	Breast and arms	Ungodly	Silver	Bear	Gihon	Medes and Persian
3	Belly and Thighs	Wicked	Bronze	Leopard	Hiddekel or Tigris	Greek
4	Legs and feet	Evil	Iron and Clay	Evil monster	Euphrates	Roman

Fig 1. Symbols as they relate to the Old Testament kingdoms and the four generations

The four heads of the river and the generations: Reference is made to the rivers because of the belief that they conceal sustainable spiritual truths that can help us to understand the revelations to John. The Pison River is symbolic of the righteous generation. This river encompasses the land of Havilah where there are gold, bdellium, and onyx stones. The geographical location of Havilah is not known.[6] The International Standard Bible Encyclopaedia records that it is a land of uncertain location. Zondervan Compact Bible Dictionary says: "There are many conjectures as to the location of the Pison River."[7] Some publications even speculate that it is the River Nile. Havilah is also the name of one of the grandsons of Ham, and the name of the son of Joktan of the lineage of the selected righteous generation of Seth. The name means "free flowing" and reminds us of what we know about the righteous man. The Holy Ghost as a river in him is freely given, and freely flows in him and with him to make him rich in wisdom and spiritual understanding. Gold is a symbol of the righteous generation (Job 23:10), and so are stones.

Havilah is said to be surrounded by the water of the Pison River. The righteous generation is surrounded by the presence of the Holy Ghost: *"The Angel of the LORD encampeth around those that fear him and delivereth them"(Ps. 34:7)*. The presence of the LORD is his primary blessing upon his people and the vehicle or glory in which the righteous person dwells and moves. Christ prayed for the glory to be returned to humanity *(Isa. 4:5)*. In the glory we are sheltered, protected, and strengthened to walk in God's favour and the dominion required of man from the beginning.

The ungodly generation and the river Gihon: *"The ungodly are not so but are like the chaff which the wind driveth away. Therefore the ungodly shall not stand in the judgement or sinners in the congregation of the righteous. For the LORD knoweth the way of the righteous; but the way of the ungodly shall perish" (Ps 1:4-6)*.

The name Gihon means "a stream." The river encompasses the land of Ethiopia. The International Bible Standard Encyclopaedia Vol. 2 states that in *Sirach 24:27 (A.V. Geon)*[8] the name is used figuratively in reference to wisdom. It is also the name of a spring in Jerusalem that is regarded as very sacred. This exposition tends to favour the wisdom aspect of the references and believes it symbolises the life of the ungodly person. Christ told his disciples in *John 7:38* that those who believe on his name will have rivers of living water flowing out of their bellies. Every Christian should have the Holy Ghost flowing like a river within their hearts. It is, however, evident that the ungodly generation, represented by the river Gihon, is to be found amongst those who have been redeemed from sin; but because they are not grounded in the word of God, the Spirit's presence in them is likened unto a stream. The Bible appropriately describes the ungodly as chaff driven about by the wind. This wind is usually associated with doctrines and dogmas contrary to the word of God. According to the parable of the sower, they are those who receive the word and it springs forth but dries up immediately. They cannot withstand in times of temptation and they easily give way to the devil. Even these people will not stand in the day of the judgement. The Bible tells us in *1 Peter 4:18*, that if it is hard for the righteous to stand what hope do the sinners and ungodly generations have of standing before God?

Those who follow Christ half-heartedly are carnally minded, are enemies of God and cheat themselves when they refuse to embrace the truth wholeheartedly. The ungodly person is not an heir of the kingdom; neither can God commit the blessings of the kingdom to that person because they are neither here nor there. The truth that should become apparent as we attempt to interpret Revelation by looking at these symbols is that God has gone to great lengths to tell us who we ought to be; and where and how we ought to serve him. The standard has been set and cannot be changed because it is backed up by the words of God and the integrity of God.

The wicked generation and the river Hiddekel or Tigris: *"Keep me as the apple of the eye, hide me under the shadow of thy wings. From the wicked that oppress me, from my deadly enemies, who compass me about. Arise, O LORD, disappoint him; cast him down: deliver my soul from the wicked, which is thy sword"* (Ps. 17:8–9, 13).

People who make up this generation belong to the kingdom of darkness and are indwelt by sin as a spirit (*Matt. 12:43–45*). These people know about God; they know they ought to serve him by turning away from sin; but for different reasons they remain unrepentant. God uses them to chastise his people to get them to return to the paths of righteousness when their sins are great (*Jer. 51:20*).

The name Hiddekel means "rapid." It is also another name for the River Tigris and by its geographical location flows towards the land of Assyria. Another symbol used to describe this generation is the leopard, a fast running animal. This is an indication of how quickly a wicked generation can degenerate to an evil and adulterous generation, if there is no repentance from sin.

The evil generation and the river Euphrates: This is a river that flows through Babylon. The name means bursting. Whilst we are told the boundaries of other rivers, nothing is said about the boundaries of this river in the related script. Geographically the river has boundaries and its location is known; but spiritually it symbolises sin as a spirit, in the evil generation found all over the world. These people are of the kingdom of darkness and totally reject God:

"But he answered and said unto them, an evil and adulterous generation seeketh after a sign; and there shall no sign be given to it, but the sign of the prophet Jonas." (Matt. 12:39–41). *"But draw near hither, ye sons of the sorceress, the seed of the adulterer and the whore"* (Isa. 57:3).

The Devil uses the people of the kingdom of darkness to perpetuate evil throughout the world. Like the human flesh they cannot inherit eternal life without repentance:

"Surely there shall not one of these men of this evil generation see that good land, which I swear to give unto your fathers." (Deut. 1:35). As it was with Israel so shall it be with the evil generation of any period. Referring to this river as sin, *Isaiah 11:15* says:

"And the LORD shall utterly destroy the tongue of the Egyptian sea, and with his mighty wind shall he shake his hand over the river, and shall smite it in the seven streams, and make men go over dryshod."

The seven streams of this river, which the Euphrates symbolises, are the seven devils of sin which rule in the kingdoms of the world. Christ spoke about them as of the unclean spirit in *Matthew 12:43–45*. According to Vines Expository Dictionary, there is only one devil but many demons.[9] The seven devils cast out of Mary Magdalene to prepare her to spread the good news of Christ's resurrection was obviously the unclean spirit called sin. The Bible is not written to glorify the devil;

therefore they are not listed together in any one place; but can be uncovered from his works in the Bible. They are:

The spirit Sin: *Romans 6:14*

The spirit of rebellion and witchcraft, and iniquity and idolatry: *1 Samuel 15:23*

The spirit of ignorance, and the fear of sin: *Ephesians 4:18; 2 Timothy 1:7*

The spirit of deceit, and death: *Proverbs 12:20; Ephesians 4:22; Romans 5:12*

The rivers Tigres and Euphrates, are found in Assyria and Babylon, respectively. The Northern and Southern kingdoms of Israel and Judah went into captivity under these two nations. Some things relating to natural Israel are a reflection of spiritual things that are happening to the Church. One is inclined to believe that the mystery of the location of the first two rivers is another confirmation of the journey of man, and is reminiscent of the reality of the bondage of sin and his work in the lives of God's people. None of the captives of the Northern Kingdom returned. So it is with the ungodly generation who does not repent, there can be no place in the eternal kingdom of God for them. The hidden truths of these revelations should not be clouded with a search for proofs provided by men, as long as they can be supported by other parts of the Bible. The spiritual man was in the mind of God but was not revealed, until the coming of Christ; the same can be said of the rivers and should explain the mystery of their locations. The LORD God confirmed that he judges by generations when Moses asked to see his glory:
"And the LORD passed by before him, and proclaimed, The LORD, The LORD God, merciful and gracious, longsuffering, and abundant in goodness and truth. Keeping mercy for thousands, forgiving iniquity and transgression and sin, and that will by no means clear the guilty; visiting the iniquity of the fathers upon the children's children, unto the third and to the fourth generation" (Exod. 34:6–7).

The Parable of the sower and the seed tells us the reaction of the four generations of people in the world to the word of God and confirms that it is only the righteous generation who receives the word on good ground that will bear fruit and comply with the mandate of spiritual fruitfulness required in *Genesis 1:26–28*. The ungodly generation of the kingdom are those in any period of the Church's history, who receive the word amongst thorns, then the cares of the world and the deceitfulness of riches choke the word out of the soul, causing unfruitfulness. The word thorn is a symbol of wickedness. God told Adam that the earth would bring forth thorns and thistles; this refers to the wicked and evil generations of the world.

God knows that once one generation turns away without repentance, by the time iniquity lingers to the third generation he must pronounce judgement and issue a warning, for judgement will be executed in the fourth and restoration made (*Gen. 15:16*). In the book of Joel, the fourth generation is referred to as another generation. This is the principle upon which the Book of Revelation is interpreted in this exposition. It is a spiritual concept, which the Holy Ghost is bringing to light to help the Church read God's time clock in these dark days, when man seeks sensual truths to discredit the existence of God; or the work of the Holy Ghost in time. The psalmist uses the word "river" to symbolise the work of the Holy Ghost in the life of a person. The seven streams of the river of the Holy Ghost would be as described in *Isaiah 11:2*: *"And the spirit of the LORD shall rest upon him, the spirit of wisdom and understanding, the spirit of counsel and might, the spirit of knowledge and the fear of the LORD."*

In the dispensation of the eternal state we are also introduced to another river: *"And he shewed me a pure river of water of life, clear as crystal, proceeding out of the throne of God and of the Lamb. And in the midst of the street of it and on either side of the river, was there the tree of life which bear twelve manner of fruits; and the leaves of the tree were for the healing of the nation"* (*Rev. 22:1–2*).

The children of Israel were to journey from Horeb to the Euphrates before possessing the land. The places which marked the way they should go are symbolic of the various kingdoms that would influence the lives of the Jews until the coming of Christ and down through the Church Age until the evil symbolised by the river Euphrates and the influence of sin dries up in the world. If Christians are not living with this hope, then we make the death of Christ irrelevant (*1 Cor. 15:19*). See *Figure four,* entitled *"The Progressive Journey of Israel"*.

CHAPTER THREE

THE OLD TESTAMENT KINGDOMS AND THE KINGDOM OF HEAVEN

Many natural kingdoms have ruled on the earth, but only those that have direct impact on the lives of the Jews are relevant to the context of John's revelations. These kingdoms are four: the Babylonian Empire under Nebuchadnezzar; the Medes and Persian under Darius the Mede and King Cyrus of Persia; the Grecian Empire under Alexander, who conquered Darius Codomannus; and, lastly, the Roman Empire, which was in existence until many years after the death of Christ and the coming of the Church Age.

THE NINE KINGDOMS: Their Symbols, Generations, and Archetype

Kingdoms and Churches	Symbols	Archetype
1. BABYLON Dan 7:4 (2:37-38; Rev 2:1-7)	A lion and Gold	King Nebuchadnezzar
2. MEDES AND PERSIA Dan 7:5 (2:39); Rev 2:8-17	A bear and Silver	King Cyrus
3. GREECE Dan 7:6 (2:39; Rev 2:18-3:6	A leopard and Brass	King Alexander the Great
4. ROME Dan 7:7-8 (2:40-43)	Iron and Clay	The Caesars
5. THE KINGDOM OF HEAVEN THE TIMES OF THE GENTILES Matt 13:31-32; Isa 42:1 Ephesus Church Smyrna and Pergamos Churches Thyatira Church Sardis Church Philadelphia Church THE RAPTURE OF THE TWO WITNESSES	 Gold Silver Brass Iron The rod of iron	The Kings of the Kingdom over four generations – Rev 1:5 The righteous generation The ungodly generation The wicked generation The evil generation The two witnesses – Dan 7:21-22
6. THE BEAST The Laodiceans Church This Church escorted to heaven by Christ THE SEVEN VIAL JUDGEMENTS	The Evil Man The mark of the Beast The breast plate of iron	The one world order Rev 13:1-7; 17:1-6; 18:20 Locusts
7. THE MILLENNIAL KINGDOM	The sceptre of righteousness	Jerusalem rebuilt
8. THE DEVIL AND HIS TEN KINGS Isa 26:20-21	Christ and The Rod of Iron	The devil cast into the lake of fire
9. THE KINGDOM OF GOD	The everlasting rule of Jesus the King	Entry into God's seventh day rest

Fig 2. In this table we see the natural kingdoms of the Old Testament; and the spiritual rule of the Church Age; over four generations that will rule on earth before the return of Christ.

The Roman kingdom gave way to ten kingdoms, seven of which are still in existence today but under different names. However, they are only mentioned to give better understanding of the signs of the end.

The four natural kingdoms, like the four generations, are symbolised by gold, silver, brass and iron. These symbols make it is easy to accept the natural kingdoms as a type of the rule of the four generations. The four generations called forth in the beginning (*Isa. 41:4*) belong to the two spiritual kingdoms: light and darkness that will rule on earth before the return of Christ. They will rule because the earth was given to the children of men, and each generation must rule on earth; the righteous will be rewarded whilst others will be judged according to their sinfulness. Nebuchadnezzar's dream helps us to understand more clearly how one kingdom gave way to the next. See *Daniel 2:31–35*:

"Thou, O King, sawest, and beheld a great image. This image, whose brightness was excellent, stood before thee; and the form thereof was terrible. This image's head was of fine gold, his breast and his arms of silver, his belly and his thighs of brass, his legs of iron, his feet part of iron and part of clay. Thou sawest till a stone was cut out without hands, which smote the image upon his feet that were of iron and clay, and break them to pieces. Then was the iron, the brass, the silver and the gold, broken to pieces together, and became like the chaff of the summer threshing floors; **and the wind carried them away that no place was found for them; and the stone that smote the image became a great mountain, and filled the whole earth**.*"*

Nebuchadnezzar saw the image of a man whose kingly authority is significantly reduced as one kingdom gave way to another until *"no place was found for them."* Daniel's interpretation of the dream identified Nebuchadnezzar as the head of gold, and the other kingdoms were symbolised by silver, brass and iron respectively. He stated that Nebuchadnezzar's kingdom would have worldwide influence. The dream had its fulfilment during the time of the four kingdoms but because of the symbolic reference it is also apocalyptic. The dream confirmed that there would be a time when the rule of each kingdom would change from one kingdom to the other until a spiritual kingdom set up under Christ was formed. The coming of Christ during the reign of the Roman Empire saw the emergence of the kingdom of heaven as one that would break in pieces all other kingdoms and bring in an everlasting kingdom. See *Daniel 2:44–45*:

"In the days of these kings shall the God of heaven set up a kingdom, which shall never be destroyed: and the kingdom shall not be left to other people, but it shall break in pieces and consume all these kingdoms, and it shall stand forever... For as much as thou sawest that the stone was cut out of the mountain without hands, and that it break in pieces the iron, the brass, the clay, the silver and the gold; the great God hath made known to the king what shall come to pass hereafter; and the dream is certain, and the interpretation thereof sure."

This provides a motive for the devil to seek to resist its advancement, with the aim of destroying it altogether. The ten toes of the feet of the image, which are part iron and part clay, refers to both kingdoms mingling together yet separate. Both are spread through knowledge of good or evil. The statement that *'they shall mingle themselves with the seed of men; but they shall not cleave one to another; even as the iron is not mixed with clay'* can only refer to the righteous generation who are in the world but not of the world. Therefore in unveiling the spiritual truth relating to the image, it must be associated with the four generations of people in the world as a result of Adam's sin; the decline of righteousness in the kingdom of heaven; and the increase of wickedness in the kingdom of darkness as the rule of one generation gives way to the other, as it was with the four natural kingdoms as revealed in *Daniel 7:3–8*.

It is evident that in the continued struggle between good and evil, as seen by Daniel in *Chapter 7:2–3*, and from the study of the kingdoms as shown in *Figure two*, that the peoples of the kingdom of heaven will be ruled by the kingdom of darkness for a season. This will result in the humbling of the Church and because of her failure, to maintain her ruling position, she must go through the entire period of the great tribulation. John made mention of these kingdoms in *Revelation 17:9–12:*

"And here is the mind that hath wisdom. The seven heads are seven mountains, on which the woman sitteth. And there are seven kings, five are fallen, and one is, and the other is not yet come; and when he cometh, he must continue a short space. And the beast that was and is not, even he is the eighth, and is of the seven and goeth into perdition. And the ten horns which thou sawest are ten kings which have received no kingdom as yet; but receive power and shall give their power and strength unto the beast."

The five kingdoms are counted from the kingdom of David to the Roman Empire; the sixth is the kingdom of heaven, that is and the other to come is the millennial kingdom of Christ as the seventh; the eighth kingdom is the rule of the Devil and his ten kings who will gather in war against Christ and his kingdom after the Millennium, when the Armageddon War will be fought. The Devil is still a part of the seventh kingdom, for there will still be people on earth bearing children in the Millennium.

Many Church leaders and eschatological teachers are expecting a revival of the old Roman Empire before the return of Christ. This is contrary to what is revealed in the dream of Nebuchadnezzar (*Dan. 2:31–35*). The scriptures clearly said of those kingdoms: *"the wind carried them away that no place was found for them."* They will no longer be used as God's time clock for the end of all things. When God destroys a system there is no revival except in his judgement he made allowance for it. Rather, the evil generation of the world symbolised by iron, a symbol that also relates to the Roman Empire, will be of one mind and will be the sword of the LORD to chasten the ungodly of the Church Age to return to righteousness; the wicked may also see and repent.

The kingdom of heaven and dispensations: Dispensations provide opportunity for God to deal with mankind based on his provision of increased knowledge leading to perfection. Although some difference of opinion exists about how many dispensations there are, the fact that they exist is evident. Dispensations are God's way of administering people and judging sins over generations, because of the shortage of the life span of man (*Gen. 6:3*). God has a time frame in which he will perfect creation according to his good pleasure; the dispensations serve as a guide to help man understand where we are at in time. According to Phillips:

"Each of these periods, (with the exception of the eternal state of those in heaven) has a beginning and an ending, and each one ends in failure and judgement. In most cases the end of one dispensation and the beginning of another are clearly marked by a catastrophe. In a few cases the two ages overlap somewhat for a brief period."[1]

Dispensations, therefore, make it possible for God to dispense judgement and bring about renewal movements for the fulfilment of his purpose. The Church is God's agent of change, and God has ordained that by her he will reap the greatest harvest of souls from the earth in this dispensation of grace. Bible history covers nine dispensations as can be seen below.

Dispensation	Characteristic	Duration	Conclusion	Symbol
1. The Age of innocence	Sinlessness	Creation to the fall of man	Expulsion from the Garden	The Garden of Eden
2. The Age of Conscience	Permissiveness	The fall to the flood	The Deluge	The mark of Cain
3. The Age of Human Government	Lawlessness	The flood to the Tower of Babel	The confusion of tongues	The sword of the magistrate
4. The Patriarchal Age	Pilgrimage	Abraham to the Bondage in Egypt	Slavery	A tent and an altar
5. The Age of the Mosaic Law	Disobedience	Moses to Christ	The crucifixion Of Christ	The tables of stone
6. The Church Age	Grace	Pentecost to the Rapture of the Church	Rapture of the Church	The cross of Christ
6(a) The Judgement Age	Wrath	The rapture to the vial judgements	The vial judgement	The mark of the Beast
7. The Millennial Age	Theocracy	The return of Christ	The release of the devil	A rod of iron
8. The Devil and ten kings	Anarchy	The release of the Devil and the Armageddon	The Great White Throne	A rod of iron
9. The Eternal State	Glory	Forever and ever	No end	New Jerusalem

Fig. 3. Copied with highlighted amendments: [2]

Of the nine dispensations, we will concentrate only on five for the purpose of interpreting Revelation. We will begin at the Patriarchal Age, when God chose the nation of Israel to be a model for the people of the spiritual nation, the Church, to look at and understand how God dealt with his people. The journey from Horeb (see *Figure 4*) to the Euphrates would begin at the fifth dispensation, the age of the

Mosaic Law, and end with the Millennial Age and God's final judgement on sin and death. God has hidden these truths in symbols and types to be revealed in time, that the Christian will know that it is not the will of God that the Church should be unaware of the timing of the return of Christ.

The Progressive Journey of Israel: Deuteronomy 1:6–8

After thirty-eight years of wandering in the wilderness under the leadership of Moses, the nation Israel was instructed to move out of confinement and make their way to the Mountain of the Amorites. The name Horeb means "waste," "drought," or "barren." Israel wasted thirty-eight years wandering around the mount. The Amorites is a nation over which Israel was instructed to dominate and wipe out because of their sinfulness. The mountain is a symbol of national power, or a nation consumed with fierce military energy (or national, political, or moral stability or greatness).[3] See *Jerimiah 51:25*. It may also refer to the Church Age (*Isa. 2:1–2; Rev. 8:8*). The mountain of the Amorites would be a place of national dominion over sin through continued obedience to the words of God. They were to pass through different places leading to the mount, and each of these several locations have their fulfilment in the ruling dynasties under whose hands Israel would pass until the Church Age.

The Places and the Kingdoms they Represent

1.	The Plain	The Babylonian Empire
2.	In the Hills	The Medes and Persian Empire
3.	In the Valley	The Grecian Empire
4.	In the South	The Roman Empire
5.	By the Sea Side	The coming of Christ—Matthew 4:13–16 "And leaving Nazareth he came and dwelt in Capernaum, which is upon the sea coast in the borders of Zabulon and Nephthalim: That it might be fulfilled which was spoken by Esaias the Prophet, saying . . . The people which sat in darkness saw great light: and to them which sat in the region and shadow of death, light is sprung up."

THE KINGDOM OF HEAVEN, THE CHURCH AGE AND THE TIMES OF THE GENTILES

6. The Land of Canaan	*The spiritual rule of the four generations of men in the earth until the time the Beast and the Antichrist will be bound and cast into the Bottomless pit.*
7. Lebanon	*The Millennial reign of Christ—Isaiah 29:17–21; Psalms 92:12–13*
8. The River Euphrates	*The kingdom of the ten kings—after which sin will be totally dried up in the world—Genesis 15:18; Revelation 16:12*
9. Possession of the land	*The eternal reign of Christ—Psalms 105:10–11*

Fig. 4. The Journey of Israel ending in the Church Age.

The message was to **all Israel**, which includes the Church Age. Both nations were specifically instructed concerning the destination Lebanon. The name means "white." When God spoke to Joshua he said "this Lebanon," meaning the natural city, but to Moses he said "Lebanon to the Euphrates." Israel's possession of the land and permanent rest will come at the end of the Church Age. Natural Lebanon is famous for its cedar trees; spiritual Lebanon will contain the righteous as "cedar trees" *(Isa. 41:19; 61:3)*. The cedar tree is a symbol of kingly authority. Phillips explains the meaning of the symbol thus: *"human greatness. It speaks of man as displayed to the best advantage and in his finest most impressive form" (Num. 19:6)*.[4]

The Church age is still passing through a type of Canaan experience, where we wrestle not for possession of land, but that we may possess eternity with Christ. It may be easy to accept these places as symbols of the Old Testament Kingdoms and a type of the Church Age, but how does one explain what "by the sea side" meant to Christ and the Jews? To do so, we must turn to the prophetic words Jacob spoke on his death bed: *"Naphtali is a hind let loose: he giveth goodly words" (Gen. 49:21)*. There may not seem to be much to be excited about in these words, but there is a great deal to be learnt. Every good thing Jacob said of his sons find fulfilment in Christ. According to Pink, "this expression has a double meaning." In the Hebrew the word signifies, first, "sent" or "sent forth," just as a stag driven from its cover goes forth, scattering her pursuers. But the word also means:

"Let loose," or "let go." It is the term used of Noah when he "sent forth," the raven and the dove from the ark; as also of the priest, when at the cleansing of the leper, he let go or let loose the living bird. The word expresses the joy of an animal

that has been made captive and, in its recovered liberty; bounce forth in gladness, just as we have often seen a dog jumping for joy after it has been unchained. Jacob, then picture Naphtali rejoicing as a freed hind. Then he foretells the joy which the tribe shall express after its escape—"goodly words" he shall give forth. After it regains its liberty, the tribe shall sing a Song of Praise.

"But if this tribe is interesting to us from its Old Testament association, it has far deeper interest for us from its New Testament connections. Zebulun and Naphtali were closely linked together, yet each had a separate interest. The land of Zebulun provided a "haven" or rest for the Lord Jesus during the first thirty years that he tabernacle among men; but it was in the bounds of Naphtali in the cities of Capernaum, Bethsaida, Chorazin, and other places, that he went about doing good and ministering the Word of Life. In his preaching of the Gospel to the poor were the "goodly words" of which Jacob spoke!"[5] Christ dwelt in Capernaum, which is upon the seacoast, fulfilling what is meant 'by the sea side.'

CHAPTER FOUR

THE FATE OF THE KINGDOM OF HEAVEN

Christ told many parables about the kingdom of heaven. Some of them give startling revelations about its fate. *Daniel 7:21–22* tells us that a time came when the saints possessed the kingdom; therefore there must have been a time when the saints wrestled for the kingdom (*Dan. 7:3*). The following are some of the parables of Christ that are of particular significance.

The Parable of the Sower and the Seed: The sower is Christ the Son of Man and the seed is the word of God. The word brings forth fruit: thirty, sixty, and one hundred-fold, according to the way a person hears, believes, lives by, and communicates God's word to others. As it is for the word, so it is also for the individual and the churches. God calls one person in righteousness but his focus is on a holy nation, based on the principle of one individual, one family, one generation, one community, one nation, and one kingdom.

One old person hears (30), believes and practices (60), and teaches them (100)
One old person tells his children (30)
Children tell their children (60)
Children tell another generation (100)

Christ appeared in John's vision as an old man full of age and his message to the Church as the corporate body as well as to individuals is: *"Ye that hath an ear to hear let him hear what the Spirit says unto the Churches."* As the message is for one old person so it is also for the generations of the Church Age; to the intent that the word is never unproductive and multiplies increasingly when the message is conveyed by each generation. When one generation fails to tell, by the time the silence reaches the fourth generation the message is totally lost and that generation becomes a stranger to the truth and the covenant; hence they are not seen as children but as "another generation." (See *Joel 1:1–3*.) In the case of the Church Age, Christ referred to the Sardis Church as "having a name that she is alive but dead," and deadness means she has become as another generation. This remark singles this church out as one that exists in a kingdom with more ungodly people than are righteous.

The Church of Ephesus: *the old people, believed, taught and practiced them:* (AD 001–500)
The Churches of Smyrna and Pergamos: *the old people tell the children:* (30) (AD 500–1500)
The Thyatira Church as *children telling their children:* (60) (AD 1500–2000)
Their children telling *another generation:* (100) (AD 2000–AD(?))

The greatest harvest for the Church should come at the point of the 100 fold return; significantly, the time of the Sardis Church. As it was with the children of Jacob, the greatest harvest of God's promise to Abraham was in the time of Jacob's children when they greatly multiplied in Egypt. However, through the devices of the devil they were subjected to slavery, and demonstrated the idolatry, immorality they were exposed to in Egypt in their wilderness journey, therefore, their sins were judged and the dispensation of the Mosaic Law began. The devices of the devil have not changed and one can see the evidence of these sinful traits in the Church Age. The leopard symbolises the devil's rule in the lives of the wicked generation of the world. His influence on the lives of the children of the kingdom of heaven has not changed. The time of the greatest harvest for the Church is now, and as God's divine intervention to fulfil his promise to Abraham came at the time of Christ, so also God will divinely intervene in the affairs of the Church to protect the harvest of the end times.

Jesus also used the many parables to relate what the spiritual climate in the churches would be like in the same periods. By commendation, rebuke, and warning, the people of God were exhorted to remain faithful even in adversity. Christ sealed the prophecy of the book of Revelation with the authority of the name of God as the "Alpha and Omega," the Almighty God whose kingdom is over all.

The letters to the seven Churches reflect the teachings of Christ on forgiveness in: *"Moreover if thy brother shall trespass against thee, go and tell him his fault between thee and him alone: if he shall hear thee, thou hast gained thy brother. But if he will not hear thee, then take with thee one or two more, that in the mouth of two or three witnesses every word may be established. And if he neglects to hear them, tell it unto the church: but if he neglect to hear the church, let him be unto thee as an heathen man and a publican. . . Again I say unto you, that if two of you shall agree on earth as touching anything that they shall ask, it shall be done for them of my Father which is in heaven. . . Then came Peter to him and said, Lord how oft shall my brother sin against me, and I forgive him? Till seven times? Jesus said unto him, I say not unto thee, Until seven times: but until seventy times seven. . . So likewise shall my heavenly Father do also unto you, if ye from your heart forgive not everyone his brother their trespasses"* (Matt. 18:15–35).

The forgiveness of Christ towards the Christian 'his brother' is demonstrated in the seven Church ages:

The Ephesus Church	The golden age of the Church as **one brother**
The Smyrna and Pergamos Churches	The silver age of the Church as **two more**
The Thyatira Church	Tell the **Church of the renewal** and restoration movements but she tolerated the doctrine of Jezebel and was judged for her compromise
The Sardis Church Age	The time when judgement will restore righteousness.
The Philadelphia Church Age	The Church of **the two witnesses in agreement** shall ask and receive the counsel of the Holy Ghost that restores agape love. This is also the time of the fulfilment of Daniel's seventy weeks of years.
The Laodiceans Church	Experiences the seven times forgiveness. Note also that the jailed servant in the narrative was still in jail at the end. So will it be for those who are not part of the seventh trumpet resurrection.

In the divine nature of Christ he is both a brother to the Jews in flesh and in spirit. From the time of David's kingdom the Jews were given seventy weeks of years to be restored to the favour of Christ. The Jews sinned against him as the eternal "Word of God" when they turned away from the commandments, laws, statutes, and ordinances given them by God. The final week will be in the day of the Philadelphia and Laodiceans Churches. These churches will emerge after the judgement of the Sardis Church Age brings restoration of the order. In his prayer to the Father Christ prayed for the unity of the body. See *John 17:11, 20–21*:

"And now I am no more in the world, but these are in the world, and I come to thee, Holy Father, keep through thine own name those whom thou hast given me, that they may be one, as we are... Neither pray I for these alone, but for them also which shall believe on me through their word. That they all may be one, as thou, Father art in me, and I in thee, that they also may be one in us; that the world may believe that thou hast sent me." He forgives his brethren of the Church Ages seven times.

In the book of Joel, because of the failure of the fathers to "tell" in their generation, we see judgement passing from one generation to another until the Sardis Church Age. In other words: that which the palmer worm has left of the Church of Ephesus (symbolised by gold) the locusts of the churches of Smyrna and Pergamos (symbolised by silver) will eat; and that which the locusts have left the canker worm of the Thyatiran Church (symbolised by bronze) will eat; and that which the canker worm has left the caterpillar of the Sardis Church (symbolised by iron) will eat. This really confirms that there is very little this Church can do without divine intervention because a caterpillar eats and eats until it falls asleep. The Parable of the Wheat and the Tares teaches that it is a dangerous thing for the people of God to sleep in a bed of ignorance.

In *Genesis 6:2–3* God said: *"My Spirit will not always strive with man for man is evil from youth."* *Daniel 7:2* also speaks of a time when the four winds of heaven: characteristics of the Spirit of God at work in man, strove upon the great sea. The world of humans as the four generations is the great sea. Human striving caused by the devil will cease only because God divinely intervenes to establish his chosen saints as his holy nation according to his pre-ordained plan. See *2 Timothy 2:17–19*:

"And their word will eat as doth a canker; of whom is Hymenaeus and Philetus. 18. Who concerning the truth have erred, saying that the resurrection is past already, and overthrow the faith of some. Nevertheless the foundation of God standeth sure, having the seal. The Lord knoweth them that are his. And let everyone that nameth the name of Christ depart from iniquity."

God has given Christ and his Church three periods known as days to put down all rebellion. The first day began with the covenant God had with David and ended with the death of Christ. The Church is in the second of the three-day period, which is this day of grace. The third will be the millennial day of Christ. In this day, Christ has set forth the Church to watch during the twelve hours and into the night season (*John 11:9*) according to the hour of the watches practised in the Old Testament. The seven churches must take their turn to watch:

The Churches	**The six watches**
The Ephesus Church	06—09 first
Smyrna and Pergamos Churches	09—12 second
Thyatira Church	12—03 third
Sardis Church	03—06 fourth
Philadelphia Church*	06—09 fifth
Laodiceans Church*	09—12 sixth

- *These churches exist at a time when darkness is great.*

In the parable of the Ten Virgins, Christ tells of the coming of the bridegroom at midnight. His parables are important pointers to the activities of the Church, and the end time plan of God for the Church as the bride of Jesus.

The Parable of the Leaven: *"The kingdom of heaven is like unto leaven, which a woman took and hid in three measures of meal, till the whole was leavened"* (*Matt. 13:33*).

In this parable, Christ reveals that the kingdom of heaven, which he started, will become corrupt because of the work of the evil one, whose evil wisdom is described as a woman. The Bible speaks of the wisdom of God in the feminine gender. It is obvious that the evil wisdom of the world will also be referred to in the feminine gender; because evil wisdom is also productive she is referred to as the one who flatters with her words.

"When wisdom entereth into thine heart, and knowledge is pleasant unto thy soul; discretion shall preserve thee, understanding shall keep thee... To deliver thee from the strange woman, even from the stranger which flattereth with her words" (*Prov. 2:10–16*).

"Get wisdom, get understanding, forget it not; neither decline from the words of my mouth. Forsake her not, and she shall preserve thee: love her, and she shall keep thee" (*Prov. 4:5–6*).

Uniformly the scriptures refer to leaven as a secret activity corrupting moral and doctrinal values. Christ said in *Matthew 16:6*: *"Take heed and beware of the leaven of the Pharisees."* The leaven of the Pharisees means the things they believe, say and do. Paul refers to the leaven of malice and wickedness. Evil wisdom is the woman who sows the leaven of malice, hypocrisy, and materialism; some of the faults found in the churches as roots of evil. See *1 Corinthians 5:6-8*:

"Your glorying is not good. Know ye not that a little leaven leaveneth the whole lump. Purge out therefore the old leaven that ye may be a new lump, as ye are unleavened for even Christ our Passover is crucified for us. Therefore let us keep the feast, not with old leaven, neither with the leaven of malice and wickedness, but with the unleavened bread of sincerity and truth."

Another leaven that threatens the kingdom is immorality. Christ said as it was in the days of Sodom, so shall it be at the end. If Christians fail to show those in the world the nature of God, then there will be no one to influence change. The three measures of wheat in which the leaven is hidden is a mystery that has to be worked out by identifying the symbols. Wheat is symbolic of the word of God; the three periods as days given to Christ to accomplish his mission are days within which the word of God will be measured to mankind. However, when Christ has put down all rule of evil the wisdom of the world will cease to exist because sin will be destroyed forever.

Three things are responsible for the rebellion of God's creatures: wrong worship, wrong wisdom, and the world. Lucifer sought to be worshipped; Eve sought wisdom but was deceived when she listened to the counsel of the devil against the counsel of God (*Isa. 30:1*). Christians are seeking to be like the world. As it was in the beginning so shall it be at the end. The kingdom of heaven has many people in it who are only nominal Christians, and who can be easily influenced. They have some knowledge of the word but are not grounded in the truth. They are the ungodly generation of the many "called." They believe those parts of the Bible that benefit them. They, like Judas, claim to be friends of Christ, but like the wicked servant who hid his talent, their good work is minimal. It is at the hands of the ungodly generation that the wicked and evil generations are motivated to influence the affairs of the kingdom. *"An ungodly man diggeth up evil, and in his lips there is a burning fire" (Prov. 16:27).* They are like the generation of silver in Nebuchadnezzar's image.

The Parable of the Wheat and the Tares sets this out more graphically:

"The kingdom of heaven is likened unto a man which sowed good seeds in his field. But while men slept, his enemy came and sowed tares among the wheat, and went his way. But when the blade was sprung up, and brought forth fruit, then appeared the tares also. Let both grow until the harvest: and in the time of harvest I will say to the reapers, Gather ye together first the tares, and bind them in bundles to burn them: but gather the wheat into my barn" (Matt. 13:24–30).

Once the devil has sown one antichrist thought in the heart of one person and that influence is sustained, he can go away and do nothing more but wait for its multiplication. What began with one blade turns out to be bundles, which unfortunately must grow together with the wheat until the time of harvest at the end of the world. The question every person in the kingdom of heaven should be asking of her or him-self as the time of Christ draws near is: "Am I of the wheat or the tares?" *Matthew 13:37–43* explains the meaning of the parable to the effect that the tares are the children of the wicked one and they will be gathered out of the kingdom of heaven, not of darkness, and shall be cast into a furnace of fire, and there shall be weeping and wailing and gnashing of teeth. This is really not a time to be casual about one's spiritual life style.

The Parable of the Net: *"Again the kingdom of heaven is like unto a net, that was cast into the sea, and gathered of every kind: Which, when it was full, they drew to shore, and sat down, and gathered the good into vessels, but cast the bad away. So shall it be at the end of the world: the angels shall come forth, and sever the wicked from among the just. And shall cast them into the furnace of fire: there shall be wailing and gnashing of teeth" (Matt. 13:47–49).*

Christ revealed to us that the kingdom of heaven will gather every kind of fish out of the sea of humanity, from the time it was set up until the last Church Age, when the seventh trumpet will be sounded and the righteous will be caught up to meet Christ and be escorted into heaven. The kingdom is also described as a great house in which there are vessels of gold, silver, wood, and earthenware; some to honour, and some to dishonour. It is not surprising therefore that there are so many religions and denominations claiming to be preaching Christ and are not. The fault of the Church of Sardis is that "thou hast a name that thou livest and art dead." This is all part of the work of the devil to deceive and hold people in the bondage of sin.

The advice Paul gives to the Church is worth mentioning as a note of warning to all those who are content to be of the ungodly and not of the righteous: *"Let everyone that nameth the name of Christ depart from iniquity." (See 2 Timothy 2:19).* Paul also tells us that profane and vain babbling increases ungodliness in the kingdom; therefore the wisdom of the world will work against the kingdom and will influence those who live carelessly in it.

The Parable of the Fig Tree: *"He spake also this parable: a certain man had a fig tree planted in his vineyard; and he came and sought fruit thereon, and found* none. Then said he unto the dresser of his vineyard, Behold, these three years I come seeking fruit on this fig tree, and find none: cut it down; why cumbereth it the ground? And he answering said unto him, Lord, let it alone this year also, till I shall dig about it, and dung it: And if it bear fruit, well: and if not, then after that thou shalt cut it down" (Luke 13:6–8).

In this parable, Christ has revealed the day on which he will return as being the third millennium of his first coming, counting the one thousand years of the kingdom of David as one day. The mandate to be fruitful and multiply is the basis on which every person born into the world will be judged, and those of the kingdom whose lives are spiritually unfruitful will be cast into the fire as unprofitable servants.

The Parable of the Pearl of Great Price: *"Again, the kingdom of heaven is like unto a merchant man, seeking goodly pearls; Who when he had found one pearl of great price, went and sold all that he had, and bought it" (Matt. 13:45–46).* A pearl cannot be divided and remain valuable. So is the kingdom of heaven to all who must possess it: a precious pearl that must not be divided. Knowledge of the fate of the kingdom should put a compulsion in the hearts of every believer, to ensure that he or she will not form part of that which will cause the pollution or division in the kingdom of heaven. Christ told his disciples, *"Woe unto the man by whom the son of man is betrayed."* The same woe awaits those who will hand the kingdom over to the wicked and evil generations of the world.

The fate of the kingdom does not mean that it is not to be desired by all those who fear God. Hear the ***Parable of the Hidden Treasure:*** *"Again, the kingdom of heaven is like unto treasure hid in a field; that which when a man hath found, he hideth, and for joy thereof goeth and selleth all that he hath, and buyeth that field" (Matt 13:44).* This parable tells us that we should value the kingdom and do all that is necessary to become part of it.

Whilst waiting for its appearance in the world, Israel passed through different eras of natural governments. Similarly, the Church Age is God's medium for bringing into being his everlasting kingdom and she will pass through different stages of spiritual government until iniquity is judged in the earth. It is helpful to see the overall picture from the dispensational perspective. However, in the continued struggle between good and evil *(Dan. 7:2–3)*, it is evident from the study of the kingdoms as shown in *Figure two*, that the peoples of the kingdom of heaven will be ruled over by the Devil, Lucifer, and the false prophet for a little while and this will result in the humbling of the Church. Therefore, no one should read the revelations of the prophets and be caught unprepared, for their rule will be severely torturous and oppressive.

The Kingdom of Heaven and the Riding Horsemen: Dispensationalists view the seven churches as seven periods through which the Church must pass before the millennial reign of Christ. This view is adapted for the purpose of interpreting the books of Revelation. The events surrounding the rule of the seven churches are revealed as seven seals are opened. A summary of these events and their likely dates are shown in *Figure five*. It should be noted that these dates are hypothetical in stance, although they are in agreement with the watches of each of the seven Churches. However, no one really knows the actual time of the end though we may discern the season.

The Seven Seals; the Seven Churches and the Riding Horsemen of Revelation Chapter 6

Churches/Seals/Symbols	Comments	Criticisms/Commendations
Seal One – Rev 6:1-2 The White Horse Bow and crown The Ephesus Church	Likely period: AD 001-500 Rider: the righteous generation The horse: The doctrines of truth The name means: Desired Bride	Went forth conquering to conquer Persevere and have patience; be faithful until death; to eat of the tree of life
Seal Two - Rev 6:3-4 The Red Horse A great sword Silver 1. The Smyrna Church	**Likely period**: AD 500-1000 Rider: the ungodly generation The Horse: Mixed doctrine The name means: Myrrh Known works and tribulation	To take peace from the earth Gracefully bear suffering, fear no evil Be ready for tribulation.
Seal Two – Rev 6:3-4 2. Pergamos Church	**Likely period**: AD 1000-1500 Many doctrines The name means: Marriage, adultery and compromise. Known works. Know you dwell where Satan is seated. But holds fast the name of Christ	 Tolerates false doctrine, immorality, idolatry and heresies. Keep faith. Reward is certain.
Seal Three – Rev 6:5-6 The Black Horse Pair of balances Brass The Thyatira Church	**Likely Period**: AD 1500-2000 Rider: the wicked generation Horse: evil wisdom The name means: Continued sacrifice Tolerates evil wisdom Judgement is coming	Scarcity and famine Children will be killed with death Will pass through the entire period of the great tribulation.
Seal Four – Rev 6:7-8 The Pale Horse The Sardis Church **Seal Five** – Rev 6:9-11 The Philadelphia Church	**Likely Period**: AD 2000 to Anti-Christ Rider: Death – the evil generation Horse: evil wisdom Hell followed with death The name means: Remnant A dead Church. A faithful remnant The required repentance will give birth to a vibrant Church of two witnesses The name means: Brotherly love Known works. Receives an open door. Rebellious Jews will come and worship with the Gentiles.	Power to kill one-quarter of the Earth's population Hunger: famine causes many death Sword: evil wisdom kills souls Death: disasters and diseases Beasts: terrorism and war - many die Repent: Many will die, the faithful will be clothed in white The souls of those killed during the Sardis Church Age will rest under the altar until their fellow servants are killed as they were To reveal the desired bride "Be faithful until death" These words suggest death is inevitable

Seal Six – Rev 6:12-17	Black Sun Blood Moon Stars fall from heaven: Lucifer and his angels	The Holy Spirit's restraint removed The Word of God will become judgemental
The Laodiceans Church	The name means: Judgement of the people Neither hot nor cold Those who die will rest in graves waiting for the sounding of the seventh trumpet	To be spewed out of the mouth of Christ. Those who overcome will be honoured.
Seal Seven – Rev 8:1-13	The seven trumpets given To the angels. Their sounding will reflect as things past, present and and future	The seven angels in the vision prepares to sound progressively in time, to mark the various in-gatherings.
	The seven vial judgements	Will be poured out after the Church is taken away and the Day of the Wrath of God begins.

Fig. 5. Likely period for the rule of the seven churches and the riding of the horsemen. .

Although the Church Age may have began in AD 34, Christ's learning years as a priest would have began much earlier, probably when he was five years old, as it was with Samuel, who was lent to the priesthood at the same age. At the age of twelve Christ was seen amongst doctors and lawyers professing to be about his Father's business. Hence it would be correct to begin to count the Ministry of the Church from those early years for Christ is the head of the Church and first-born of the new creation.

John spoke about things past, present, and future, therefore, some of the events relating to the churches and the riding of the horsemen would have already taken place by the time of the actual gathering of the saints around the Tabernacle in Heaven, and the dates assigned are only a basis for reasoning. At the time of John's vision, when the seventh seal was opened, the seven angels prepared themselves to sound in sequence of time. This means their assignments would be over a period of time to come, and the first trumpet judgement for the ingathering, according to this exposition, was sounded at the beginning of the rule of the Sardis Church, and after the progressive restoration movements which began in AD 1500–2000.

Dr. Bill Hamon, likens the true position of the Church restoration movements to *"a hard snowball rolling it down the steep, smooth slope of a snow-covered mountainside, it begins to get bigger and go faster. "The Protestant Movement was the making of the snowball at the top of the mountain. Then, with each restoration movement, the snowballing Church has become greater and the movements are happening faster. For instance, there was a thousand years of Dark Ages, then Church Restoration began in 1500. Three hundred years, later, in 1800, the Holiness Movement came. Then a hundred years later, in 1900, the Pentecostal Movement appeared. Fifty years later the Latter Rain/Charismatic Movement was born. And* now, since 1950, there has been a new restoration move or spiritual renewal every decade, (1000–300–100–50–10)."[1]

The Bible and dates: In many instances the Bible is consistent about dates but we struggle to link dates together because of the inadequacy of records. However, a careful and diligent search can give a rough idea of dates, and for the benefit of this exposition the genealogy of Christ as recorded in *Matthew 1:17* serves as an aid:

"So all the generations from Abraham to David are fourteen generations; and from David until the carrying away into Babylon are fourteen generations; and from the carrying away into Babylon unto Christ are fourteen generations." (See *Genesis 15:13, 16*.) *"And he said unto Abraham, Know of a surety that thy seed shall be a stranger in a land that is not theirs, and shall serve them; and they shall afflict them four hundred years; But in the fourth generation they shall come hither again: for the iniquity of the Amorites is not yet full."*

According to the above scriptures, a generation in the eyes of God's is 100 years. In the eyes of mankind, as sin increases, the years were reduced. Nonetheless, God's standard of judgement stands over generations even if years are shortened.

Abraham to David   *14 generations*
David to Babylon   *14 generations*
Babylon to Christ   *14 generations*
Christ to the renewal movement of AD 1500

> *It is interesting that Islam came into existence in AD 610 and by AD 2000 has lasted almost fourteen generations.*
> *Since past dynasties have lasted fourteen generations there is every likelihood that the time is ripe for another divine intervention from God in the history of world.*

Although none of the above figures give a conclusive guide, they do show that numbers play a significant role in events of the past; and such consistency is likely to be reflected amongst the rule of the generations to the end of time. The children of Israel under Zerubbabel returned to Jerusalem in 538 BC, which would be approximately 534 years from the reign of King Saul including the 70 years of the Babylonian exile. Also from Egypt to the end of the reign of Solomon would be 520 years, and from the divided kingdom in 930 BC to 400 years before Christ when the voice of God was silent is 530 years. Within the first five hundred years of the Church Age nearly all the Roman Empire was converted to Christianity. God promised to restore to David the years that the locusts had eaten in Joel's prophecy. For reasons that are unclear, God restores in folds and a four-fold restoration is assumed in this instance. These varied events and number of years serves as a reference point for the estimated 500 year rule of each Church; again, this is only a basis for reasoning. After AD 500 many denominations came into being plunging the church into a dark period of 1000 years, until AD 1500, when the various revival movements began and have continued since that time.

CHAPTER FIVE

AN OVERVIEW OF THE BOOK OF REVELATION

The book of Revelation will be unveiled chapter by chapter from a spiritual perspective. On the following pages, it is divided into four parts with each chapter briefly summarised to give readers an overall perspective of the book.

PART ONE: Revelation Chapters 1–12

Chapter 1 — **Introduction of Christ**

Chapters 2–3 — **Letters to the Seven Churches**

The seven Churches were all located in Asia; all seven represents seven periods through which the body of Christ will pass before the end finally comes.

Chapters 4–5 — **A Preview of the Time in the Future When:**

The Ancient of Days sits in judgement

The gathering of the saints around about the Throne

The four and twenty elders

The four fathers as the four beasts

The Lamb as Christ in the midst of the gathering

The Church as the bride of Jesus the Son

The angels as the Seraphim

Chapters 6–7   **The Travail of the Church Leading to the Great Tribulation:**
Scenes of Seals One to Six: A revelation of the Church's travail in the kingdom of heaven up to and including the time of the great tribulation through to the time the day of the Wrath of God begins: i.e. after the Laodiceans Church is called up to heaven.
The sealing of the twelve tribes: they form part of the Philadelphia Church as one of the two witnesses who will be killed for their testimony.

Chapters 8–10   **The Beginning of the Tribulation Period**
The sound of a trumpet summons John to heaven; the throne and tabernacle have been set up.
All things are now ready. Jesus promised to go and prepare a place for his bride. John saw the place in the vision and was inspired.
A revelation of the seven angels to whom authority was given to blow the trumpets at various times during the Church Age.
The Angel with the Golden Censer: he appears to be Christ our eternal High Priest. As our eternal High Priest he offers up prayer for the saints of the Laodiceans Church: those left behind after the rapture of the two witnesses, seen in the gathering around the throne in heaven.

The Seven Trumpet Judgements in Time:

The first trumpet	The reign of the Sardis Church
The second trumpet	The reign and the fall of the Philadelphia Church
The third trumpet	The fall of Lucifer to the earth
The fourth trumpet	The reign of Lucifer when a third part of the sun, moon, and stars are smitten and the days shortened
The fifth trumpet	Lucifer and the keys to the bottomless pit—locusts as demons upon the earth.
The sixth trumpet	The judgement on the river Euphrates.

Chapters 11–12

John commissioned to reveal the vision to the Church by letters.

Revelation of the fate of the two witnesses as the Church with plucked eagle's wings and the first rapture
The seventh trumpet: the resurrection of the dead in Christ and the second rapture of the Church.

The Church appears before the Throne of God in heaven.

The Dragon and the Antichrist as the Man of Sin

The Dragon resists the Son's right to his bride

The Dragon and his host cast down to earth

PART TWO: Revelation Chapters 13–14

Lucifer and the Antichrist assumes rule on earth over a one world order—after the first rapture of the Church

The rise to prominence of the Man of Sin

The rule of the Laodiceans Church

The seventh trumpet and the second rapture of the saints

The Lamb Crowned King of Kings and is given 144,000 servants who will serve him forever

PART THREE: Revelation Chapters 15–18

Seven angels given the seven last plagues to be released on Earth after the second rapture of the Church
The pouring out of the vial judgment upon the Earth as God's judgement on evil
The destruction of Jerusalem and the protection given to the remnant Jews

PART FOUR: Revelation Chapters 19–22

Scenes of the marriage supper of the Lamb

The fate of the Beast Lucifer and his false prophet

The Devil bound for a thousand years

The Millennial reign of Christ

The Great White Throne Judgement

The New Jerusalem

A New Heaven and a New Earth

PART 2
THE RULE OF THE SEVEN CHURCHES

CHAPTER SIX

THE GOVERNMENT OF THE CHURCH

The Church is the medium God is using to reap the harvest of souls in the earth. She is of the kingdom of heaven and is responsible for promoting it on earth. According to the Spirit-Filled Life Bible Commentary, the "dispensational interpretation sees the prophetic application in the letters suggesting they outline seven stages of Church history, culminating with the two end-time stages seen in Philadelphia and Laodiceans Churches."[1] Some of these chapters will be linked together according as they relate to each other. Others will be unveiled individually.

"For unto us a child is born, unto us a son is given: and the government shall be upon his shoulder: and his name shall be called Wonderful, Counsellor, The mighty God, The everlasting Father, The Prince of Peace. Of the increase of his government and peace there shall be no end on the throne of David, and upon his kingdom to order it and to establish it with judgment and with justice from henceforth even forever. The zeal of the LORD of hosts will perform this" (Isa. 9:6–7).

"And it shall come to pass in the last days, that the mountain of the LORD's house shall be established in the top of the mountains, and shall be exalted above the hills, and all nations shall flow unto it" (Isa. 2:2).

Revelation Chapter One:

Rev. 1:4–8. "John to the seven churches which are in Asia: Grace be unto you, and peace from him which is, and which was, and which is to come; and from the seven Spirits which are before his throne. And from Jesus Christ, who is the faithful witness, and the first begotten of the dead, and the prince of the kings of the earth. Unto him that loved us, and washed us from our sins in his own blood; And hath made us kings and priests to his God and his Father; to him be glory and dominion forever and ever. Amen. . . 'I am the Alpha and the Omega, the beginning and the ending,' saith the LORD, 'which is, and which was and which is to come, the Almighty.'"

"I, John, who also am your brother and companion in tribulation, and in the kingdom and patience of Jesus Christ, was on the island that is called Patmos, for the word of God and for the testimony of Jesus Christ. I was in the Spirit on the Lord's day, and I heard behind me a great voice, as of a trumpet, saying 'I am the Alpha and the Omega, the first and the last, and What you seest, write in a book, and send it to the seven churches which are in Asia. . . I am he that liveth, and was dead; and behold, I am alive for evermore. Amen; and have the keys of hell and of death. Write these things which thou hast seen, and the things which shall be hereafter'" (Rev. 1:9).

The book of Revelation is addressed to the seven churches that were in Asia at the time it was written. The letters are addressed to the Church because Christ has committed the spiritual government of the nations of the world to the keeping of the Church. The salutation at the beginning of each letter reveals much of the concern of Christ for the particular Church in its time. God is identified as the God of all ages: him that was, that is, and that is to come.

According to *Isaiah 2:2*, the spiritual government of the Church is above the governments of the World and above all leaders in the social order. And the Church submitted to Christ is God's mandated agent of change, therefore, Christ watches over his Church to perform the will of God. She is in this vantage position because of the Spirit at work in the sons of God. Spirit must have dominion over spirit, however, this can only be so when the Christian abide in fruitfulness or in the love of God.

The sevens of Revelation: The book contains a series of "sevens," beginning with the seven churches as the seven golden candlesticks. There are seven seals which when opened reveal seven scenes of things pertaining to the seven churches, some of which by the time of the actual gathering of the saints around the tabernacle in heaven, would have already taken place on earth. There are seven trumpets that will be sounded to mark the times of the various ingathering of the harvest and the judgements pertaining to each season. There are seven thunder judgements the secrets of which are sealed up. Finally there are seven vial judgements that will take place on earth after the Church is escorted to heaven by Christ.

The one who walketh in the midst of the seven golden candlesticks: The candlestick is the symbol that Christ uses to describe the Church over her seven stages. The fact that they are golden; means that at every stage there will still be people who are demonstrating the righteousness of God on earth. Christ is seen in the midst of the seven golden candlesticks, because he has promised that he will be with his Church always even unto the end of the world (See *Matthew 28:19–21*). Christ committed the government of the Church to his apostles as administrators and leaders of the righteous and ungodly generations of the kingdom of heaven, and look to them to fuel its growth conscientiously and progressively through preaching to win souls, teaching and mentoring to replicate leadership and help the ungodly conform to the image and likeness of God, so that the rule of the Church will be progressive.

The seven seals and seven trumpets hold secrets of the government of the seven churches and the seven judgements that will contribute to the establishment of the everlasting kingdom of light on earth. The seven churches are seen as benchmarks to navigate the Church Age into God's end time plan. The things at which Christ was appalled were evident in the individual church at the time. They were the roots of evil which when addressed lethargically have the disposition of gathering momentum; and as such have manifested themselves as spiritual strongholds against the Church in the kingdom of heaven. The parables of Christ underline the fact that righteousness in the kingdom will decline. At each stage of decline Christ addresses the angel or spirit of the Church. Christ reveals the identity of the seven angels as the seven stars.

"The mystery of the seven stars which thou sawest in my right hand, and the seven golden candlesticks. The seven stars are the angels of the seven churches; and the seven candlesticks which thou sawest are the seven churches"(Rev.1:20).

John 4:24 states that, "that which is born of flesh is flesh and that which is born of spirit is spirit." Since the Spirit is one, all who are of Christ in the Church are addressed as one spirit. *"There is one body and one Spirit" (Eph.4:4)*; therefore, the Church of the righteous generation is one spirit or one body.

The Father, the Son, and the Holy Ghost are united in sending these letters; they are addressed to servants because only servants who understand the past and are children of God can understand the spiritual things and the prophetic secrets that the Spirit unfolds about the present and the future. According to *2 Chronicles 7:*14; it is the righteous generation that is called upon to repent and turn away from their wicked ways, to seek healing of the land. The Father is the covenant keeping God who promised to make of Abraham a great nation and, as the Almighty God, has the power to fulfil the counsel of his will. The seven spirits before the throne of God represent the Holy Ghost as he is revealed in *Isaiah 11:2*.

The position of the Church in the kingdom of heaven means that there can only be one Church governing in strength or existing in weakness, throughout the dispensations of Grace and Judgement. It is obvious that where she fails God will also look to leaders to give an account of their stewardship. (See *Ezekiel 34:2*). If leaders were not necessary, Christ would have gone directly to the people instead of spending three and a half years developing those whom he had chosen to become leaders. Moses would have gone directly to the people in Egypt without the elders. It should not be thought of for a moment that Christ had nothing to say to the people of this or any other Church Age, because if we judge righteously, we will admit that the ways of the people of God today cannot be entirely pleasing to him. What's more, the government of the Church must continue until God changes the status quo, and because history reveals that man is always falling prey to sin, it is presumptuous to think that the present state of the Church is acceptable to God. It is, therefore, understandable that the letters are addressed to the entire body of Christ over seven periods through which the Church must pass before his return.

The seven periods may not be proportionate in length, and views vary as to the actual dates ascribed by history to each period. However, because the Church is at the core of the kingdom of heaven, the letters relate specifically to the decline of righteousness in the kingdom. The dates ascribed to each church in this study are proportionate in length, except for the churches in the days when evil rules and time will be shortened because of the judgement expected. The first letter describes the Church as having departed from her first love and counsels her to return to the path from which she has strayed, which is to be led by the Spirit as sons of God.

Christ also addressed himself by many titles to put to rest all speculations or denial about his identity. The Jews did not all accept him as the true witness; some did not even believe in the resurrection. His rejection was such that even until this day the Jews as a nation are still looking for the promised Messiah. Jesus reminded them that he is the first to be born sinless, and the last; he is the first to be born of a virgin, and the last; the first Messiah, and the last. Jesus clearly stated that he was not yet a king but the prince of the kings of the earth, that his witness is true, and that he was raised from the dead as the first begotten Son of God and the firstborn of the new creation whom God sought from amongst the people of the earth. John saw things as they were in the past, as they were with the churches then; and things which are to come pertaining to the Church; and the kingdoms of the world.

Christ addresses the churches as *"He that holdeth the seven stars in his right hand."* God promised Abraham children as stars and as dust. Angels are referred to as stars; Jesus is the Bright and Morning Star *(Gen. 15:5; Job 38; Rev. 22:16)*. Angels as stars are spirits, and the letters are written to the seven spirits or seven stars, who are the righteous generation of the seven churches, over each period *(Rev. 1:20)*.

The different titles of Jesus in the letters to the churches serve as evidence of his kingly authority. The hand symbolises the spiritual authority of Christ over the Church at any stage to execute judgement or give rewards. The power in his possession is described as being of his right hand and speaks of his total dependency on the counsel of the Holy Ghost. The events of chapters two and three are synonymous with the four horse riders of *Chapter six* of Revelation, and the opening of the first six seals reveal the activities surrounding each church in its time.

By the time John wrote the Apocalypse between AD 95 and 96, the Church Age had been in existence for approximately sixty-two years. All the apostles except John had been killed. Christians were severely persecuted and afraid of the future; they had grown weary of waiting for the return of Christ. The letters came at a time when the churches needed encouragement. Within five of the seven churches were major sins and weaknesses for which the righteousness of God demanded repentance.

Christ's message to each church addressed the unacceptable practises and conducts within it. While alluding to its strengths, the message also showed the influence of the Church as a body growing weaker and warned of its eminent decline due to the increasing degree of disobedience and false doctrines manifesting amongst them.

By implication he warned that these changes would lead to the final judgement for the corporate body if there was no repentance.

At the end of each letter there is a definite promise made to the church sealed in the name of the one who is the Alpha and Omega: this supports the general application of the letters and agrees with the fact that they are confined to definite periods in the history of the Church. For example, *Revelation 3:12* says, *"I will write upon him the name of my God, and the name of the City of my God, which is new Jerusalem, which cometh down out of heaven from my God and I will write upon him my new name."* This promise is applicable to the bride of Christ: *"And they shall see his face, and their names shall be in their foreheads"* (Rev. 22:4).

Before commencing the unveiling to give a detailed explanation of the enigma contained in the book of Revelation, the brief introduction to some chapters will guide the reader into a wholesome encounter that will enhance the understanding of the mysteries as they unfold. I will also consider some of the circumstances relative to the writer John at the time of his writing, and attempt to explain the signs that are consistent with the book of Revelation and corroborated by other parts of the scriptures. In addition, an examination of the distinguishing qualities associated with the writer will enlighten and help to capture vividly the degree of his appreciation and reactions to the vision that the Lord gave to him.

The Apostle John

John addresses himself as our brother and fellow companion in tribulation. As we are all servants of Christ in his kingdom John also speaks as one who is part of the kingdom of heaven. From the study of the gospels it appears that John was a reserved and quiet man. He rarely spoke when he was with Christ; it could also have been because of his youth. He was always in the background, observing and contemplating the profound truths of his expositions. John seemed to be a very sensitive man, one who loved Christ. He was advancing in age and no doubt deeply concerned about the preservation of the kingdom for Christ, especially since all the other apostles were already dead.

He was taken through seven scenes, showing the decline of righteousness in the kingdom of heaven, and the events of the great tribulation period through which the Church must pass, ending with the destruction of the Antichrist during the day of the wrath of God, from which the Church will be saved. The first scene in chapter four was intended to encourage and motivate him, to show him that there is indeed a glorious ending even though the Church was severely persecuted at the time. These scenes doubtless prompted him to ask many questions in the vision, and I believe some of the explanations given by the angels were in response to the thoughts of his heart.

It is understandable why he was the person Christ chose to bring the revelation of the end times: because characteristically he would listen intently and absorb the information entrusted to him for the Church. It was to this same John that Christ committed his beloved mother when he was leaving. It shows John as a caring and reliable person; a friend who had proven he was a brother in the tribulation of Christ. Here also the crucified but risen Christ was entrusting these sacred truths into his hands for his beloved bride.

This same John is identified as the person who wrote the gospel of the New Testament bearing his name. In writing the book John selected certain miracles which he calls "signs" that point to different aspects of the eternal truth of the words of God. These "signs" point to the greater spiritual miracle and to this end we can understand that the symbols used in Revelation are consistent with the meanings they convey in the other works of John. He states that he used these signs for a specific purpose, which is that the readers of his books may believe.

John was writing to a depressed, confused, bewildered, and persecuted people who, at that time, had developed cold feet concerning the return of the Lord Jesus, with doubt enveloping their minds. Some of the lessons we learn from the signs of John's writing authenticate the fact that Jesus is the Christ the Son of God, that he is the fulfilment of all the Old Testament prophecies, and the perfection of the true Son of God, the firstborn among many.

The scene in heaven recorded in *Chapter Four*, showing the victorious Church gathered around the throne of God, is a **sign** to the Church that there is definitely a new gathering of God's people around his throne as Israel once gathered around the tabernacle of his presence in the wilderness. It is a sign that should encourage the Church of all ages as she passes through one kind of tribulation or another. It is also a witness of the truth of Christ, which, if the reader believes, he will not only have eternal life but have patience to wait for his return.

John's revelation reminds those who are partners with Christ in tribulation that though the persecutions of the redeemed may last a long time, the victory is already won and the end is determined, and that the only way of resisting the continuous assaults of the enemy is by being faithful to the message of Christ. The Christian should also always be ready, like Christ, to suffer for the sake of the gospel.

The Bible is the testimony of God to his people; one chapter testifies of the other: world events do not influence what is written in the book; rather the book tells us about world events that will testify of the reality of God and the truth of the prophecies of the Bible. The people of the world cannot accurately and spiritually interpret them because they are addressed to the children of the kingdom. Christ told his disciples in *Mark 4:11* that:

"It is given to them to understand the mysteries of the kingdom." We are told in *Daniel 12:10 "Many shall be purified, and many made white, and tried; but the wicked shall do wickedly: and none of the wicked shall understand; but the wise shall understand."*

It is inadvisable to apply worldly wisdom alone to interpret something that is written by the Holy Ghost at the hands of chosen individuals and which holds truth for generation after generation. Only those filled with the Holy Ghost are open to understand the mysteries of the book of Revelation. To expect the wisdom of the world to provide correct interpretations of its contents is to trivialise the importance of the book to the Church. Paul reminds us that:

"The natural man receiveth not the things of the Spirit of God: for they are foolishness unto him; neither can he know them, because they are spiritually discerned" (*1 Cor. 2:12–14*).

Jesus Christ told his disciples many things saying, *"Now that I have told you before it comes to pass that when it comes to pass you might believe."* The unveiling of God's truths always puts an end to speculation and opens up the way for people to make informed choices. The Bible tells us about these things that when we see them come to fulfilment, those who are wise will believe the Bible and, adhere to the words of God to make sure of their eternal security in Christ.

John saw him clothed in a priestly garment with a golden girdle about his loins. *"His hair on his head was as wool and as white as snow; and his eyes were as a flame of fire."* John saw Christ always with his Church; he saw him also as a man well advanced in age, with white hair different from the Christ whom he saw ascending up to heaven in the youth of his days. This was a sign that he would tarry before his return. His garment tells of the position he now occupies in heaven. His golden girdle signifies his position of power and strength with the Father. He saw him not as the prophet he was whilst on earth, but in his new and permanent office as our eternal High Priest. Further in the book of Revelation we see Christ returning to earth as King of the kings of the Earth forever. However, as of now he is still a prince in heaven, for there can be only one King on the throne of heaven: God the King of Kings.

On his first appearance to the Jews, he was one like the Jews; no one could differentiate between him and his disciples. The book of Revelation, being a sign, speaks significantly about each event. The entire image of the Son of Man is a sign to the world. His feet of fine brass tell us that judgement is determined, and possibly indicate the time when the Church would be judged, i.e. beginning at the brass age of the kingdom. Brass can also be nearly black and depicts the colour of the Hamites who will champion the gospel just before the return of Christ: those whose "feet are 'shod' with the preparation of the gospel of peace." One may choose to agree or disagree with this concept, but the land of Ham has always provided a place of refuge for God's chosen people. Abraham sojourned in Egypt in the days of famine; Joseph was sent to Egypt probably to protect him from his brethren; Moses the deliverer was born in Egypt; Christ was sent to Egypt for protection from Herod. Furthermore, looking at the whole spectrum of Christianity on a global basis in these times, one would agree that the Hamites, the race with dark skins, are more readily displaying resounding enthusiasm and commitment towards the spreading of the gospel in these end times. This does not mean that there are no other races actively involved and committed to the work; the knowledge is significant only because it is a sign to the Church. Those whom God will bless in such a way should not think of themselves more highly favoured than any other race, but learn a lesson from the Jews; and execute the task with every commitment, grace and humility, so that no one neglects their responsibility and becomes a castaway. The Bible tells us in *Romams 11:21* that *"those who were grafted in can be grafted out again."*

The four stages of government during the Church Age: There are four stages of government during the Church Age, according to the four generations of people in the world. As I wrote this piece, it occurred to me that there is a set pattern of government since the kingdom of David. David's kingdom according to Joel, passed through four stages before the nation went into captivity. Four kingdoms ruled over Israel *"and the wind carried them away that no place was found for them."* This statement is significantly saying that God is not using natural kingdoms as his time clock for end time events. Rather he is using the four generations of the two spiritual kingdoms. If the world wants to know where we are in time they should look at the quality of the government of the Church Age. Similarly, if the Church Age wants to know where we are in time they should look back on God's dealing with the Nation Israel.

Number of years of David's kingdom before Judah went into captivity: 1050–586 = 464 years; 464 + 70 years of exile = 534 years

God promised to restore those years and he does so in the Church Age.
Joel 2:25, ends with the palmer worm which indicates there will be a restoration of the righteousness of the kingdom before the end comes. 500 x 4 = 2000 years.

God's time line for bringing Christ back is drawn. One can discern that there is a window of opportunity open to the Church for a short while to conform to Christlikeness before the release of his judgement on sin and vessels of sinfulness, beginning at the house of God—the kingdom of heaven. To bring in the government of the new Church Age, God must do a cleaning up exercise to shake out some of the deadness that is apparent in the kingdom (*Rev. 3:1–3*). We are informed that righteousness and judgement are the habitation of the throne of God. Whenever righteousness declines, judgement will bring in restoration, for when his judgements are in the earth his people will learn righteousness (*Isa. 26:9*). The government of the Church Age is at its end and this is a crucial time for the people of God to return to him with all their hearts; the Church Age, according to *Revelation 3:1–6, Revelation 7:7–8, and Revelation 8:7–8*, is ripe for judgement. If this is so with the Church, it also holds true for the world, since both are operating within the same time frame.

CHAPTER SEVEN

THE GOLDEN AGE OF THE CHURCH

This exposition looks to the Bible to provide support for any conclusions reached in the unveiling of the secrets of any of the chapters of the Book of Revelation. In an earlier chapter it was stated that the Book of Genesis holds many foundation principles revealing the pattern of God's relationship with man generation after generation. Pink rightly observes that Chapter five of Genesis is worthy of close attention for in many instances we find the phrase: *"these are the generations of..."*[1] There is another comment from Pink which throws some more encouraging light on the generation concept. He observes that *"Chapter 5 of Genesis ends with listing of the godless generation of Cain to seven generations and then closes with an account of the birth of Seth—the appointed successor of Abel and the one from whom the Messiah would come."*[2] Here we see an interesting parallel with the seven Churches. After Christ has dealt with the sinfulness of men in these seven Church Ages he will be established as king over all the Earth forever. Chapters two and three reveals the contents of seven letters to the Churches of Asia and connect them with the four riders of Chapter six and the opening of six of the seven seals. There are four governments in the Church Age and the four beasts in heaven are called to bear witnesses to the things being communicated to John for the Churches.

Revelation Chapters Two and Six:

Ephesus Church: Revelation 2:1–7, Matthew 13:8
Scenes from Seal One: Revelation 6:1–2

"And I saw when the Lamb opened one of the seals, and I heard, as it were the noise of thunder, one of the four beasts saying: Come and see".

John spoke in the past tense and this means that his revelation is certain; although, at the time of the vision, some things had yet to take place. It is believed, according to this exposition, that the spiritual rule of this first church lasted approximately 500 years, and its natural existence for much less time.

The white horse and the rider: The horse is symbolic of strength, power, or conquest.[3] John Phillips interprets horse as successful power of war.[4] The white horse represents the strength of the doctrines of truth by which the Church is empowered. It is the pure unadulterated word of God which Christ left with his Church; it represents the counsel of the Holy Ghost as the power to the Church (*Acts 1:8*). One generation is commissioned to tell the next, and where this teaching and preaching is not done according to the power of the Holy Ghost the righteous person gives way to sin and departure from the agape love of God.

"And in thy majesty ride prosperously because of truth and meekness and righteousness; and thy right hand shall teach thee terrible things. Thine arrows are sharp in the heart of the king's enemies; whereby the people fall under thee" (*Ps. 45:4–6*).

The rider of this horse is the righteous generation led by Christ as the head of the Church as she exercises dominion in the Earth. Christ as the Word of God and the counsel of God *(Rev. 19:13)* and the head of the Church goes forth with his Church to make followers of all as they demonstrate the love of God in the world consistently relying on the counsel of the Holy Ghost as the arrows to their bow. Agape love must be the motivating factor and the spirit of this church; hence, she was seen has having departed from her first love, which means men were no longer being led by the Holy Ghost as is required of sons of God (*Rom. 8:14*). Without the hearing of the counsel of the Holy Ghost, as the life more abundantly which Christ came to give, it is impossible to ride in dominion over all principalities and powers for without faith: hearing the counsel of the Holy Ghost, it is impossible to please God (*Heb. 11:6*).

The bow and crown: The rider had *"a bow and a crown"* given unto him. He went forth *"conquering to conquer."* The bow symbolizes far-reaching authority—pride, deceit, and falsehood[5]—and can relate to any of the four generations. Its far reaching authority is the great commission and spiritual authority given to the Church to go into the world and preach and teach the gospel of truth to all nations, baptizing them in the name of the Father and of the Son and of the Holy Ghost.

The bow is without an arrow because the arrow is the counsel of the Holy Ghost that gives the Christian power to live by faith and practice agape love. The righteous person who will receive the counsel of the Holy Ghost as the arrow to his bow must conquer his own insecurities and internal conflicts of unbelief and strife by submitting his thoughts and imaginations to the obedience of the word of God. He must develop his relationship with God through prayer and fasting, thus making it possible to hear the counsel of the Holy Ghost. *"Through thee will I push down my enemies. For I will not trust in my bow, neither shall my sword save me"* (*Ps. 44:5–6*). The psalmist here alludes to the fact that it is only through the counsel of the Father that he can push down his enemies. He does not trust in his kingly authority, or his own understanding of the truth, for he sees only through human eyes.

The rider also has a choice to make either to use his bow (spiritual authority) to prevail over evil and resist the devil in his walk to gain his crown; or to live in the deceitfulness of sin with his pride, lust, anxiety and lies. Ever since Eden, people have been given a chance to choose between the tree of life and the tree of the knowledge of good and evil. Thus he goes forth 'conquering to conquer.' This means the Christian must conquer internal struggles with sin before being able to conquer, or have dominion over the devil. Often times as Christians we choose the way of pride, deceit and falsehood when we seek after the riches of the world instead of living in pursuit of righteousness to triumph over sin. Counsel empowers the righteous to dominate over the challenges and adversities of life. Paul sums this up clearly for us when he says in *2 Corinthians 10:4–6*.

"For the weapons of our warfare are not carnal, but mighty through God to the pulling down of strong holds; Casting down imaginations, and every high thing that exalteth itself against the knowledge of God; and bringing into captivity every thought to the obedience of Christ. And having in a readiness to revenge all disobedience, when your obedience is fulfilled."

It is clear that the deceit and falsehood associated with the bow is demonstrated when the righteous person turns away from obeying the words of God. Jesus said in *John 15:10*, *"If ye keep my commandments, ye shall abide in my love; even as I have kept my Father's commandment and abide in his love."* Those of any church age whose righteousness endure to the end shall receive a crown of glory (*Prov. 4:9*).

The Ephesus Church

Ephesians 1:4: *"According as he has chosen us in him before the foundation of the world, that we should be holy and without blame before him in love."*

The name Ephesus means "desirable." The true Church made up of the righteous generation in any Church Age, is still the desired bride of Jesus. She has an assignment for the world which must be fulfilled; therefore, she must continue working until his return in *Mark 16:15–16*:

"Go ye into all the world and preach the gospel to every creature. He that believeth and is baptized shall be saved; but he that believeth not shall be damned."

Departed from first love: Christ called the church to remember the point at which she began (*Acts 1:8*). *"By whom also we have access by faith into this grace wherein we stand, and rejoice in hope of the glory of God . . . And hope maketh not ashamed for the love of God has been shed abroad in our hearts by the Holy Ghost which is given us"*(*Rom. 5:2-5*).

The first works is that which was required of Adam and Eve: which was to obey the counsel of the Father and *"be fruitful, multiply and replenish the earth."* Spiritual fruitfulness means *"abiding in agape love."* Agape love is a demonstration of obedience to all truths, which include obeying the logos and listening to hear and obey the counsel of the Holy Ghost.

"Woe to the rebellious children saith the LORD, that take counsel but not of me, and that cover with a covering but not of my Spirit, that they may add sin to sin. That walks to go down to Egypt, and have not asked at my mouth, to strengthen themselves in the strength of Pharaoh and trust in the shadow of Egypt. Therefore shall the strength of Pharaoh be your shame" (Isa. 30:1–2).

The counsel of Christ to the Church is revealed in *John 15:7–10*: *"If ye abide in me, and my words abide in you, ye shall ask what ye will, and it shall be done unto you. Herein is my Father glorified, that ye bear much fruit; so shall ye be my disciples. As the Father hath loved me, so have I loved you: continue ye in my love. If ye keep my commandments, ye shall abide in my love; even as I have kept my father's commandment and abide in his love. These things I have spoken unto you that my joy might remain in you, and that your joy might be full."*

A step by step analysis of what Christ said will reveal the grave consequences of not abiding in agape love:

> *If ye abide in me:* Christ said of himself, *"I am the way, the truth, and the life."* And *"Blessed are the undefiled in the way, who walk in the law of the LORD"* (Ps. 119:1). The Christian who receives a divine revelation of Christ as the representation of all the commandments, testimonies, statutes, precepts, judgements and 'word' of God as the counsel of the Holy Ghost all referred to as "the way," will immediately understand the sins of the Ephesus Church Age.

> *And my words abide in you:* Christ lived for the mandate (*Gen. 1:26–28*), and those who are of him must meditate upon it as something appointed or authorised by God for each person, saved or unsaved, which must be done by every one that is born into the world. *"I will meditate upon thy precepts and have respect upon thy ways"*(Ps. 119:15). Although this Church's work may have been good yet they had departed from the "counsel of the Holy Ghost" or turned away from God as their first love (*Deut. 7:5*), which is the first commandment; and the second is like it: *"and thy neighbour as thyself."* Christ is a living expression of a true neighbour; by loving him we can through him love our neighbours who may be hostile to us, or the sinner who desperately need salvation. Christ is both the power and wisdom of God and to reject him is to reject the counsel and wisdom and knowledge of God.

> *Ye shall ask what ye will, and it shall be done unto you:* Those who abide in Christ or in the 'way' will be led by the Spirit and are able to pray for things according to the will of God and the leading of the Spirit. The people of the Church Age as John saw them, were

no longer seen as seeking God with their whole heart *(Ps. 119:2)*; they had forgotten the counsel of the Father and his counsel (joy) was no longer abiding in many hearts *(Ps. 119:11, 16; Ecc. 2:26)*, therefore, many had departed from agape love. To depart from the "way" or the counsel Christ came to give is to render his death irrelevant. Surely this is a serious offence that calls for the repentance requested by Christ from the Churches.

"I know thy works, and thy labour, and thy patience, and how thou canst not bear them which are evil: I know you have tried them which say they are apostles and are not and has found them liars; I know thou hast borne; I know thou hast patience; I know thou hast laboured for my name's sake and have not fainted; but thou hast left thy first love—repent and do the first works" (Rev. 2:2).

There are four kinds of love by which a person can live: *"agape love that values and esteems; God's love as seen in the gift of his Son,"* or the Holy Ghost to man. It is also practiced in obedience to the absolute truth of the counsel of the Holy Ghost. The apostle were instructed to tarry in Jerusalem until they received power from on high, but they rejected the counsel of Christ and went back to fishing. Hence the question Christ asked Peter concerning agape love: *"Lovest thou me more than these?"* The reason Christ came to die for sinners, is to restore fallen man to the glory of the presence of God, so that we can receive the guidance of the Holy Ghost, as it is written :

"Thou art my hiding place; thou shalt preserve me from trouble; thou shalt compass me about with songs of deliverance. I will instruct thee and teach thee in the way which thou shalt go; I will guide thee with mine eye" (Ps. 32:7–8).

The next is *"'phileo' is to be distinguished from agape in that it is more nearly represents 'tender affection'"*[6] or brotherly love, as seen in Peter's response to Christ (*John 21:16; Titus 3:4*). Sincere *philial* love as in Peter's first response to Christ is man's reaction to the relative truths of the word of God. These two kinds of love are generally common to the children of the kingdom of light who live in obedience to the word of God. Conjugal love; or love between individuals is obedience to the personal truths of the word of God that creates a cordial environment between two or more persons in any relationship; finally, there is *eros*, which is obedience or response to sensual truths or feelings, much of which is in the world. Agape love overcomes the world, because it is not found in the world. The walk of agape love was not possible to all the people of God until after the death of Christ and the coming of the Holy Ghost.

In an environment where the Devil rules by deception and lies, sons of God need to hear the counsel of the Holy Ghost to do the work we are commissioned to do successfully. Christ confirmed this in *John 14:10–12*. However, it is possible to obey the commandments we know and continue living for a season as in the days of Israel of the Old Testament. Counsel is like a supply of oxygen to someone in a closed compartment. If the supply ceases, the person will die slowly when the oxygen in the container is spent. Therefore, the departure from love was a serious offence which, if left alone, would eventually lead to spiritual death, as in the case of Adam and Eve.

The removal of candlestick: Christ's indictment against the Ephesus Church shows that there was a definite shift in the focus from the fruitfulness of abiding in the agape love of God. After the first five hundred years the unrepentant Church was snatched out of her ruling position to reap the judgement written, which is that *"I will come unto thee quickly, and will remove thy candlestick out of his place, except thou repent."* Inevitably, after she is removed out of her place, without repentance she will continue to fall. The call to repentance addressed to the Ephesus Church is corporate and the zeal of the LORD will cause it to happen before the end comes. The call occurs several times in the history of the Church Ages and the case of the churches in Ephesus and Sardis deserve close attention because they mark two significant stages in the revelations to John: the point of departure and the point of judgement. The disheartening thing about this revelation is that there is sufficient evidence to show that the unrepentant Church will be judged before she is finally taken to heaven because of what Christ said to the Smyrna Church.

CHAPTER EIGHT

THE SILVER AGE OF THE CHURCH

The Churches of Smyrna and Pergamos: Revelation 2:8–17

These two Churches are archetype of the rule of the Medes and Persian kingdom of the Old Testament. The two letters are addressed to a Jewish and Gentile congregation respectively.

Scenes From Seal Two—Revelation 6:3–4

"And when he had opened the second seal, I heard the second beast say, Come and see. And there went out another horse that was red: and power was given to him that sat thereon to take peace from the earth, and that they should kill one another: and there was given unto him a great sword."

In Nebuchadnezzar's dream, the silver age of the Old Testament kingdoms was during the reign of the Medes and Persian kings. This seal also covers the period relating to the two churches of the silver age of the kingdom of heaven. When it was opened, John saw what would happen in the life of these Churches in the future.

The red horse and his rider: The red horse is the strength of the warped doctrinal knowledge tolerated by the church in this era. Paul spoke of the falling away from the truth, and this falling away happened between AD 300 and 500 and lasted for 1000 years to AD 1500, when Martin Luther's reformation movement began. The rider is the ungodly generation of the kingdom of heaven. ***The great sword*** is the strength of the doctrines of men as they prevail against the true doctrines of the kingdom; and the power sin gave to this generation to take "peace" from the earth - *John 14:27*

"Peace I leave with you, my peace I give unto you, not as the world giveth, give I unto you."

"For the word of God is quick and powerful and sharper than any two edged sword, piercing even to the dividing asunder of the soul and spirit and the joints and marrow, and is a discerner of the thoughts and intent of the heart" (*Heb. 4:12*).

The counsel of the Holy Ghost as the word of God gives life; it convicts the world of sin and of righteousness and this does not always bring peace except through obedience. Red is the colour of blood, symbolising bloodshed and judgement; or the sin of humanity as seen in the eyes of God (*Isa. 1:18*). The assignment of the rider is definitely to take the word of God and the knowledge of Jesus out of the Church and the hearts of generations. According to A. W. Tozer:

"To accept Christ it is necessary that we reject whatever is contrary to him . . . Our Lord calls men to follow him but he never made the way look easy. Sometimes he said things to his disciples or prospective disciples that we today discretely avoid repeating when we are trying to win men to Christ . . . If any man will come after me let him deny himself and take up his cross and follow me. . . Think not that I am come to send peace on earth: I came not to send peace but a sword."[1]

The sword of the Spirit, as the counsel of the Holy Ghost, cuts sin away from the soul. The great sword given to this rider is not from God but is the evil doctrine of the devil by which "they should kill one another"—one dead soul killing another soul with words that lead to death. These corrupt doctrines eventually led to the falling away which Paul warned of. There were those false teachers in early times who taught that the resurrection had passed and even now there are still those amongst the Jews who have not accepted Christ as the Messiah. The indictment against the two churches that are of the silver age concerns the kind of teachings that seduced the minds of the people of God into idolatry and immorality.

There is a popular belief that the Church will not go through the great tribulation: this is the counsel of men. The words spoken by Christ against the Church of Smyrna; state that the Church must have tribulation ten days. The number "ten" speaks of entirety or wholeness. (See *Revelation 2:10*). God warns of imminent judgement to give people time to repent; or conversely, to drink progressively from the judgement cups, viz-à-viz the cup of the Lord's right hand, the cup of astonishment and desolation, the cup of fury, the cup of trembling and finally, the cup of his wrath. In six of these church ages there will be those who will drink progressively from these cups until after the rapture of the saints of the Laodiceans Church. According to *1 Corinthians 10:21*: *"Ye cannot drink the cup of the Lord's table, and of the table of devils."* Therefore some things revealed at the opening of the second seal will not be completely fulfilled until the time of the Church of Pergamos, for both are symbolised by silver, or the river Gihon.

The Smyrna Church: Revelation 2:8–11

"I know thy works, and tribulation, and poverty, (but thou art rich) and I know the blasphemy of them which say they are Jews, and are not, but are of the synagogue of Satan. Fear none of those things which thou shalt suffer: behold, the devil shall cast some of you into prison, that ye may be tried; and ye shall have tribulation ten days; be thou faithful unto death, and I will give thee a crown of life" (Rev. 2:9–10).

Biblical history confirms that the Smyrna Church was located in a city commercially prosperous and wealthy with a large Jewish population many of whom were apostates. She was a financially poor church and was undergoing great persecution for her faith, which she was encouraged to bear gracefully and be faithful even unto death to earn her crown of life.

Sometimes when Christ spoke to his disciples, he spoke of the end of a thing, even though it could be interpreted as relating to the present. For example, he spoke of a time when angels will be visibly ascending and descending upon the son of man. Since this was not seen at his first coming, it can only be relative to his millennial reign. *"Be faithful unto death"* can be taken as a reference to the natural passing of the soul out of this world or the time of the church of the two witnesses because Christ already knew their fate according to this exposition.

The specific problem of this church is that she had those with her who were of the 'synagogue of Satan.' Naturally, she went through ten intensive periods of persecution by the Roman Emperors between AD 64 and 340. Willmington says: *"The instigators of the persecution were apostate Jews who were in reality instruments of Satan."*[2] However, the thrust of this unveiling is that where there is a natural context there is also a spiritual one; and the things relative to the churches were the roots of evil which, given the slightest chance, would often repeat themselves. In much the same way, the Jews were betrayed by their apostate brethren, so also the righteous generation of the kingdom of heaven will be betrayed by their ungodly brethren, for it is the same devil that is at work in the world seeking to destroy the righteousness of the believer.

Christ introduced himself as the one who was dead and yet alive; by so doing he reassured the Jewish Christians of his resurrection to dispel rumours that there was no resurrection from the dead (*Matt. 28:14*). The reassurance is also to the present day Church: though some may die for the cause of the gospel, because he is alive, all will live. *"Ye that over-cometh shall not be hurt with the second death"* (*Rev. 2:11*). It was not unusual for churches in those days to be poor, yet poverty can be experienced in the natural or spiritual. This church was poor in the natural sense but rich in faith. *"Hath not God chosen the poor of this world, rich in faith, and heirs of the kingdom which he has promised to them that love him?"* (*James 2:5*).

The name Smyrna means myrrh. Myrrh was used for many things in the scriptures: for purification of women and for embalming. It was one of the components of the anointing oil. The name speaks of the mixture of things happening to the Church: purification and sleepiness; it could also mean that this church is still the anointed of God; and the power of the Spirit was still being experienced amongst them to a measure even though they existed amongst those who were agents of Satan. The parable of the wheat and the tares would reflect what was happening in this Church:.

"The kingdom of heaven is likened unto a man which sowed good seed in his field: But while men slept, his enemy came and sowed tares among the wheat, and went his way. . . Let both grow together until the harvest: and in the time of harvest I will say to the reapers, Gather ye together first the tares, and bind them in bundles to burn them: but gather the wheat into my barn." (Matt. 13:24–30).

The parable speaks of a time when men would sleep and alludes to the fact that the unwholesome situation of righteousness and ungodliness existing together in the kingdom of heaven will continue until the time of the final judgement but the fate of the unrepentant Church is already determined. (See *Revelation 2:10*.)

The promised crown of life is not only for the few persons of this Church but for all who will gracefully bear suffering and live unto Christ throughout the Church Age. Two things in this verse support the application of this letter to the global Church over different periods: the word "ye" refers to the entirety, as does the ten-day tribulation. The number ten is used in reference to an entire nation, or an entire period. In Abraham's intercession for Sodom he stopped at ten. From generation to generation God warns of judgement, but he does not execute the judgement determined until his people become as "another generation." This means that he judges during the time that wickedness rules, but executes his judgement in the day that evil takes over; he begins with the people of the kingdom of heaven first because judgement must begin at the house of the Lord.

The Church of Pergamos: Revelation 2:12–17.

Scenes From Seal Two cont'd. (See Revelation 6:3–4.)

"I know thy works, and where thou dwellest even where Satan's seat is . . . But I have a few things against thee, because thou hast there them that hold the doctrine of Balaam, who taught Balac to cast a stumbling block before the children of Israel . . . So thou also them that hold the doctrine of the Nicolaitanes, which thing I hate. Repent or else I will come unto thee quickly and will fight against them with the sword of my mouth . . . to him that overcometh will I give to eat of the hidden manna, and will give him a white stone" (Rev. 2:13–17).

"Whosoever transgresseth, and abideth not in the doctrine of Christ, hath not God. He that abideth in the doctrine of Christ, he hath both the Father and the Son" (2 John 1:9).

Biblical history reveals that Pergamos was the oldest city in the province of Rome and the official seat of the Roman Government. The name means marriage, adultery, and compromise. Adultery can be spiritual or natural: spiritual adultery is departure from the truth. The scriptures quoted above confirm the falling away of the Church from the doctrines of the kingdom and the rejection of the work of the word of God and the Spirit of God in the lives of its people. When the nation of Israel departed from God she was referred to as an adulterous nation. The difficulties experienced by the Church of Pergamos were mainly connected with the religious system known as "Emperor worship," which the Christians refused to take part in. Antipas, one of their members was the first Christian to be martyred there. The message from Christ was that he would judge those who denied him through idol worship or persecution of his saints; but that he would reward those who were faithful even until death. This was not a new counsel to believers. The Apostle Paul wrote in *2 Timothy 3:10–13*:

"But thou hast fully known my doctrine, manner of life, purpose, faith, longsuffering, charity, patience. Persecutions, afflictions, which came unto me at Antioch, at Iconium, at Lystra; what persecutions I endured: but out of them all, the Lord delivered me. Yea, and all that will live godly in Christ Jesus shall suffer persecution. But the evil men and seducers shall wax worse and worse, deceiving and being deceived."

This letter came as a gentle reminder to the Church that it is an honourable thing to be counted worthy to suffer for the sake of the gospel. The fact that Christ began to teach that the Church should be faithful until death should remind Christians in every age that there is a time in the future when all the words of the prophets will be fulfilled and God is faithful to deliver those who trust in him and live according to his timing.

The one who has the sharp sword with two edges: In this scene Christ spoke as the one who has the word of eternal life.

"Let us labour therefore to enter into that rest. Lest any man fall after the same example of unbelief. For the word of God is quick and powerful and sharper than a two edged sword, piercing even to the dividing asunder of soul and spirit, and joints and marrow, and is the discerner of the thoughts and intent of the heart" (Heb. 4:11–12).

Christ spoke to remind the Church of the need to hold fast to the truth of the word of God. He also spoke as the one who would execute judgement by the words of his mouth on those who persecute his saints: *"But with righteousness shall he judge the poor, and reprove with equity the meek of the earth: and he shall smite the earth with the rod of his mouth, and with the breath of his lips shall he slay the wicked"* (Rev. 1:16–17, 2:16, 19:15; Isa. 11:4).

Dwells where Satan is seated: The city was known as the seat of Satan because it was also the center of the worship of Asclepius the god of healing symbolised by a serpent which Christians regarded as satanic; it was said that the church of Smyrna had those among their number who claimed they were Jews but were of the synagogue of Satan. Spiritually, this church knowingly tolerated false doctrine and had not dissociated herself from the ungodliness that was around her in the world. The corporate repentance required of the Ephesius Church is reiterated to this Church, which means the judgements against the Church as the body of Christ are accumulative.

The hidden manna: The promise to this church of the hidden manna refers to the restoration of the counsel of the Holy Ghost from which the Ephesus Church had departed. (See *Psalm 32:8*). However, the restoration will not be made until the corporate repentance required of the Ephesus Church is made. In any generation it is the counsel of God that will withstand iniquity. When sinfulness of man is great in the world God withholds his counsel from the people as it was in the days of Eli. In the counsel of the Holy Ghost there is life and if it is not withheld people will "eat" of it and live on in a perpetual life of sinfulness. When the counsel is withdrawn, the life will slowly ebb away, to produce repentance and judgement. (See *Genesis 3:22*). For the same reason God will also withhold his counsel from the hearts of many in the Church Age; releasing only that which is necessary to keep the body until the fullness of his time. *Amos 8:11* warned that there would be a time when there would be a famine for hearing of the word of God. Even in the present day church, although the word of God is with us as the logos, yet the direct revelation from God coming to the Church is restricted to a few chosen individuals; there is also a prevailing general lack of understanding even of the logos, which is most times applied to individual lives, without its general application to the Church as a movement of God's people.

"The people that walketh in darkness have seen a great light: They that dwell in the land of the shadow of death, upon them hath the light shined. Thou hast multiplied the nation, and not increased the joy: they joy before thee according to the joy in harvest, and as men rejoice when they divide the spoil" (Isa. 9:2–3).

God sent his Son to restore humanity to the glory of his presence where the counsel of the Holy Ghost can be received as the joy of the LORD or the hidden manna that gives strength to dominate over evil. There will be full restoration when God divinely intervenes to reinforce the integrity of his word, which will be in the time of the rule of the militant church. Thereafter Christ's eternal reign will eventually bring freedom from sin and usher in the universal rule of the Kingdom of David under Christ, when once again there will be unlimited access to the tree of life, as the counsel of the Father.

The things that will occupy the minds of the people in the world around the church of the age are fornication, prostitution, idolatry, false religions, sexual immorality, and the love of money. These things will be manifested in all kinds of vices that affect people's way of life. The parables of *Matthew 13* reflect the activities of the seven churches; and in them Christ was already revealing what the fate of the kingdom would be because of the failure of the Church. The parable of the mustard seed reveals some things about the kingdom in which the Church exists:

"Another parable put he forth unto them, saying: The kingdom of heaven is like unto a grain of mustard seed, which a man took, and sowed in his field: which indeed is the least of all seeds but when it is grown, it is the greatest amongst herbs, and becometh a tree, so that the birds of the air come and lodge in the branches thereof" (Matt. 13:31–32).

The kingdom began on a small scale with a handful of people, including the twelve apostles, but it gathered momentum as more and more people converted to become the branches of this great tree. Birds symbolise good or evil spirits and therefore the "birds of the air" are not necessarily good birds. The parable of the net suggests that the kingdom gathers a mixed multitude of people many of whose minds are not perfect towards God. Those with imperfect hearts have roots of evil in them and are enemies of the kingdom (*1 Tim. 6:10*). Notwithstanding, the one with the sharp sword with two edges has the ability to reward good and pronounce judgement on evil.

The call to repentance: This Church was called to repent, even for the things happening in the world around her, for she has been given the responsibility to bring Christ to the world, and only the Church can repent to cause healing in the land (*2 Chron. 7:14*). Christ told Adam that the earth would bring forth thorns and thistles: wickedness and evil. It is therefore up to the righteous to do something about the wicked and evil generations because of their relationship with God, but if ungodliness persists amongst them, like thorns among the shoots of genuine plants, the life of God can slowly be choked out of many souls. The sharp sword in the mouth of Christ means he will eventually decree the judgement determined on the unrepentant Church.

CHAPTER NINE

THE BRASS AGE OF THE CHURCH

In Chapter *1:14–15* Christ appeared as the one who executes judgement *(John 5:22)*, with feet as fine brass. Brass is a symbol of judgement. In the history of the Jews, their sinfulness was usually judged in the third generation and judgement executed in the fourth. In the day of Solomon as the third generation king, his kingdom was judged, but judgement was executed in the day of his son. When he gave the letter for this Church he also appeared with eyes like flame of fire and feet like fine brass; and his counsel to this third generation Church in essence was to prepare for judgement: *"Behold I will cast her . . . and them that commit adultery with her into great tribulation."*

The Thyatira Church: Revelation 2:18–29.

Scenes of Seal Three: Revelation 6:5–6

"I know thy works, and charity, and service, and faith, and thy patience, and thy works; and the last to be more than the first. Notwithstanding I have a few things against thee, because thou sufferest that woman Jezebel, which calleth herself a prophetess, to teach and to seduce my servants to commit fornication, and to eat things sacrificed unto idols. And I gave her space to repent of her fornication; and she repented not. Behold I will cast her into a bed and them that commit adultery with her into great tribulation, except they repent of their deeds" (Rev. 2:19–20).

"And when he had opened the third seal, I heard the third beast say, Come and see. And I beheld, and lo a black horse; and he that sat on him had a pair of balances in his hand. And I heard a voice in the midst of the four beasts say, a measure of wheat for a penny and three measures of barley for a penny; and see thou hurt not the oil and the wine" (Rev. 6:5–6).

In this vision the third beast speaks. He invites John to come and bear witness to the continued fall of the Church. The fall began in the Ephesus Church Age through to the Smyrna and Pergamos Church Ages. John is called to bear witness to the judgement pronounced on the Church as Ezekiel was called to bear witness to the wickedness of the elders of Israel before the time of God's judgement (*Ezek. 1:15–16*).

The complaint—suffers Jezebel to teach: Jezebel of the Old Testament was the Gentile wife of King Ahab. She successfully introduced idolatry and immorality in Israel. See comments on this and other doctrines in chapter fifteen. Although the things spoken about this church are somehow encouraging, it is obvious that the adultery committed by the former churches has not been repented of and the doctrines of the times are still tolerated.

The black horse and his rider: The black horse is the false doctrine tolerated by the Church Age. The rider is the wicked generation of the world as they wield influence over the Church. *The pair of balances:* In the day of Daniel, Belshazzar was said to have been weighed in the balance and found wanting. This is the position with the church of this age. The pair of balances in the hand of the rider are those with which the people of God ought to weigh themselves; those who do not take heed and stand strong will give way to sin and the influence of the wisdom of the world and will be found wanting.

A measure of wheat for a penny; and three measures of barley for a penny: The prophet Amos used the fruit of the fig tree to speak prophetically concerning the Nation Israel. Here also Christ uses the product common to both Old and New Testament saints to speak prophetically into the Church Age. Barley and wheat are symbols of words. In the Old Testament wheat was regarded as a very valuable product, three times as valuable as barley. Wheat was cultivated abundantly in Egypt and Palestine. Referring to his death and resurrection Christ said, *"Except a corn of wheat falls to the ground and dies it abideth alone."* Abraham was as a *"grain of wheat"* taken out of Mesopotamia. The particular specie of wheat referred to in the passage is the one with many heads; which says something about the lineage of Abraham for it was said that kings would be of his lineage. *"A measure of wheat for a penny,"* insinuates that in the time when the wicked generation rule in the world, during the age of the Thyatira Church onwards, many will preach the gospel to make a living, but not because they are committed to its cause. She *"suffers Jezebel as evil wisdom to seduce the servants of God."*

Barley on the other hand, is a hairy and bristling thing with rough prickly beard: a symbol of the wicked generation, or corrupt doctrine. Barley was considered inferior to wheat. It was used to feed asses and a primary food of Egypt *(Exod. 9:31)*, a type of the world. The word "ass" is a symbol that describes the ungodly generation *(Job 1:14)*. As food, barley was held in low esteem and was believed to be a symbol of poverty. Three measures of barley for a penny: insinuates that over the same period the gospel preached in the Church Age will produce more sinners than righteous; and love for money will be very much a part of the problem of the Church Age. A time of economic hardship when, a person's whole salary can scarcely feed the household, will eventually develop, resulting in famine in many parts of the Earth. *See thou hurt not the oil and wine:* The people of the church are carriers of the anointing and the Holy Ghost which produce a great people and a strong who must continue to work until the Philadelphia Church produces the greatest harvest of souls the world has ever witnessed.

A penny was considered as one man's wage *(Matt. 20:10)*. The obvious conclusion to be drawn from the statement concerning the wheat and the barley is that in this Church Age, the emphasis for the preaching of the gospel would be on money and not on love for God; and the true gospel will be thrice outweighed by the false. Comparing the following two parables of the kingdom of heaven to which the Church belongs with what was revealed when the third seal was opened in the vision one will agree that they correspond with the experiences of the Thyatira Church Age *(AD 1500–2000)*.

"He answered and said unto them, He that soweth the good seed is the Son of Man; the field is the world; the good seed are the children of the kingdom; but the tares are the children of the wicked one; the enemy that sowed them is the devil; the harvest is the end of the world; and the reapers are the angels" (Matt. 13:37–39).

"Again the kingdom of heaven is like unto a net, that was cast into the sea, and gathered of every kind: Which when it was full, they drew to shore, and sat down, and gathered the goods into vessels, but cast the bad away. So shall it be at the end of the world: the angels shall come forth, and sever the wicked from among the just. And shall cast them into the furnace of fire: there shall be wailing and gnashing of teeth" (Matt. 13:47–50).

The kingdom of heaven began with good seeds of the word of God and produced righteous men and women but as time went by the other seeds were sown introducing tares amongst the wheat, and they began to wield influence in the kingdom. The second parable definitely confirms that this unwholesome situation will be found also in the Leodecian Church Age the time of the end of all things when the angels will be commissioned to sift from amongst the righteous those who will be cast into the furnace of fire. Hence the judgement pronounced on the Church in this Age will not take place until much later in time.

The Thyatira Church Age

The name Thyatira means continual sacrifice, and speaks of this Church as a body of people who never give up. The two symbols associated with Christ in this part of the vision are: eyes like flames of fire, and feet as fine brass, which speak of judgement. In accordance with the judgement pronounced on the former church, *"Repent or else I will come unto thee quickly and will fight against them with the sword of my mouth."* Christ spoke as the one who will pronounce the judgement determined when wickedness rules. The prophet Isaiah seems to have something to say about this Church Age: *"A voice of noise from the city, a voice of noise from the temple, a voice of the LORD that rendereth recompense to his enemies. Before she travailed, she brought forth; before her pain came, she was delivered of a man child"* (Isa. 66:6).

According to Hamon: the restoration movement of AD 1500 restored to the Church the gospel of 'repentance from dead works' and this gospel endured for a period of 300 years before the second was restored to Church Age. Although her work was found to be better than those of the last two churches before her, still the corporate repentance required of the Ephesus Church was not made. Nevertheless the restoration movement of AD 1500 was a great noise from the Church; with Martin Luther's *"The just shall live by faith'* movement. Individually each person's body should be a temple of the Holy Ghost. There was a corresponding noise from individuals in the restoration periods with renewal of spiritual gifts to the Church Age, such as the evidence of speaking in tongues, healings, and miracles.*"Though I speak with the tongues of men and of angels and have not **charity**, I am become as a sounding brass or a tinkling cymbal" (1 Cor. 3:1).* Many people were drawn to the Church movement because the healing and miracle experience, but not out of a sincere desire to conform to Christ-likeness or even love for God. Since the genuine return of the entire body, to the agape love of God was not achieved in the Thyatira Church Age, it means the judgement pronounced would be executed in the Sardis Church Age as a *"noise from the one who renders recompense to his enemies."*

Hamon comments that: "Historically, the protestant movement came into existence at that time because Martin Luther, John Knox, Thomas Cranmer, and various others fought for and established the right to be churches separate from Catholicism. By restoration, the movement came into existence because the Holy Spirit initiated it for the Church. The Protestant churches brought back into the Church the revelation, proper application and re-establishment of the first doctrine of Christ – repentance from dead works, and the teaching that we are justified by the mercy and grace of Jesus Christ through faith, and nothing else.[1]

This is the time the wicked generation of the kingdom of darkness, symbolised by the leopard or the river Hiddekel, begins to influence the lives of the people of the kingdom of heaven. Both symbols are identical in meaning: "rapid" and "swift." Undoubtedly, this indicates that wickedness of evil wisdom will swiftly influence the kingdom and righteousness will rapidly decrease. Consequently, this Church is judged in the Bronze Age, but the judgement *"I will kill her children with death,"* will greatly manifest by the next Sardis Church Age *(Rev. 3:1–3)*. This is not the first time God has judged a nation or even a person without ending the tenure of service abruptly. In the case of King Saul, God had rejected him, and though David was anointed as king, yet Saul was allowed to continue until his sin was full. Also in the case of the kingdom of Judah, the sign God gave to King Ahaz of the rejection of the kingdom of Judah was not to Ahaz alone but a prophetic sign to the house of David that God would fulfil his promise to David in the Church Age *(Isa. 7:11–16)*. In the days of Ahaz God knew that the nation was already beyond remedy and judgement was pronounced; and the rejected kingdom would be restored in the Church Age *(Matt. 3:1–3)*. Even though Judah was judged at that time; and was seen to have recovered some sanity during the reign of King Josiah, it was years later before she was carried away captive to Babylon. Here again history seems to be repeating itself as the Church awaits the fullness of time when she will go through the great tribulation. Paul warns the Church of the danger of unbelief and departure from the ways of God as he reminds us of the similar failure of the Jews and the consequences in *Hebrews 3:10–13*:

"Wherefore I was grieved with that generation and said they do err in their hearts, and they have not known my ways. So I swore in my wrath they shall not enter into my rest. Take heed, brethren, least there be any of you with an evil heart of unbelief, in departing from the living God."

Albeit, there is something encouraging about this church: her *"love, service, faith and patience are greater than at first."* One cannot deny that the various restoration movements are responsible for these changes. Nevertheless, the human ideology that has replaced the truth will slowly kill the souls of many Christians and many will have their names erased from the book of life (*Rev. 3:1–6*). The great commission given to the Church is to preach the gospel to the ends of the world according to the power of the Holy Ghost. This programme cannot be altered; and wherever there is a departure the judgement of God must run its course. The judgement of the great tribulation is, therefore, pronounced upon the entire body of Christ, but will not begin just yet.

The promise of the Morning Star: The promises to this Church will be fulfilled after the corporate repentance required has been made. It should also be understood as a warning to get ready for the return of Christ.

"And I will kill her children with death; and all the churches shall know that I am he which searcheth the reins and hearts: and I will give unto everyone of you according to your works. But unto you I say, and unto the rest in Thyatira, as many as have not this doctrine, and which have not known the depths of Satan, as they speak; I will put upon you none other burden. But that which you have already hold fast till I come . . . And he that overcometh, and keepeth my works unto the end, to him will I give power over the nations" (*Rev. 2:22-26*).

The judgement pronounced means that the Church Age will go through the entire period of the great tribulation. Although the judgement is pronounced and is certain, it will not begin at the Thyatiran Church in view of what Christ said in his admonition (*Rev. 2:24*). The righteous remnant of this Church Age has enough to cope with just resisting the evils of the day, but there is still the warning that her children will be killed. The person who endures to the end will be given power over nations. This implies that judgement will be individual as well as corporate, and that there is yet a time when the militant church will exercise authority over the nations of the world, when the counsel of the Holy Ghost as the hidden manna is restored. They will also endure to become the bride of Jesus who is the Morning Star.

CHAPTER TEN

THE IRON AGE OF THE CHURCH

In this segment, the spiritual and natural activities within and surrounding the last three churches are revealed. From a dispensational perspective, and according to this exposition, the tenure of this Church Age is not expected to be as long as others before, because the days are evil. The fourth beast calls John to come and see the secrets of seal four. The great tribulation will begin during this Church Age. The counsel to the previous Church was "be watchful, judgement is coming."

The Church of Sardis: Revelation 3:1–6

Scenes from Seal Four: Revelation 6:7-8
The Time of the Sounding of the First Trumpet: Revelation 8:1-7

"*And I looked and behold a pale horse: and his name that sat on him was Death and Hell followed with him. And power was given unto them over the fourth part of the earth, to kill with sword, and with hunger, and with death, and with the beast of the earth*" (Rev. 6:8).

This is also the iron age of the kingdom and the archetype of the Roman Empire. The rider is Death. He is one of the spirits of the devil; he works together with deceit and is the last enemy to be destroyed. Death and hell are given power over one quarter of the earth to kill the souls of many through deception and lies, and hold them bound in death (*Rev. 3:1–3*). Famine will cause hunger and many will die of starvation; there will be terrorism and war instigated by evil human beings as the beasts of the earth. This will cause great upheaval in many countries of the world.

"And unto the angel of the church in Sardis write these things saith he that hath the seven Spirits of God, and the seven stars; I know thy works that thou hast a name that thou livest, and art dead. Be watchful and strengthen the things which remain, that are ready to die; for I have not found thy works perfect before God. Remember therefore how thou hast received and heard, and hold fast, and repent. If therefore thou shalt not watch, I will come on thee as a thief and thou shalt not know what hour I will come upon thee. Thou hast a few names even in Sardis which have not defiled their garments; and they shall walk with me in white; for they are worthy. He that overcometh, the same shall be clothed in white raiment, and I will not blot out his name out of the book of life, but will confess his name before my Father, and before his angels"(Rev. 3:1–6).

To come as a thief refers to an unexpected historical judgement not the second coming.[1] The various scriptures that relate to this period seem to agree that this will be a very trying time for the Church. She is about to reap the accumulative judgement pronounced upon her in *Revelation 2:10*. Moved out of her ruling position, she has reached the end of the generation trail and Christ will fight against her with the sword of his mouth, as the judgement pronounced is now being implemented, *"which is to kill her children with death."* This is the mission of the rider of the fourth horse and a time of judgement for the Church. Phillips comments that: "The beasts are closely linked with pestilence caused by destructive creatures such as rats. *Rats menace human food supplies which they both devour and contaminate, especially in the more underdeveloped countries which can least afford to suffer loss.*"[2] However, in view of what is revealed when the fifth seal was opened: souls of those who were slain for the testimony which they held, the beasts are more than just rats: but human agents as the sword of the LORD (*Ps. 17:13*). Their activities are likely to take the form of terrorism in resistance to the Church and the word of God. Rats, pestilence and diseases will kill whoever eats or comes in contact with contaminated food and the infectious diseases carried by rodents, irrespective of their belief or religious inclinations.

Be watchful, repent and strengthen the things which remain that are about to die: Christ addresses the church as the risen Son of God who is also weighing the activities of the seven churches in his hands; hence his complaint: *"I know thy works, that thou hast a name that thou livest and art dead."* The people that despise the good wisdom from above in favour of the wisdom of the world will be deceived into death. The wisdom from above gives order and purpose to life and because the new creation has access to the seven spirits of the LORD to teach, instruct and guide, she should be operating in the more abundant life given to the saints in Christ. As children of God we have the ability to discern good from evil and therefore the next counsel to the church is extremely important.

Things are sometimes referred to as "souls" (*Luke 1:5*). Christ counsels the righteous generation of this Church Age to be watchful, repent, and strengthen the souls amongst them that are ready to die. To be watchful means to be prayerful and this kind of prayer would require humility to acknowledge one's faults, repentance, and supplication for restoration of the counsel of the Holy Ghost as the promised hidden manna (*2 Chron. 7:14*). The two vital components that keep the Church alive are: praying unceasingly and ever increasing knowledge of the will of God. The church that rejects the wisdom of God cannot pray effectually; and the fact that they are asked to remember what they have heard confirms that the doctrines have now developed into strong-holds against the truth. Christ gave similar counsel to his disciples the night on which he was betrayed. *Matthew 26:40–41: "Could ye not watch with me one hour? Watch ye and pray that ye enter not into temptation."* Again, he said in *Luke 18:1 "men ought always to pray and not to faint."*

He that hath the seven Spirits of God and the Seven Stars: The message is from Christ, the perfect specimen of the sons of God who lives by the seven Spirits of the Father; this is the way he expects the church of this age as sons of God to live. The various renewal movements that have affected the Church Age from AD 1500 have seen the various gospels of *Hebrew 6* restored to the Church. According to Dr. Bill Hamon, the last doctrine to be restored and which concerns the church of this age is *"resurrection from the dead."*[3] The number seven speaks of perfection which means that this Church is sufficiently equipped with the seven Spirits of the Father to become a living expression of the manifestation of the sons of God on earth. Yet she is still handicapped and encumbered with dead works because the days are evil. Willmington, quoting McGee, writes about Protestantism: *"The great truths which were recovered in the Reformation have been surrendered by a compromising Church."*[4] There is no reason for this church to fail because angels that excel in strength live by the seven characteristics of the Holy Ghost. The seven stars are the righteous generation of the seven churches who must live by the seven characteristics of the Holy Ghost. This is a mature church over which Christ is both the "Lion" and the "Lamb."

The Sardis Church

The name Sardis means remnant: *"Thou hast a few even in Sardis which have not defiled their garments."* Sardis was noted for its great wealth. The message suggests that during her rule she will be seriously compromised in her quest for the wealth and materialism of the world around her. And because the evil generation of the world is influencing the activities of the church in the kingdom, genuine believers are few. If Christ should come now, not many believers will make it to heaven. Divine intervention at this stage of the Church will be necessary to protect the integrity of the words of Christ when he said the gates of hell as wickedness and evil, or thorns and thistles, will not prevail against his Church.

"He that over-cometh the same shall be clothed in white raiment, and I will not blot his name out of the book of life, but I will confess his name before my Father, and before his angels" (*Rev. 3:5*).

"When the righteous turneth from his righteousness, and committeth iniquity, he shall even die thereby" (*Ezek. 33:18*).

If the Church takes note of the warnings of Christ to return to godliness, then there will be fewer casualties and many will be purified and prepared for the next stage of the Church Age, but many will also die. The souls of the righteous who will die in this period were seen under the altar in heaven when the fifth seal was opened.

The sounding of the first trumpet: The first trumpet marking the beginning of the ingathering will be sounded in this Church Age. The first six trumpets will not be heard on earth, but will alert heaven that the time of God's judgement on the earth and the beginning of the ingathering is about to take place.

"The first angel sounded, and there followed hail and fire mingled with blood, and they were cast upon the earth: and the third part of trees was burnt up, and all green grass was burnt up" (Rev. 8:7).

Hail and fire speaks of judgement. Christ confirms his position as the one who is empowered to execute God's judgement on unrighteousness. He referred to this time as "the beginning of sorrows." John bore witness of these things in a vision, but by the time of the actual gathering of the saints around the heavenly tabernacle takes place some of these things will be in the past. For example, the first three or four trumpets would have already been sounded.

Trees and green grass: These are symbolic references to people. Trees are symbols of the children of the kingdom of heaven. There are good trees and corrupt trees according to the scriptures:

"Even so every good tree bringeth forth good fruit; but a corrupt tree bringeth forth evil fruit" (Matt. 7:17).

"Now also the axe is laid unto the root of the trees: every tree therefore which bringeth not forth good fruit is hewn down and cast into the fire" (Luke 3:9). And where the tree falls, there it will lie forever.

Grass refers to sinful mankind. There is clear evidence that the mixed doctrines of the present age cannot bring to pass the plan of God for a militant church. There has to be a return to Christ-likeness and the *"hail and fire"* of this age means the fire will also have a purifying effect on many souls. God will not use the old nature of the flesh to do that which he proposed to be accomplished in the new nature of the spirit. If the revelation given about this period was simply to tell the Church what will happen to the vegetation then humanity would seem to be insignificant in the scheme of things. The people of the world are as the "grass," and one quarter of the world's population will be killed. Many Christians (as "trees") will die, and some will have their names erased from the Book of Life.

The famine in many parts of the world at this time requires that the Church be discerning of the deceit of the devil so that the corporate responsibility to the poor and needy does not becloud her true responsibility of wining souls for the kingdom. The scripture of *Matthew 25:31–46* must be looked at in its spiritual context as well as in the physical. Sheep and goats are symbols of the righteous and ungodly generations respectively. Christ's response to the rich young ruler shows that, although he had done all the things to satisfy the needs of the poor and needy, and was not lacking in any of his social responsibilities, nevertheless he had done nothing to inherit eternal life. Christ gives the following counsel to the Church in *Matthew 24:6–9:*

"And ye shall hear of wars and rumours of wars: see that ye be not troubled: for these things must come to pass, but the end is not yet. For nation shall rise against nation, and kingdom against kingdom: and there shall be famines, and pestilences, and earthquakes in diverse places. All these things are the beginning of sorrows. Then shall they deliver you up to be afflicted, and shall kill you: and ye shall be hated of all nations for my name's sake."

As in the time of Jeremiah, when the prophets and priests were deluding the people that God would not destroy the temple, so now there are those who believe the Church will not be judged for her failure to uphold righteousness. The belief that the Church will one day be carried off to heaven without being accountable for her failures is not being true to the knowledge of who God is, for righteousness and judgement are the habitations of his throne. Even though many will die as a result of the famine and harshness of life, the end is not yet here. The Church must first manifest the fullness of the power of the children of God on earth before the end comes because it is the will of God for her. From the beginning of time the mouth of the LORD has commanded humans to: **be fruitful, multiply, replenish the earth, and have dominion.**

This should be a time of self-examination for everyone belonging to this Church Age, for the judgement promised is as individual as it is corporate and is about to take place. It ought to be a time when the righteous should mourn for the restoration of the joy or counsel of the Holy Ghost and for state of the Church and the evil things that are happening in the world; only then revival will come at this point in time.

"Blessed are they that mourn: for they shall be comforted" (Matt. 5:4).

"To proclaim the acceptable year of the LORD, the day of vengeance of our God; to comfort all that mourn; To appoint unto them that mourn in Zion, to give unto them beauty for ashes, the oil of joy for mourning, the garment of praise for the spirit of heaviness; that they might be called trees of righteousness, the planting of the LORD, that he might be glorified" (Isa. 61:2–3).

Part of the mandate of Christ is to restore counsel to the Church as the "oil of joy" to those who mourn. Isaiah spoke of mourning even before Christ gave the beatitude. Obviously the poor in spirit are the righteous generation of any Church Age. If the Ephesus Church had not departed from her first love, there would be no need to mourn where the Holy Ghost is fully functional, because the poor in spirit is totally reliant on God, even as the poor people of the time of Christ relied on him to be fed. Taken together, all scriptures addressing this Church Age at the time when "Death" rules and her works are imperfect; calls her into the place of mourning required of the righteous for godliness to be restored (*2 Chron. 7:14*). The statement of Christ and the signs of the times should cause the righteous to weep for the state of the world as Christ wept at the tomb of Lazarus. He did not weep for the death of Lazarus for he knew he would wake him but for the fate of his brethren who would die in their sins because they had rejected him as the Messiah.

Death and Hell reaping great harvest: *"If you will not watch I will come as a thief."* Judgement will surely come to the Church in the Sardis Church Age and the stage is already set. How sad it is to note that many of the souls who die during this time are bound for hell. The pale horse who features in this period reflects what is happening physically on earth as a result of what has taken place in the spiritual realm. The unrepentant disposition and evil conviviality of the Church since she departed from her first love precipitates the judgement (*"and I will kill her children with death"*). However, the corporate repentance required of the Church from the beginning will be made by the Sardis Church, for the zeal of the LORD will cause it to happen. As a result the greatest revival the world has ever seen will take place; and for the first time in the history of the Church the world will see the true manifestation of the sons of God on a level not witnessed before. Although many will be killed during the time of the Sardis Church, the time of the rapture is not just yet. However, events to bring Christ back will be rapidly stepped up as the wickedness of mankind increases and the man of sin is revealed.

It has been said that the struggle of the kingdom of darkness with the kingdom of light is to take the peace (the word) of God from the world. However, after the Sardis Church repents, God will pour out of his Spirit upon his servants and handmaidens as promised in *Joel 2:28–32*, thus giving birth to the Philadelphia Church. There is something uniquely encouraging about the ultimate fate of the Church: the promise of power over nations. *"And he shall rule them with a rod of iron; as the vessels of a potter shall they be broken to shivers: even as I received of my Father. And I will give him the morning star" (Rev. 2:28).* This is a statement of assurance to the Church that it is not over and that the plan of God for the Church to rule over nations will yet be accomplished in the Philadelphia Church Age.

CHAPTER ELEVEN

THE CHURCH OF THE TWO WITNESSES

God has not totally rejected the Jews as his people, and because he is God of all age, who spoke concerning the destination of Israel from Horeb to the Euphrates, he must bring them back in the Church Age to complete the final week of Daniel's seventieth weeks of years. After the corporate repentance of the Sardis Church is made, he will show mercy and return the fullness of the Holy Ghost to the body of Christ with the birth of this Church. This is referred to in Joel 2:29.

Scenes from Seal Five: Revelation 6:9-11
The Time of the Sounding of the Second Trumpet: Revelation 8:8-9
The Philadelphia Church: Revelation 11:1-13; 3:7-13

"And to the angel of the church in Philadelphia write; These things saith he that is holy, he that is true, he that hath the key of David, he that openeth, and no man shutteth; and shutteth, and no man openeth; I know thy works: behold I have set before thee an open door, and no man can shut it: for thou hast a little strength, and hast kept my word, and hast not denied my name. **Behold I will make them of the synagogue of Satan, which say they are Jews, and are not, but do lie; behold I will make them to come and worship before thy feet, and to know that I have loved thee.** *Because thou hath kept the word of my patience, I also will keep thee from the hour of temptation, which shall come upon all the world, to try them that dwell in the earth. Behold I come quickly; hold fast that which thou hast, that no man take thy crown. Him that over-cometh will I make a pillar in the temple of my God, and he shall go no more out."*(See *Isaiah 61:4-7*).

The Unveiling: Truths of the End Times

This Church is made up of the 144,000 Jews who were sealed in *Revelation 7:1–8* and the remnant of the Sardis Church as Gentiles coming together as brethren, and for the first time the world will witness the true corporate manifestation of the power of the Sons of God coming from the body of Christ (*Rev. 3:9*). The exploits of this Church will be so great that the entire world will be united against her. (See *Matthew 24:6–9*).

The witnesses of God at any time are only two, namely the Word of God and the Spirit of God at work in the hearts of a man *(John 14:23–24)*. Corporately, all who are indwelt by them are only two witnesses and one body *(Isa. 6:8)*. Christ spoke to remind the Church in as many words that the way back to God and perfection can only be one of holiness; through a life lived according to the truth of the word of God; and in the manifestation of the love of God in the life of the believer. One could even say he is reminding the Church how much he loves her, as his bride, or even that he is our brother, the firstborn, who cares for his brethren deeply. He also confirms that the way to the revealed knowledge of God was opened through the "veil" of his flesh and the price of his blood.

"Remember ye the law of Moses my servant, which I command unto him in Horeb for all Israel, with the statutes and judgements. Behold, I will send you Elijah the prophet before the coming if the great and dreadful day of the LORD" (*Mal. 4:4–6*).

This Church will go forth in the spirit and power of Moses and Elijah: Moses because many will be redeemed from Sin; and Elijah because of the manifest power of sons of God as in the time of Jezebel. At one time in the Old Testament, when the nation of Israel lapsed into apostasy, God raised up Elijah as a prophet and he destroyed the prophets of Baal and restored the righteousness of God in Israel. This was also the case in the days of John the Baptist whom Christ acknowledged as one who came in the spirit and power of Elijah. The decadent and apathetic state of the Church of Sardis required a final intervention from God (*Joel 2:29*); thereafter, this Church was born. This is the first Church of the night watch and her tenure will be very short. She comes into being in the morning of the third millennium of the death of Christ. Christ rose from the dead in the morning of the third day to assume his glorified position with the Father; even so it shall be with this church, this is affirmed by what Christ said: "*behold I come quickly.*" As the body of Christ she will also be delivered from death to be translated to the glorious position Christ has prepared for her with the Father.

The identity of Christ in this letter reveals much of what can be expected of this Church.

> ***He that is Holy:*** Christ spoke as the living and holy Word of God that was with the Father in the beginning, by whom he created all things, and by whom he perfects all things and will judge all things. He identified himself with a restored holy people, for the scriptures affirm that he is coming back for a bride without spot or blemish.

Him that is true: He spoke as the counsel and truth of the word of God by which human beings are made perfect.

He that hath the key of David: The one who has authority over all principalities and powers to do whatever is necessary to restore order, structure and godly government in the earth; and the one who will sit on the throne of David forever. The love David had for God is the key that gave him recognition and the authority by which he lived and ruled as king over the Kingdom of Israel and the influence he had over other nations; so that his throne before God is an everlasting kingdom. This Church, like David will walk in compelling power and authority and must have great impact in the world because the counsel of the Holy Ghost is restored and she can walk in agape love; and as a result of her exploits, many false religions will crumble. Counsel is the hidden manna promised to the Pergamus Church; it is the mystery hid in God from the foundation of the earth: i.e. "Christ in you the hope of glory." Christ being the representation of the counsel of the Holy Ghost. The counsel of the Holy Ghost is the key that opens the door to man's heart; it is also the truth that overcomes the world because it is "absolute truth" that is not found in the world system. David's habit of seeking the counsel of the LORD always was the key to his success.

He that openeth and no man shutteth: The door which no one can shut has been opened by Christ through his death on the cross so that those who seek wisdom, knowledge and counsel from God will find it. He has power to open the prophecies that have been sealed up until the end of time; he also gives an open door to people's hearts to hear the counsel of the Holy Ghost, which is the power of God unto salvation to those who believe. He also has the ability to open the gates of the nations of the world to receive the gospel of the kingdom. He has power to close the hearts of men that they cannot hear and repent when their iniquity has been judged. This may refer specifically to the Jews as a nation, of whom Paul said they have been grafted out of the covenant for a season so that the Gentiles could be grafted in. It is also said no one comes to the Father except the Holy Ghost draws them.

He that shutteth and no man openeth: In the parable of the friend at mid-night Christ spoke of a time during the Leodecian Church Age when the door to the counsel of the Father will be shut to the Church Age: *"And he from within shall answer and say, Trouble me not: the door is now shut, and my children are with me in bed; I cannot rise and give thee"* (Luke 11:7). It was also Christ as the

Word of God in the mouth of the Father who instructed John to seal up the seven thunder judgement, and Daniel to shut up the book until the time of the end *(Dan. 12:4)*. It might therefore be wise to view some past interpretations of the book of Daniel as conveying human wisdom rather than revelation knowledge that is required to change things.

Isaiah 61:5 refers to the Gentile Christians as "strangers" for indeed we were strangers to the commonwealth of Israel *(Eph. 2:12);* the sons of alien will be those of the tribe of Ishmael for whom Abraham interceded *(Gen. 17:18,20)*. The greatest blessing God can give to any one is a place of eternal rest in his presence. There is no doubt God has blessed Ishmael with wealth in the natural, but *"that he might live before you"* certainly refers to a time in eternity. The phrase *"sons of alien"* seem to refer to a time when God will reap through this Church Age, a great harvest from amongst the Ishmaelite.

Christ spoke about the violence of the world against the kingdom of God in *Matthew 11:11–12 "And from the days of John the Baptist until now the kingdom of heaven suffereth violence, and the violent take it by force."* John the Baptist the fore-runner of Christ came preaching the kingdom of heaven and he was violently killed by King Herod to satisfy the frivolous request of his step daughter, engineered by her mother. The combination of words used in this statement may be interpreted in two ways:

(a) Those who belong to the kingdom will be victims of violence coming from the world, because the world cannot withstand the manifest power demonstrated by the sons of God. Even from the days of Elijah this has proven to be true. After Elijah had demonstrated the power of heaven over the prophets of Baal, Jezebel sought for his life: John the Baptist came in the manifest power of Elijah, and suffered the same fate: *Matthew 11:14;* Christ came and demonstrated the power of the Son of God on earth and was killed by the World: *Isaiah 53:3;* The apostles were killed by the world: *Matthew 10:1, 16–26; 38–39; Matthew 11:11*. The two witnesses will be killed by the world: *Revelation 11:1–12;*

(b) The kingdom advances by the force or might of the counsel of the Holy Ghost to the son. This means he will be given what to say in order to enforce the will of God on earth, which sometimes causes them to do unpleasant things which the world is not able to bear *(Matt. 10:24–40; Prov. 8:14; 11:14; 12:15; Prov. 24:6)*. *"For by wise counsel thou shalt make thy war; and in the multitude of counsellors there is safety."*

The fate of the two witnesses who will advance the kingdom in the spirit and power of Moses and Elijah is tied up into these verses. The exploits of this Church will be so great that the entire social order will be united against her. (See *Matthew 24:6–9)*.

Scenes from Seal Five: Revelation 6:9-11

"And when he had opened the fifth seal I saw under the altar the souls of them that were slain for the word of God, and for the testimony which they held: And they cried with a loud voice, saying, How long, O Lord, holy and true, dost thou not judge and avenge our blood on them that dwell on the earth? And white robes were given unto everyone of them; and it was said unto them, that they should rest yet for a little season, until their fellow servants also and their brethren, that should be killed as they were, should be fulfilled".

When this seal was opened, John saw under the altar in heaven, the souls of those saints who had been killed for their testimony of Christ when the great tribulation began during the time of the rule of the Sardis Church. They were told to rest a little season until their fellow servants and also their brethren, that would be killed as they were, should be fulfilled. This revelation alludes to the killing of the two witnesses as saints of the Philadelphia Church. The identity of these two witnesses will become clearer when chapter eleven is unveiled.

The Second Trumpet: Revelation 8:8

"And the second angel sounded, and as it were a great mountain burning with fire was cast into the sea, and the third part of the sea became blood. And the third part of the creatures which were in the sea and had life, died and the third part of the ships were destroyed."

A mountain is symbolic of strength and power, especially national power, moral stability and greatness. *Isaiah 2:1–2* refers to the government of the Church Age as the mountain of the LORD's house. The second trumpet judgement is against the Church of the two witnesses. The great mountain ablaze with the fire of the Holy Ghost is representative of the Philadelphia Church and the one hundred and forty-four thousand Jews are one of the witnesses. She receives the second outpouring of the Holy Ghost promised in *Joel 2:29*. Her children will be given into the hands of their enemies in the world; and this is evidently the time when the false Prophet gains world recognition because he would have featured prominently in the persecution and killing of the two witnesses (*Dan. 8:5–12*). The saints of the resurrected Church will stand around the throne of God as the bride of Jesus his Son and the body of Christ the Messiah. Satan will challenge the Son for his bride and it is for this reason he will be cast out of heaven.

The first prophecy of the fate of the Church is given in *Genesis 3:15:* "*And I will put enmity between thee and the woman, and between thy seed and her seed; it shall bruise thy head, and thou shalt bruise thy heel.*" From the fall of Adam there has been enmity between the generations who belong to the kingdom of light and those of the kingdom of darkness; even in times of apparent peace, the devil does not change. Christ is the seed of the woman as the wisdom of God. At his first coming Christ bruised the head of the serpent by taking the keys of death and hell from him and putting him under the authority of the Church because he is the head of all principalities and powers; but the devil has been bruising the heel of Christians since Pentecost, when through the spirit of ignorance and deceit he has prevented the saints from living fulfilled Christian lives; or that Christians die before leaving this earth. He will also bruise the heel of Christ in this Church Age by the killing of the two witnesses. One aspect of the mandate of Christ is to set at liberty those who were bruised by death began after his resurrection when many souls were raised from the dead with him, and will be complete at his second coming. The heel of Christ is really the weakest part of him which is the Church as his 'Achilles heel.' This is not a message the body of Christ wants to hear, even though it is true; it only goes to confirm that the power of deception is strong in this Church Age also.

The sad part of this revelation is that there will come a time when this door will be shut and no one will be able to open it. This revelation, or indeed any other, should not come to the Church simply as knowledge, but as a reawakening to righteous living; for the holiness of God means that no sin can enter into his presence. We see that there are those of the Church of Sardis whose names were blotted out of the book of life. This should make those believers who teach eternal security return and evaluate this truth; for without holiness no one can enter into the kingdom of God. More will be said on the two witnesses in Revelation Chapter eleven.

CHAPTER TWELVE

THE LAST CHURCH AGE

Unveiling of Chapters Eight and Nine

Different events take place in this Church Age. Trumpets three to six will be sounded as seal six is opened to reveal the end of all things. After the two witnesses, as the Philadelphia Church are called up to heaven the devil and his angels will be cast down to earth. Both chapters eight and nine as they relate to the trumpet judgements will be unveiled in this last Church Age.

Revelation Chapters Eight and Nine

Scenes from Seal Six
The sounding of the third trumpet: Revelation 8:10–11
The Laodiceans Church Age: Isaiah 1:21–31; Revelation 3:14–22:

"And unto the angel of the church of the Laodiceans write these things saith the Amen, the faithful and true witness, the beginning of the creation of God; I know thy works; that thou are neither cold nor hot. So then because thou art lukewarm, and neither cold nor hot, I will spew thee out of my mouth. Because thou sayest, I am rich, and increase with goods, and have need of nothing and knowest not that thou art wretched, and miserable, and poor, and blind, and naked: I counsel thee to buy of me gold tried in the fire, that thou mayest be rich; and white raiment, that thou mayest be clothed, and that the shame of thy nakedness do not appear; and anoint thine eyes with eye-slave, that thou mayest see. As many as I love I rebuke and chasten: be zealous and repent"(Rev. 3:14–19).

This letter from the: *'The Amen.* It is the only letter addressed to a people rather than a place. It is addressed to the church of Jews and Gentiles who will be left behind after the Church of the two witnesses are called up to heaven. The title of Christ in this scene tells us that the end of all things has come. Indeed he appeared to John as The Alpha and Omega: the first to do many things and the last. He spoke to say that everything that has a beginning has an ending. The journey of the Church may have been long but now the end of all things has come.

The faithful and true witness: He spoke also in his name as "the Word of God," the faithful and true witness, and one who has endured all things with his Church as he walked amongst the seven candlesticks. He also spoke in fulfilment of his words in *Matthew 28:20*, *"and lo I am with you alway even to the end of the world."* When he returns with the saints, they also, will be called faithful and true witnesses.

The beginning of the creation of God: He is the firstborn of the new creation and the firstborn among many brethren; and the firstborn Son of God from among the human race.

The call to this church (Rev. 3:18–19): Donald Guthrie comments that: *"The advice given is devastating, yet in some sense reassuring. They are to 'buy' from Christ gold, clothes and eye ointment, the very thing they thought they could depend on obtaining from the city."*[1]

The city of Laodicea was noted for the production of a type of black clothing, made from the wool of the local breed of sheep, and for the production of medical ointment for ears and eyes; thus they were asked to anoint their eyes that they may see the events that are taking place, and have ears to hear what the Spirit is saying to the Church Age. The promise of a reward for those who endure to the end means that some people of this period will still make it to the marriage supper of the Lamb. Speaking to his disciples who later constituted the Church, Christ said in *Matthew 24:15*:

"When ye therefore shall see the abomination of desolation, spoken of by Daniel the prophet, stand in the holy place (whoso readeth, let him understand)."

To stand in a holy place is addressed to a church that is living according to the Word and the Spirit. In the Old Testament the Holy place was in the center of the tabernacle where the shrewd bread and the candlestick were to be found. The Holy place pre-figures the human mind where the word of God and the Spirit work to bring about perfection; it can also mean to put on Christ likeness; or to let the word of God abide in hearts and live by them because the days are evil. What Christ is saying here is that the saints should continue to live a holy life unto God by abiding in his image and not corporate with sin when the persecution is great. Christ also promised that those days would be shortened for the sake of the elect, i.e. those who are left behind after the church of the two witnesses is taken away. In ending this commentary on the churches, the words of Christ to the churches ring through with the warning that no one should ignore: *"He that hath an ear, let him hear what the Spirit saith unto the churches."*

Before Christ came people had sinned and fallen short of the glory of God. Christ's intercession was that the glory would once again be restored to him and by so doing all who are of him would benefit through the coming of the Holy Ghost (*John 17:4–5*). But this time will be even worse than it was before the coming of Christ; as the glory is once again withdrawn. The four cardinal points are used in the Bible as significant symbols. For example: *the east means the glory of the presence of God; the north the place of the Word of God that brings mankind out of darkness into the marvellous light of the kingdom of God.* The Word of God comes to serve man in this respect but there are times when the word of God rules over man in judgement.

The restraint of the Holy Ghost will also be removed to give place to the devil to work until sin is full; and the glory of the LORD which Christ received for his bride as protection will be taken away from the righteous remnant who belong to the Laodiceans Church: and their persecution will be very great and many will pay with their lives: *"And the LORD will create upon every dwelling place of mount Zion, and upon her assemblies, a cloud and smoke by day, and the shining of a flaming fire by night: for upon all the glory shall be a defence"* (Isa. 4:5). (See *Isaiah 60:1–2*).

The judgements spoken of by the prophets will begin to take place on earth as Lucifer and his fallen angels are cast out of heaven to rule on earth: *"And there was war in heaven: Michael and his angels fought against the dragon; and the dragon fought with his angels. And prevailed not; neither was their place found any more in heaven. And the great dragon was cast out, that old serpent called the devil, and Satan which deceiveth the whole world: he was cast out into the earth, and his angels were cast out with him . . . Therefore rejoice ye heavens and ye that dwell in them. Woe to the inhabitants of the earth and of the sea! For the devil is come down unto you having great wrath; because he knoweth that he hath but a short time"* (Rev. 11:7; Rev. 12:7–9, 12).

Until this period the devil and his evil angels were the spiritual wickedness in heavenly places, and there was a place in the heavens from where they operated. Now that there is no place in the heavens for them, the obvious place for them to operate is amongst the people of the earth.

Scenes From Seal Six: Rev 6:12-17

"And I beheld when he had opened the sixth seal, and lo, there was a great earthquake; and the sun became black as sackcloth of hair, and the moon became as blood; And the stars of heaven fell unto the earth, even as a fig tree casteth her untimely figs, when she is shaken of a mighty wind. And the heaven departed as a scroll when it is rolled together; and every mountain and island were moved out of their places." (See *Revelation 16:10–12, 21*).

The sun became black as sackcloth of hair; and the moon turned into blood: Although these things may happen in reality, spiritually they could mean different things. The sun and the moon both outshine the darkness to bring light; so also the Word and the Spirit work together to bring people out of the kingdom of darkness into the kingdom of light. The moon is a symbol of the Word of God; and speaks also of Christ's position in heaven at the right hand of the Father. The moon turning into blood could mean one or all of the following things: that the word of God will become judgemental as evil wisdom takes root in people's hearts; that the light of the gospel will no longer shine in the hearts of men because many will develop a lukewarm attitude to the truth, and the gospel will no longer be preached by human beings but angels will preach and counsel people not to take the mark of the beast.

> *"But if our gospel be hid it is hid to them that are lost: In whom the God of this world hath blinded the minds of them which believe not, lest the light of the glorious gospel of Christ, who is the image of God, should shine unto them. For God, who commanded the light to shine out of darkness, hath shined in our hearts, to give the light of the knowledge of the glory of God in the face of Jesus Christ"* (*2 Cor 4:4–6*).

Those who will be saved must live by what they already know. The righteous remnant of this Church Age is also warned against using the word as the sword of the spirit to fight against their enemies as it was in the previous Church Age (*Rev. 13:10*).

The black sun and moon also means that the days will be shortened. *"And in that day, saith the Lord God, that I will cause the sun to go down at noon, and I will darken the earth in the clear day"* (*Amos 8:9*).

The Sounding of the Third Trumpet: Revelation 8:10–11:

"And the third angel sounded, and there fell a great star from heaven, burning as it were a lamp, and it fell upon the third part of the rivers, and upon the fountains of water; And the name of the star is called Wormwood: and the third part of the waters became wormwood; and many men died of the waters, because they were made bitter." (See *Revelation 12:7–9*).

The star burning as if it were a lamp is the devil: This star is emulous and full of deceit, *"burning as if it were a lamp."* The lamp stand of the tabernacle is a symbol of the Holy Spirit. Spirits are referred to as stars and the great star is the devil; he is the evil spirit sin; he is deceitful and burning as though he were a lamp shows him emulous of the Holy Ghost. The judgement of Egypt is re-enacted here but the reason is not clear.

The Sounding of the Fourth Trumpet: Revelation 8:12–13

"And the fourth angel sounded, and the third part of the sun was smitten, and the third part of the moon, and the third part of the stars, so as the third part of them was darkened, and the day shone not for a third part, and the night likewise.

This relates to the period in the latter half of Daniel's seventieth week when the days will be shortened for the sake of the elect; and after one-third of the angels are thrown out of heaven with Lucifer.

"And except those days be shortened, there should no flesh be saved; but for the elect's sake those days shall be shortened. Then if any man shall say unto you, Lo, here is Christ, or there; believe it not. "For there shall arise false Christs, and false prophets; and shall shew great signs and wonders; insomuch that, if it were possible, they shall deceive the very elect" (Matt. 24:22).

"Immediately after the tribulation of those days shall the sun be darkened, and the moon shall not give her light, and the stars shall fall from heaven, and the powers of the heavens shall be shaken"(Matt. 24:29).

The success of the previous Church is that the counsel of the Holy Ghost was restored; but in this Church Age it will once again be withheld, limited to perhaps a few as it now is. The parable of the friend at midnight suggests that a few persons will still be able to pray and get answers.

"And he said unto them, Which of you shall have a friend, and shall go unto him at midnight, and say unto him, Friend, lend me three loaves. For a friend of mine in his journey is come to me, and I have nothing to set before him: And he from within shall answer and say, Trouble me not: the door is now shut, and my children are with me in bed; I cannot rise and give thee? I say unto you, Though he will not rise and give him, because he is his friend, yet because of his importunity he will rise and give him as many as he needeth"(Luke 11:5–8).

The 'three loaves' the Christian needs to survive are the gifts of the spirit: wisdom, knowledge and counsel. Counsel gives power to live by faith or dominate over evil. However, the scripture is instructive, for it proves that though men will not publish the gospel in these days, some will be saved. In this Church Age also the man of sin would have already been identified, and becomes influential in the world (*Rev. 6:16; Isa. 1:21–31*).

The severe persecution of the Christians on earth in these times means this church will be terribly compromised because many who profess to be of the kingdom of heaven will be mockers; that is the reason Christ is not within; but he is at the door knocking. The parable of the net aptly fits this church of a mixed multitude:

"Again the kingdom of heaven is like unto a net, that was cast into the sea, and gathered of every kind: Which, when it was full, they drew to shore, and sat down, and gathered the good into vessels, but cast the bad away. So shall it be at the end of the world: the angels shall come forth, and sever the wicked from among the just, And shall cast them into the furnace of fire: there shall be wailing and gnashing of teeth" (Matt. 13:47–50).

Christ reminds those who are his to emulate him as the faithful and true witness. They are also warned not to fight with the sword (the word of God) as the church before them had been given special authority and power to do. They are to be wise and prudent living through the evil of the time because God has permitted the rule of evil in the world so that their sin will become full and ripe for judgement. *"For the mystery of iniquity doth already work: only he who now letteth will let, until he be taken out of the way"* (2 Thess. 2:3–8, 7). Whatever God permits, it is foolishness for anyone to resist.

"For I know your manifold transgressions and your mighty sins, they afflict the just; they take a bribe, and they turn aside the poor in the gate, from their right. Therefore the prudent shall keep silence in that time; for it is an evil time. Seek good and not evil; that ye may live; and so the LORD the God of hosts shall be with you as he has spoken" (Amos 5:12–14).

After Christ has offered up prayers, he fills the censer with fire from the altar, and casts it into the earth, and there are voices, and thundering and lightning on earth, accompanied by earthquakes signifying that the time has come for the earth to be judged. Thus **three woes are determined upon the inhabitants of the earth** as a result of the sounding of the next three trumpets because the devil and his host have been cast down to earth out of heaven.

Revelation Chapter Nine

Scenes from Seal Six:
The Sounding of the Fifth Trumpet: Revelation 9:1–2

"Then the fifth angel sounded; And I saw a star fallen from heaven to the earth. And to him was given the key to the bottomless pit. And he opened the bottomless pit, and smoke arose out of the pit like the smoke of a great furnace. And the sun and the air were darkened because of the smoke of the pit. And there came out of the smoke locusts upon the earth. And it was commanded them that they should not hurt the grass of the earth, neither any green thing; neither any tree, but only those men which have not the seal of God in their foreheads. And they were not given authority to kill them, but to torment them for five months" (Rev. 12:12).

The Stars from Heaven Shall Fall: Revelation 8:10-11

"The powers from heaven shall be shaken and the devil and his evil angels will be cast down to the earth."

The fallen stars are Lucifer and his angels. They come down during the second half of Daniel's seventieth week of years, to persecute the people of the next Church

Age. He was given the key to the bottomless pit; the key was previously taken from him by Christ. Now it has been returned to him for a reason: that he should let loose demonic forces walking about on earth like human beings.

"Son of man, take up a lamentation upon the king of Tyrus, and say unto him. Thus saith the LORD God; Thou sealest up the sum, full of wisdom, and perfect in beauty. Thou hast been in Eden the garden of God: every precious stone was thy covering, the sardine, topaz, and the diamond, the beryl, the onyx, and the jasper, the sapphire, the emerald, and the carbuncle, and gold: the workmanship of thy tabrets and of thy pipes were prepared in thee in the day that thou was created. Thou are the anointed cherub that covereth; and I have set thee so: thou wast upon the holy mountain of God; thou hast walked up and down in the midst of the stones of fire. Thou wast perfect in thy ways from the day that thou wast created, till iniquity was found in thee. By the multitude of thy merchandise they have filled the midst of thee with violence, and thou hast sinned: therefore I will cast thee as profane out of the mountain of God: and I will destroy thee, O covering cherub, from the midst of the stones of fire. Thine heart was lifted up because of thy beauty; thou hast corrupted thy wisdom by reason of thy brightness: I will cast thee to the ground; I will lay thee before kings, that they may behold thee. Thou hast defiled thy sanctuaries by the multitude of thine iniquities, by the iniquity of thy traffick; therefore will I bring forth a fire from the midst of thee, it shall devour thee, and I will bring thee to ashes upon the earth in the sight of all them that behold thee. All they that know thee among the people shall be astonished at thee; thou shalt be a terror, and never shalt thou be any more" (Ezek. 28:12–19:).

Ezekiel here prophesies of the fall of Lucifer from heaven which has now taken place. It may be that the image that the false prophet will make is the image of Lucifer; constructed precisely as he is described by Ezekiel.

The Sounding of the Sixth Trumpet: Revelation 9:13–21

"Then the sixth angel sounded: And I heard a voice from the four horns of the golden altar which is before God, saying to the sixth angel who had the trumpet, "Release the four angels who are bound at the great river Euphrates." So the four angels, who had been prepared for the hour and day and month and year, were released to kill a third of mankind"(Rev. 9:13).

These are spirits specially prepared for this time; it should mean a time when evil reaches a climax all over the world. These demonic agents were given power to hurt those without the seal of God on their foreheads. This battle seems to be one where the enemies of God fight against themselves. They were given a command not to kill these people but to torment them for a period of five months. At this time people will seek death but because the demons have been commanded not to kill, they will be greatly frustrated: *"And in those days shall men seek death, and shall not find it, and shall desire to die, and death shall flee from them"* (*Rev. 9:3*).

The voice is either of God or of Christ; for only they have the power to determine the time of judgement. **The four angels of the river Euphrates (Rev. 7:1):** The River Euphrates refers, symbolically; to the end of the world and the extent of sinfulness throughout the world. It is the name of a river that flows through Babylon, which is a type of the world. It also marked the end; or the boundary of the land of Canaan which the Israelites were sent to possess (*Deut. 1:7*). The name means "bursting"; used symbolically in the Bible, it is given no specific location or boundary, which could mean that it relates to evil throughout the world. The reference to angels in the Bible can mean the angels of heaven or the spirit by which angels and humankind live. These four spirits have always been at work but they were held under control by the government of the Holy Ghost whilst the Church (the Elect Lady) was on earth. They were prepared for this hour to slay the third part of humanity. They are the four characteristics of sin, namely: ignorance, fear, deceit, and death (four of the evil spiritual influences let loose in the entire world since the fall). Because Satan now has the keys of death and hell, and the judgement of God is that the soul that sins shall die, he is legally able to kill with death and many people will die.

"Behold I give you power over serpents and scorpions and nothing shall by any means hurt you" (*Luke 10:19*). During the dispensation of grace, the Church had power over serpents and scorpions *(devils and demons)* and death. However, at this time the restraining power of the Holy Ghost will be removed and the power of evil will be fully released on the earth. In this vision we see serpents and scorpions coming together. Whereas the scorpions (a symbolic name for demons) were given power to hurt, but not to kill with death, these four evil spirits were given power to kill with death in *Revelation 9:17–8*:

"And thus I saw the horses in the vision, and them that sat on them, having breastplates of fire, and of jacinth, and of brimstone... And out of their mouths issued fire and smoke and brimstone. By these three was the third part of men killed, by the fire, and by the smoke and by the brimstone which issued out of their mouths."

The fire from the mouths of these creatures is the judgement written from the beginning— *"the soul that sins shall die"* — the smoke and brimstone are evil words that kill in execution of the judgement determined (*Ezek. 18:20*). The beast will choose his army from amongst human beings. These people will be cruel and heartless and will have power to pronounce death upon anyone who offends them, for the sting of death is with them in their mouths.

PART 3
THE FATE OF THE CHURCH

CHAPTER THIRTEEN

UNVEILING OF CHAPTERS FOUR AND FIVE

In Chapters four and five, John saw the future gathering of the Church around the tabernacle in heaven in the presence of the twenty-four elders, the four beasts, and thousands of angelic hosts. The elders cast their crowns before the Almighty which means this is a special gathering in which Christ will be crowned King of the kings of the earth. Everyone belonging to the called and chosen serve to be rewarded with various crowns (*Rev 6:1-2*) but no one that is a subject of Christ will receive their crowns before him

At this stage, the Church in heaven has finished her work; therefore, it is obvious that some of the things revealed when the seals are opened are for a witness for or against the Church because they have already taken place. The Ancient of Days sits upon the throne in heaven in the presence of the Lamb who prevails to open the seven seals. The seals will confirm the journey of the Churches according as they were written and sent as a warning to the Church in the letters to the seven Churches of Chapters two and three.

Revelation Chapter Four:

Chapters four and five show the time when the Ancient of days sits in judgement. The jasper and sardine stones are the first and the last amongst the twelve stones worn by the priest; the two stones refer to one person and reveal God as "The First and the Last, the Alpha and Omega" (*Rev. 22:13*). The rainbow round about the throne is a covenant sign that shows that the God of the beginning is the God of the end.

"After this I looked, and, behold a door was opened in heaven: and the first voice which I heard was as it were of a trumpet talking with me; which said, Come

up hither, and I will shew thee things which must be hereafter. And immediately I was in the spirit: and behold, a throne was set in heaven, and one sat on the throne. And he that sat was to look upon like a jasper and a sardine stone; and there was a rainbow round about the throne, in sight like unto an emerald . . . And before the throne there was a sea of glass like unto crystal: and in the midst of the throne, and round about the throne, were four beasts full of eyes before and behind" (Rev. 4:1–6).

John is called up to heaven after he had received the letters to the seven Churches. He saw things that would happen in the Church Age as seal after seal were opened. In his revelation the seven angels with the seven trumpets were preparing to sound, throughout history. Revelation knowledge of what must happen in the Church Age is God's mercy to his faithful saints: as it is written concerning Christ that he was able to endure the cross and despise the shame through the knowledge he had of the future. Though people who are evil can use such knowledge adversely, its primary purpose is to strengthen and encourage the saints of God because he is faithful in the things he promises, even in his judgements.

Dake states, *"Everything from Revelation 4–22 must take place after the rapture of the Church."*[1] He suggests that *Revelation 4:1* confirms this theory. There are many reasons why this claim is questionable. In the first instance, the Church in heaven after the rapture has finished her work and has no need for the kind of information contained in the letters, neither can anyone be asked to repent and do the first work. Certainly we cannot presume that the Church Age, as we now know it, is so perfect that she has nothing to repent and turn away from in these days when the evil generation rules in the world. The falling away spoken of by Paul and manifested in the progressive decline of righteousness in the kingdom of heaven must be corporately repented of before the work of the Church is completed.

The four and twenty elders: No one knows the identity of these distinguished fathers; but one thing we learn from their presence in heaven is the position of honour that is given them by God. Here also is the fulfilment of the prophecy of Hannah as she sang during the dedication of Samuel to the earthly priesthood.

"He raiseth up the poor out of the dust, and lifteth up the beggar from the dunghill, to set them among princes, and to make them inherit the throne of glory: for the pillars of the earth are the LORD's and he hath set the world upon them" (1 Sam. 2:8).

The unveiling of the scriptures shows that God has been building and perfecting human beings to occupy great positions in eternity. Although their identity is not known, it is sufficient to know that they are all people who have prevailed over sin to gain and serve in their distinguished positions in the future kingdom of God on earth.

The seven lamps of fire burning: These are the seven spirits of the LORD who bear record in heaven; and by which he relates to human beings (*Isa. 11:2*). Everyone who finds themselves around the throne must have lived and will continue to live by the Holy Ghost as the sons of God.

The four beasts full of eyes before and behind: The people described as beasts are actually the spirits of the just made perfect. In the Old Testament the stationing of the twelve tribes around the tabernacle was to be precise. Four elders considered to be wise were singled out as the head of the four groups of three tribes. Here also in heaven four elders are singled out as heads of the Jews and Gentiles as one body before the throne.

"And the first beast was like a lion, and the second beast like a calf, and the third beast had a face as a man, and the fourth beast was like a flying eagle. And the four beasts had each of them six wings about him; and they were full of eyes within and they rest not day and night saying Holy, holy, holy, Lord God Almighty, which was, and is and is to come. 9. And when those beasts give glory and honour and thanks to him that sat on the throne, who liveth forever and ever. 10. The four and twenty elders fall down before him that sat on the throne and worship him that liveth forever and ever, and cast their crowns before the throne saying" (Rev. 4:7–10).

The assembly of saints before the throne: The scene is similar to the camping of Israel around the tabernacle in the wilderness. John saw evidence that the simple structure of the past is a representation of the perfect heavenly tabernacle. *"And after that I looked, and behold the temple of the tabernacle of the testimony in heaven was opened"* (Rev. 15:5). Through the eyes of John, we see the assembly of the elders and the victorious saints before God. In the days of the earthly tabernacle Judah headed the tribes on the east under the banner of the lion; Dan the tribe on the north under the banner of a man; Reuben the tribes on the south under the banner of the eagle; and Ephraim the tribes on the west under the banner of the ox. Both Ephraim and Manasseh were adopted by Jacob as his own sons. It is significant that in heaven, Ephraim stands as the father of Gentile nations; whilst the half tribe and Manasseh replaces Dan who is written out of the end time inheritance, presumably because his tribe introduced idolatry in Israel. (See *Revelation 7:3–8*). The expression that they were "full of eyes before and behind" means that by the time of this gathering, they now have perfect knowledge of God's plan for humanity, past, present, and future; secondly the things of which they bore witness in John's vision they now see manifesting before their eyes. The reference to them as "beasts" is symbolic. The Bible refers in places to fallen human beings as beasts, such as in *1 Corinthians 15:32*: *"If after the manner of men, I have fought with beasts at Ephesus, what advantageth it me, if the dead rise not."* (See *Daniel 7:17*).

Revelation Chapter Five

This chapter is a continuation of the scene in heaven. God is seated on his throne to judge the nations of the world, after the church of the two witnesses has been caught up to heaven. Christ opens the book of secrets, breaking seal after seal to show how the Church had walked until the time of her assembly around the throne of God. There are seven seals; each one reveals seven scenes, some of which will come to pass after the sounding of the seventh trumpet and the remnant Church is caught up to heaven. Therefore, the things revealed when the seals were opened in

John's vision will be confirmed by the elders as that which was communicated to the Churches out of which they will be judged.

"And I saw in the right hand of him that sat on the throne a book written within and on the backside, sealed with seven seals. And I saw a strong angel proclaiming with a loud voice, Who is worthy to open the book, and to lose the seals thereof? And no man in heaven, or in earth, neither under the earth, was able to open the book, neither to look thereon. And I wept much, because no man was found worthy to open and to read the book, neither to look thereon. And one of the elders said unto me, weep not: behold the Lion of the tribe of Judah, the Root of David, hath prevailed to open the book, and to lose the seven seals thereof. And I beheld, and, lo, in the midst of the throne and of the four beasts, and in the midst of the elders, stood a Lamb as it had been slain, having seven horns and seven eyes, which are the seven Spirits of God sent forth into all the earth" (Rev. 5:1–6).

The Lamb: The Lamb is Christ: he is also described as the Lion of the Tribe of Judah and the Root of David. This title reveals the true heritage of Christ as the one named and qualified for this honour. The book of Matthew traces his lineage. (See *Matthew 1:1–16*). He is the only one who has prevailed over sin that all may become the righteousness of God in him.

The seven horns of the Lamb: *Luke 1:68–69 "Blessed be the Lord God of Israel; for he hath visited and redeemed his people. And hath raised up an horn of salvation for us in the house of his servant David."* Christ is the Word of God *(Rev. 19:13)*; he is also the Lamb of God *(John 1:29)*. The seven horns of the Lamb is a reference to his authority over the seven Churches.

The seven eyes of the Lamb: *"Hear now, O Joshua the high priest, thou, and thy fellows that sit before thee: for they are men wondered at: for behold, I will bring forth my servant the BRANCH. For behold the stone that I have laid before Joshua; upon one stone shall be seven eyes"* (Zech. 3:8–9).

"Therefore thus saith the Lord GOD, Behold I lay in Zion for a foundation a stone, a tried stone, a precious corner stone; a sure foundation; he that believeth shall not make haste" (Isa. 28:16).

Revelation 5:6 explains the seven eyes of the Lamb as the seven spirits of God sent forth into the world. All these scriptures refer to Christ; therefore the seven eyes of the Lamb are the seven characteristics of the Holy Ghost upon the Son as revealed in *Isaiah 11:2: the Spirit of the Lord; the spirit of wisdom and understanding; the spirit of knowledge and the fear of the Lord; the spirit of counsel and might.*

Christ is the main character of this scene because by him all are made perfect. His titles reveal his true heritage as the one who was promised and who was slain before the foundations of the world. He was killed yet he is alive, and is the true witness of God; and the only Messiah for whom the Jews waited. He features as the Lion of the Tribe of Judah who prevailed over sin and the world to make the audience possible. The Bible tells us that God does nothing without revealing it to his servants the prophets. The prophet, to whom this revelation is given, is Christ Jesus; he is the prophet like unto Moses to whom the world must listen (*Deut. 18:18*). In fulfilment of this prophecy, God gives him the revelation of the end of all things to show to his servants on earth.

We also see the hopelessness of human life; and the sinfulness of all in the sight of God. We see the finished work of the making of people in the image and likeness of God and Christ as the epitome of God's perfect human being. He is above all and the only one who has demonstrated the holiness of God characteristically and consistently; who was made sin for us, and died for us; not because he sinned but that the plan of God for the redemption of humanity and their completion in him might be fulfilled.

Those who reject the truth of the word of God should understand that life is about overcoming sin and sinfulness in order to conform to the image of God in Christ. There is only one God and one way back to him. God is constant and he will not confuse people by giving several routes to return to him. The blood of Christ is God's solution for recovery from the state of sinfulness. Christ has paved the way back to God and everyone must take advantage of the sacrifice of God's perfect Lamb and receive the word of God which brings salvation. The word of God to all is: *"Repent for the kingdom of heaven is at hand" (Matt. 3:2)*. It is impossible to repent without admitting that the root of all sins is the devil and that the only way back to God is by practising true righteousness and holiness which can come only through Christ Jesus. It was because all had failed God that Christ came as *"the first and the last,"* in this case the first to die for sin and the last.

The Cherubim

The cherubim as human beings in their angelic bodies are able to sing with the seraphim with such anointing because they are the "true worshippers" God sought from amongst his human creation *(John 4:24)*. In the Old Testament people worshipped God on altars of stone because Christ had not yet died to make God's preferred worship possible.

"And they sung a new song saying. "Thou art worthy to take the book, and to open the seals thereof: for thou wast slain, and hast redeemed us to God by thy blood out of every kindred, and tongue, and people, and nation" (Rev. 5:9–11).

After God sent Adam out of the glory of his presence, he replaced what humanity had become with what humanity must become in Christ *(Gen. 3:24)*. On the few occasions when the cherubim are mentioned in the Bible they are seen as angelic beings in the glory of the presence of the LORD. They are also described as strange beasts with two, four, or six wings. Images of them were embroidered on the inner curtain of the tabernacle and statues of two of them as angels were made over the mercy seat in the Holy of Holies, and each had only one head and two wings.

"And thou shall make two cherubim of gold, of beaten works shalt thou make them in the two ends of the mercy seat and make one cherub on one end and the

other cherub on the other end: even of the mercy seat shall ye make the cherubim on the two ends thereof" (Exod. 25:18–20).

In Ezekiel *Chapter one*, they were seen as having four faces and four wings. Those with four wings reflect the imperfection of the Old Testament saints as opposed to the finished work in Christ when human beings live by the Holy Ghost with his six characteristics. (See *Isaiah 11:2*.) The difference in the number of wings could mean one or all of many things as follows:

> It might simply mean that whereas in Revelation God's plan of restoration to his presence is fully accomplished, in Ezekiel it was not yet so.
>
> In the New Testament human beings have received the fullness of the Spirit to exercise great authority; but in the Old Testament individuals could not hear the counsel of the Holy Ghost to walk in his might, except for a few chosen ones.
>
> The vision of Ezekiel revealed God's absolute moral perfection against human imperfection; and God showed himself as spiritually and morally superior to members of Israel's corrupt and compromising society.

The cherubim of the Old Covenant were made of gold beaten into shape, symbolising the righteous generation from both covenants; those whose lives have been shaped through the things they suffer and have come out of great tribulation from the world through the ages to find their place once again in the glory of the presence of the LORD. The obvious conclusion is that the cherubim are God's new species of human being whom he has redeemed in Christ and restored to the glory of his presence (Ps. 18:9–10). The psalmist sees God riding upon a cherub with darkness under his feet. One may see this as related to the Messiah, who became sin for us, and upon whom the Holy Spirit rested *(Isa. 11:2)*; he delivered his people from the kingdom of darkness, and under his authority the kingdom of darkness is now made subject.

The symbols of the four faces represent the various tribes in their groupings around the tabernacle. They also reflect the four characteristics of Christ evinced in the synoptic gospels: the lion king; the servant ox; the perfect man and the Mighty God as an eagle. Since all living creatures must reflect the sovereignty of the Almighty God, it is inconceivable that he would create any creature with more than one head. As it is with the angels, their six wings show their position of reverence, service and worship. See *Isaiah 6:1-2 "Above it stood the seraphim: each one has six wings; with twain he covered his face, with twain he covered his feet, and with twain he did fly."*

The story of the Bible is about God and human beings having corporate rule over the earth through the Trinitarian relationship of Father, Son, and Holy Ghost. Therefore, each time God appears to judge the people of the earth he reveals his plan to them according to his desire for them to occupy the position he has for them in Christ. When he came down to pass judgement on Sodom he revealed his plan to Abraham as his friend and a father on earth. Divine unity is God and humans working together to accomplish his purpose on earth. Revelation will show in a later chapter the part the beasts play in the final destruction of the earth.

Other angelic beings who have not sinned according to the similitude of Lucifer or Adam are the seraphim. When the prophet Isaiah saw them as creatures in reverence, service and worship of God he did not see any human representation amongst them even though men like Enoch, Moses, Elijah and even father Abraham were already in heaven. This is because our completion is in Christ. He then concluded that he was a man of unclean lips, dwelling amongst a people of unclean lips. In the Old Testament only the High Priest and chosen men could stand before God in worship of him. Once in the presence of the Holy God, Isaiah realised people's unworthiness to worship him from the heart.

It is interesting to note that even in the presence of God, before Christ finishes the work to make restitution of all things to God; fallen human beings are still referred to as beasts. This tells us that no one can make it to the presence of God on account of his or her own righteousness, it is only by the righteousness of Christ, the only one found worthy to open the book because he was without sin.

The revelation of the saints around the throne in worship was to encourage John, and reassure the Church, that the promises of God in Christ were real and would be fulfilled one day; and to exhort Christians to pray for patience and grace to endure to the end whatever might be necessary to win the promised crowns.

CHAPTER FOURTEEN

THE FALL AND DECLINE OF THE CHURCH

Isaiah 2:2: "And it shall come to pass in the last days, that the mountain of the LORD's house shall be established in the top of the mountains, and shall be exalted above the hills; and all nations shall flow into it."

The government of the LORD's house must emanate from the Church, administered by leaders serving in the five-fold ministry of apostles, prophets, teachers, pastors and evangelists. Leaders must co-operate with the LORD God the Father, Christ the Son as the Word of God, and the Holy Ghost as their Counsellor to remain relevant throughout the Church Ages (*John 14:10–14, 23–24*).

The Church is God's plan for reaping a harvest of souls from the earth. However, history proves that there has been a falling away from the Bible doctrines that lead to maturity (*Heb. 6:1–2*). The falling away has occurred through the emergence of three antichrist doctrines that have resulted in the decline of righteousness in the Church Age. Dr Bill Hamon a teacher on the prophetic, states that the falling away began as early as AD 300.[1] The parables of Christ, concerning the kingdom of heaven, predict that the falling away will emanate from within, resulting in various stages of decline within the kingdom. These stages of decline are comparable to those of the kingdom of Judah, from the prosperous reign of King David to the carrying away of Judah into Babylon, and in line with the four families of locusts of Joel (*Joel 2:1–2*).

Biblical history supports the fact that other great kingdoms of Old Testament times have waxed great and have, likewise, fallen after so many years of greatness. From the point of view that all these kingdoms have been governed and rule over by some of the most intelligent human beings of history, it seem predictable that the kingdom of heaven would suffer the same fate if the focus was taken away from the Word of God and the Holy Ghost as the two witnesses of God with man. Subsequent to the falling away, God initiated various renewal and restoration movements to restore the doctrines, ministry offices and gifts of the Spirit to the Church.

Whilst pondering the rise and fall of kingdoms I was led to contemplate the various stages of decline of companies regarded as great in the book written by the Author of Good to Great, Jim Collins titled *How the Mighty Fall*. Collins has suggested a framework of five stages to the rise and fall of an organization built for greatness which bear remarkable resemblance to the fate of the seven Churches in the kingdom of heaven.[2]

Collins comments on companies in their five stages of decline do not seem to differ much from Christ's comments about the churches; and the symbols that describe them show their declining position in the kingdom of heaven: gold, silver, brass and iron. There are lessons that can be learnt from the five stages of decline relative to the various organisations studied by Collins that will help to strengthen the arguments for the decline of righteousness in stages in the kingdom of heaven, and what must be done for restoration. In the book of Matthew, when Christ was asked about the signs of the end, he referred to the fig tree as a sign. All truths are parallel, and one could as well look at the decline of these organisations in Collins' graph, to learn a lesson about the Church as a movement governed by human beings.

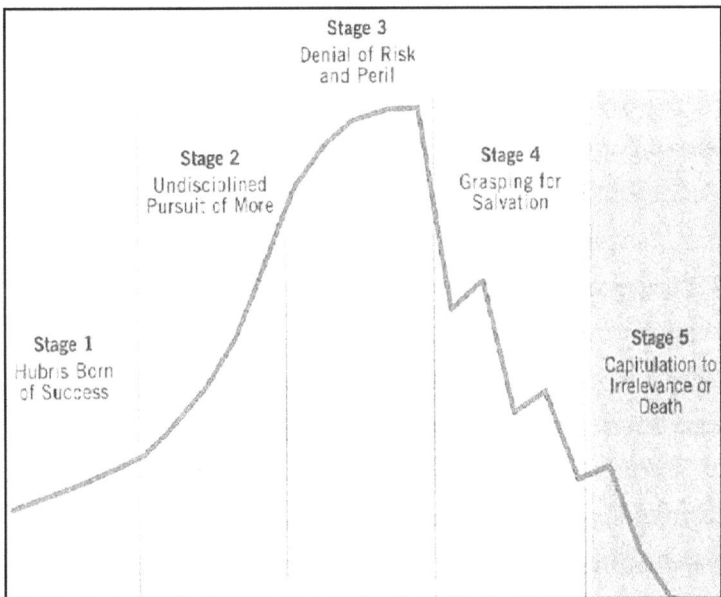

Fig.6. Collins five stages of decline[3]

With the rule of the kingdom of heaven also came the Church Age. It covers the period of the watches of the seven churches. The righteous generation of the Church were to continue ruling in the spiritual realm through their obedience to the word of God and submission to the Holy Ghost. Christ looked amongst the churches and warned of the implications of the serious imperfections amongst them. Daniel's vision in chapter seven gives a glimpse of the events that occur in the world during the time of the rule of the Church of Philadelphia to the end of Age.

Daniel's Account of the End Time: Daniel 7:2–5

"I saw in my vision by night, and behold, the four winds of the heaven strove upon the great sea. And four great beasts came up from the sea, diverse one from another. The first was like a lion, and had eagle's wings: I beheld till the wings thereof were plucked, and it was lifted up from the earth, and made stand upon the feet as a man, and a man's heart was given to it. And I behold another beast, a second, like to a bear, and it raised up itself on one side, and it had three ribs in the mouth of it between the teeth of it: and they said thus unto it, Arise, devour much flesh. After this I beheld, and low another, like a leopard, which had upon the back of it four wings of a fowl; the beast had also four heads; and dominion was given to it. After I was in the night visions, and behold a fourth beast, dreadful and terrible, and strong exceedingly, and it had great iron teeth, it devoured and break in pieces, and stamped the residue with the feet of it: and it was diverse from all the beasts that were before it; and it had ten horns. I considered the horns, and behold, there came up among them another little horn, before whom there were three of the first horns plucked up by the roots: and, behold, in this horn were eyes like the eyes of man, and a mouth speaking great things." (See also *Zechariah 4:1–11, 6:1–8; Micah 4:11–13; Revelation 11:1–14*.)

Daniel's vision 'by night' speaks specially about the events surrounding the Church of the night watches, which are the Philadelphia and Laodicean Churches. In relation to the entire Church Age, the symbolic reference of the lion, the bear, and the leopard, speaks of the decline of righteousness in the Church Age, as power and influence passes from one generation to the next until the rule of the fourth kingdom of the devil, Lucifer and the false prophet. It highlights events that will take place on earth even to the rule of the eighth dynasty, which is of the Devil and his ten kings. The righteous generation is symbolised by the lion; and the bear and leopard the ungodly and wicked generation, respectively.

The Lion: *Daniel 7:4 "The first was like a lion, and had eagle's wings: I beheld till the wings thereof were plucked, and it was lifted up from the earth, and made to stand upon the feet as a man, and a man's heart was given to it."(Rev. 2:1–7; Rev. 3:7–13).*

The symbol of the lion speaks always of the righteous generation. It can also relate to the Ephesus Church, but in this instance refers to the newly empowered, Philadelphia Church of the two witnesses. The mourning of the Sardis Church Age restored righteousness and a revived Church emerged in the power of sons of God. Daniel saw that the Church was called up to heaven to join those who are already made perfect in Christ.

The message conveyed in *Zechariah 4:1–11* finds its spiritual fulfilment in the day of the Militant Philadelphia Church, referred to as the *"golden candlestick." "And the angel that talked with me came again, and waked me, as a man that is wakened out of his sleep. And said unto me, what seest thou? And I said I have looked, and behold a candlestick all of gold, with a bowl upon the top of it, and his seven lamps thereon, and seven pipes to the seven lamps, which are upon the top thereof: And two olive trees by it, one upon the right side of the bowl, and the other upon the left side thereof. So I answered and spake to the angel that talked with me saying, What are these, my Lord? Then the angel that talked with me answered and said unto me, knowest thou not what these be? Ad I said, no my Lord. Then he answered and spake unto me saying. This is the word of the LORD unto Zerubbabel, saying not by might, or by power but by my spirit, saith the LORD of hosts. Who art thou O great mountain? Before Zerubbabel, thou shalt become a plain: and he shall bring forth the headstone thereof with shouting crying, Grace, grace unto it. Moreover the word of the LORD came unto me, saying. The hands of Zerubbabel have laid the foundation of this house; his hands shall also finish it; and thou shalt know that the LORD of hosts hath sent me unto you. For who hath despised the day of small things?"*

In the iron age when the evil generation rules over both spiritual kingdoms and philosophy and science, seek to prove the non-existence of God and the generations of post-modernity argue that there is no absolute truth; a new Church will be empowered to take control as sons of God are made manifest. The vision of Zerubbabel has natural and spiritual significance. The hands of Zerubbabel laid the foundation of the moderate temple, which was beautified and extended in the day of King Herod. But the sign was also one relating to the beginning of the Church Age, that which began very small would become a great mountain in the earth *(Isa. 2:2)*. But in the day of its greatness, it would be levelled to the ground as the Church of the two witnesses. The two olive trees on each side of the candlestick represent the two nations of Jews and Gentiles coming together to form the Philadelphia Church.

The headstone of the Church is Christ; and the church age consisting of seven Churches and four generations of people are given two periods of grace, which would be followed by two other periods, one in which the Church Age would be judged and the other in which judgement would be executed. As a testimony of the certainty of the fulfilment of the prophecy, the hands of Zerubbabel laid and did finish the temple.

The righteous generation and the Ephesus Church	Grace
The ungodly generation and the Smyrna and Pergamos churches	Grace
The wicked generation and the Thyatira Church	Judgement
The evil generation and the Sardis Church	Judgement executed
The birth of the Church of the two witnesses:	*Zechariah 4:14*

There are a few management principles that can be applied to support the four generation concept of declining rule, and the failure of the Church Age. These principles show the rise and fall of an organization in stages. Man may have discovered them, but they have always been in existence because God is the master of all wisdom. When decline is eminent to avoid death, there must be a return to the values and principles of the visionary. This is the advice Christ gave to the seven Churches, beginning with the Church of Ephesus: to return to her first love or the counsel of the Holy Ghost. Human intelligence alone, without God, in a world where the devil rules as mammon by evil wisdom, pride, arrogance, and deceit, cannot achieve lasting success either inside or outside of the kingdom of heaven.

According to the Spirit-Filled Life Bible Commentary, the "dispensational interpretation" sees the prophetic application in the seven letters suggesting they also outline seven stages of Church history, culminating with the two end-time stages seen in Philadelphia and Leodecian Churches."[4] With this in mind, whatever God will do to restore the Church to the good path, must be done and completed at stage four *(the Sardis Church)*, when decline gives rise to purging of the saints and judgement on ungodliness, before restoration and empowering for dominion over sin.

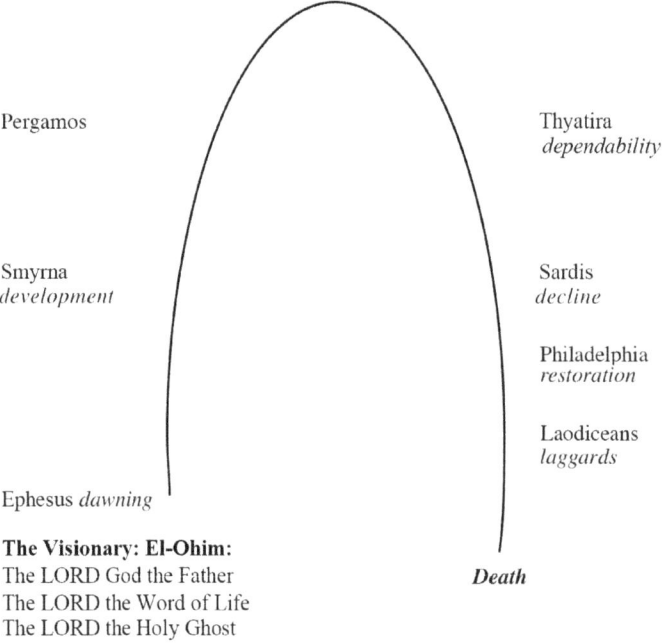

Fig 7. An adaptation from:
The theory of the five 'ds' adapted from Mike Puddicombe (growth+declinecycle_png (901x501)[5]

God of the beginning designs with purpose and principles in mind. One of the principles of God is that he will not hide any truth, good or bad from those who must do a thing: *Gen 18:17–19*. The geographical locations of the seven churches are intriguing and revealing. There is no doubt that God positioned the Churches in those locations as a testimony of his wisdom and foreknowledge. The churches are positioned so that they form a semi-circle as an arch similar to one that portrays the rise and fall of any other organization run by human beings without God at its center.

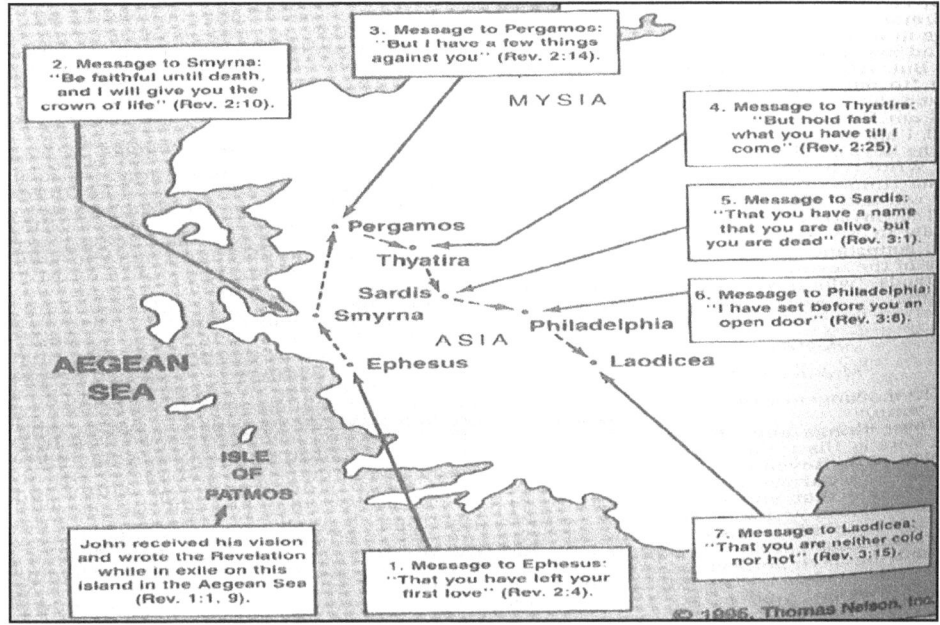

Fig. 8. The Positioning of the seven Churches[6]

Christianity is one life lived deliberately and conscientiously using godly principles and precepts to do the same things we would normally do in a life time; living that life unto God and prospering in the world so that life is lived virtuously to the praise of God and for the good of all mankind. As it is with individual organizations in the social order, so it is with the Church Age. The reason for these inclusions in the unveiling is to highlight the need for the Church Age to return to Christ-likeness and holy living as the only hope of recovering her power and strength for the completion of the work. In his book *How the Mighty Fall*, Jim Collins wrote the following about the Chief Executive of Xerox:

"When Anne Mulchay became Chief Executive of Xerox in 2001, she inherited a company mired in Stage 4. Digesting a $273 million loss, Xerox stock had dropped 92 percent in less than two years, wiping out more than $38 billion in shareholder value... Mulchay could have perpetuated a stage four loop doom by setting out to utterly smash the culture and revolutionize the company overnight. But instead, she retorted to those who said she would need to kill the culture to save the company, 'I am the culture. If I can't figure out how to bring the culture with me, I'm the wrong person for the job.' For Mulchay it was about Xerox, not about her ... For 2000 and 2001 Xerox posted a total of nearly $367 million in losses. By 2006 Xerox posted profits in excess of $1 billion and sported a much stronger balance sheet."[7]

The picture painted of Xerox is identical to what has been happening to the Church over her various stages of existence. In the fourth generation of the Church

Age, righteousness in the kingdom is at an all-time low. The righteous generation would do well to understand that they carry the culture of the Church with them, and must bring the culture of Christ-likeness to bear on the activities of the Church otherwise we are not worthy of Christ for everything is about him: *John 14:10–14*. Whenever there is decline, restoration will come only by returning to the culture and values upon which the organization was built. For the Church it is righteousness, holiness, love, prayerfulness and Christ-likeness. According to Collins, *"A great nation can decline and recover; great companies fall and recover; great social institutions fall and recover, and individuals fall and recover."*[8] He states that at the stage where decline is eminent is time to preserve the core values in order to stimulate progress. Is there any wonder then that the Sardis Church Age is counselled to *"remember how thou hast received and heard, and hold fast, and repent." – Rev 3:3*.

Stage four rescue: According to Collins' five stages of decline of an organisation, the Sardis Church Age at Stage 4 will require divine intervention and a return to her values and virtues to affect the social order. However because God is still dealing with the assets of the Church as "people with a free will," it is obvious that the unity required for corporate repentance will have to be forced with judgement. See reproduction of Collins Stage 4 graph below:

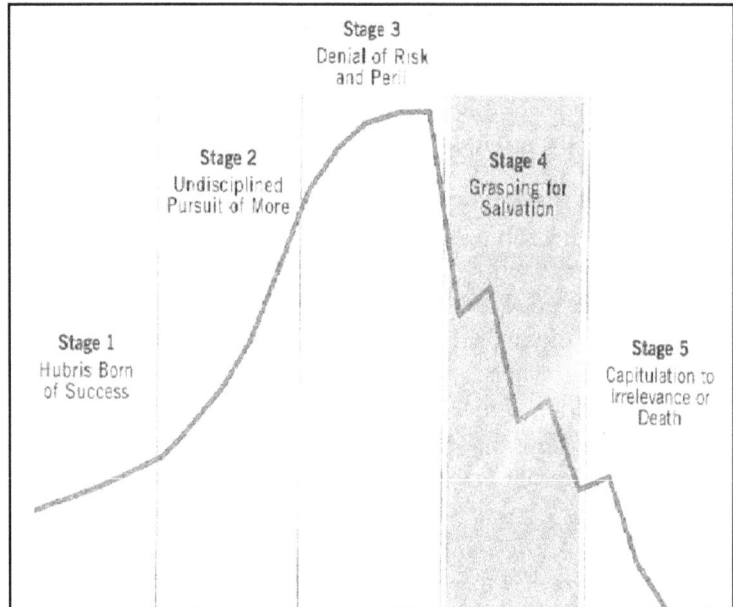

Fig. 9. Collins' Stage 4 decline[9]

Interestingly, Collins agrees that an early decision to rectify problems would have saved an organisation from decline. "No company we studied was destined to fall all the way to Stage 5, each company could have made different decisions earlier in the journey to reverse its downward slide. But by the time a company has moved through Stages, 1, 2, 3, and 4, those in power can become exhausted and dispirited, and eventually abandon hope. When you abandon hope you should begin preparing for the end. "But hope alone is not enough, you need enough resources to continue to fight. If you lose ability to make strategic choices, forced into short term survival decisions that cripple the enterprise, then the odds of full recovery become increasingly remote."[10] God's plan for every Christian who is indwelt by the Holy Ghost, is that our relationship with him will be so close that we will individually receive the counsel of the Holy Ghost as the life more abundantly which Christ came to give, and the route to agape love.

The restoration movements from AD 1500 to 2000, were God's intervention to save the Church from her downward fall: as she departed from her first love. The movements restored a measure of hope but did not totally correct the fault or avert the judgement. Stage 4 renewal and restoration graph will show how judgement will be God's hope of restoring righteousness to the Church Age to reap the greatest harvesting of souls from the earth, through a youthful generation of people.

Collins' Stage 4 "Well founded hope" graph reflects the fruit of the corporate repentance of the Sardis Church Age after the judgement which claimed the lives of the souls under the altar.

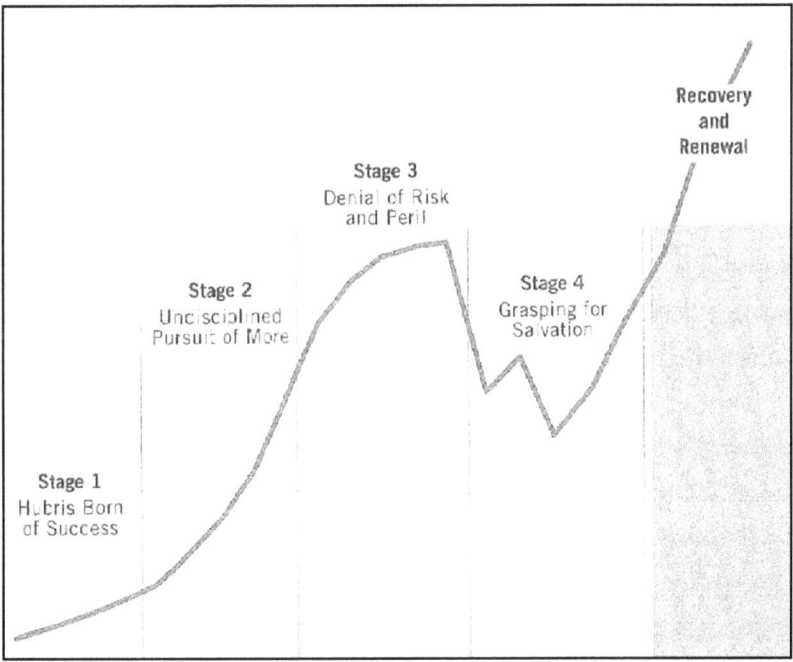

Fig. 10. Collins' Stage 4 decline and recovery: Well founded hope[11]

Stage 4: Well founded hope for the Church. This hope is satisfied with the empowering of the Philadelphia Church Age. This divine intervention from God, following the judgement on the Sardis Church Age, will result in the combined Church Age of Jews and Gentiles as the "well founded hope" for the Church Age to reap the greatest harvest from the earth because of the renewed co-operation between the Father, the Sons of God and the Holy Ghost thereby living out the scripture that says it is God who works in us both to will and to do of his good pleasure. According to Collins:

"If we discover that organisational decline is a function first and foremost of forces out of control—and if we discover that those who fall will inevitably keep falling to their doom—we could rightly judge in despair. But that is not our conclusion from this analysis, not if you catch decline in Stages 1, 2 or 3. And in some cases Stage 4 as long as you still have enough resources to get out of the cycle of grasping and rebuild one step at a time. And if you have already taken a fall and you do... the sooner you break the cycle of grasping for salvation the better. The path to recovery lies first and foremost in returning to sound management practices and rigorous strategic thinking."[12]

The counsel of Christ to the Sardis Church Age is to "watch, remember how thou hast received and heard and hold fast and repent." The Church that departs from the counsel of the Holy Ghost will fail to live by faith, for faith comes by hearing what the Spirit says unto the son—*Rm 14:8*. The mandate of Christ given in *Isaiah 61:1–11* speaks of a time when mourning will restore *"the oil of joy"* to the Church Age; even to the time when the Jews and Gentiles will unite to form the Church of the two witnesses. The well founded hope of the Church Age is Christ's resolve to build his Church and the gates of Hell will not prevail against the work. The inevitable decline of righteousness in the kingdom is because men turned away from the guidance of the Holy Ghost but restoration in this Church Age will result in the double anointing promised to the Jews in: *Isaiah 61:7 and Joel 2:28–29*.

CHAPTER FIFTEEN

DOCTRINES RESPONSIBLE FOR THE DECLINE

Matt 24:14 "And this gospel of the kingdom shall be preached in all the world for a witness unto all nations; and then shall the end come." Rm 14:17 "For the kingdom of God is not meat and drink; but righteousness, peace and joy in the Holy Ghost. For ye that in these things serveth Christ is acceptable to God, and approved of men."

The three doctrines that the Churches have entertained over the four stages of decline are: the Nicolaitanes, Balaam, and Jezebel. It takes wisdom and knowledge to change or destroy a soul, therefore, if the gospel of the kingdom of God is not preached to save souls, the gospel that promotes the world kingdom will be preached. The scripture confirms that whosoever serves Christ by preaching the gospel of the kingdom is acceptable to God and approved of men.

The kingdom of God is the wisdom, knowledge and joy of the Holy Ghost by which he teaches, instructs and guides his children (*Ps. 32:8*). That is to say whosoever, preach and teach the wisdom, knowledge and counsel of the Father serves God acceptably and is approved of men. Whenever these three things are replaced by any other doctrine then death will come to the soul, which is the assignment of the Devil (*John 10:10*). Righteousness according to Vines *"was formerly spelled 'right-wiseness'"*[1] which clearly expresses its meaning. The joy of the Holy Ghost is the counsel of the will of God to man; when man departs from the counsel of the Holy Ghost, love is not perfected in his heart, and neither can he please God for without the hearing of faith it is impossible to please God (*Heb. 11:6*). The righteousness of God therefore is the wisdom of God; the peace of God is the commandments of God that give man knowledge of the laws, statutes and judgements of God which, when they are kept in love establishes peace between God and man.

There are different views on the nature of these doctrines. It would appear that they are symbolic names for: *the world (Col. 2:6–8), wrong worship (1 John 2:15–17), and wrong wisdom (James 3:15–17).* They introduce into the Church the ways of the world which takes the commandments, laws, statutes and judgements of God out of the hearts of mankind; and sinful mankind cannot hear the counsel of God of himself, and where the counsel of God is lacking, man will listen to the counsel of the devil, that bewitches the soul and leads to wrong worship. They are one and all of the three temptations of God's living creatures. They are reflections of the three temptations of Christ that the devil threw at him. Lucifer sought to be worshiped; Eve sought wisdom but was deceived when she listened to the counsel of the devil against the counsel of God *(Isa. 30:1)*. The new creation, is seeking for the things of the world instead of the Kingdom of God *(Matt. 6:33)*.

In order to propagate the truth, there must be a preacher or teacher, who serves as a prophet between God and sinful mankind; someone who can hear God for the people *(Rom. 10:14)*. Bible scholars agree that the Church can be a single individual or corporately as a body of people. The devil seeks to corrupt minds and as it is with one individual, so it will be for the Church as the body of Christ. The Church, through the people, seemed to have succumbed to these three temptations. There is no record of the individual Church having corporately repented of the things for which each one was convicted, and there can never be loose ends where sin is concerned. The testimony of God when he revealed his glory to Moses is that he forgives, sins, transgressions and iniquities and *"will by no means clear the guilty" (Exod. 34:7–8)*. These are strong words that cannot be ignored in any age.

The Nicolaitanes:

The Rider of the White Horse; Revelation. 6:1–2
The Church of Ephesus: Departed From First Love; Revelation. 2:4

Col. 2:6–8 "As ye have therefore received Christ Jesus the Lord, so walk ye in him: 7. Rooted and built up in him, and stablished in the faith, as ye have been taught, abounding therein with thanksgiving. 8. Beware lest any man spoil you through philosophy and vein deceit, after the tradition of men, after the rudiments of the world, and not after Christ." Rev. 2:3 4 "Nevertheless, I have somewhat against thee, because thou hast left thy first love."

During the Ephesus Church Age, the doctrine of the Nicolaitanes was identified as developing but ignored. It seemed to have affected men as leaders who are the mouth-peace between God and sinful mankind. In this Church Age, some of those who said they were apostles and were not had departed from the counsel of the Holy Ghost that enables the Christian to practice agape love and were found to be liars. The doctrine continued until the Pergamus Church Age, when it took root and to it was added the doctrine of Balaam; and by the time of the Thyatira Church

Age sin had increased and the third doctrine of Jezebel was also added. Now in this Sardis Church Age all three are working together against the advancement of the kingdom of God.

The name Nicolaitanes is made up of two Greek words: *niko* meaning "to conquer" and *laos* meaning "people." To conquer people speaks about leadership. The doctrine seems to relate to the leaders of the Church movement. Nicodemus was a ruler of the Jews; his name means "conqueror of the people."[2] Leadership is God's idea, which means that leaders have a great impact on the people they lead in any movement, and the obvious place for the devil to begin his assault against the advancement of the Church movement, is with its leaders. One of the original seven deacons chosen to do arms was called Nicolas. It is believed that the doctrine is a derivative of his name. According to Willmington, *"Many believe John was speaking of the growing distinction between the clergy and the laity."*[3] The name may therefore be a symbol describing leaders of the church movement who became influenced by the ways of the world – *Col 2:8. The Spirit-Filled Life Bible Commentary* on the Nicolatanes says: "apparently the group claimed some kind of superiority status that permitted idolatry and immorality."[4] By AD 96, when John wrote the Apocalypse, these traits were in the Church but really blossomed into a problem about AD 300 when the leaders of the Catholic Church ruled that the Bishops should have authority over all the churches. Seeds of righteousness will grow into trees; so also will seeds of ungodliness. Even in the day of Christ he warned against false prophets who would seek to mislead the people. -

"Beware of false prophets, which come to you in sheep's clothing, but inwardly they are ravening wolves. Ye shall know them by their fruits. Do men gather grapes of thorns, or figs of thistles? Even so, every good tree bringeth forth good fruit; but a corrupt tree bringeth forth evil fruit. A good tree cannot bring forth evil fruit, neither can a corrupt tree bring forth good fruit. Every tree that bringeth not forth, good fruit is hewn down, and cast into the fire. Wherefore by their fruits ye shall know them" (Matt. 7:15–17).

Throughout the Bible God speaks to leaders of the people for the people. The devil sought to sift Peter as wheat. He was the eldest apostle and one of the three closest to Christ whom he called "a stone" or a strong leader. Wheat is a symbol that describes the righteous man – *Matthew 3:12*. By this statement Christ revealed that the plan of the devil is to sift the righteous generation, or even leaders of the Church Age as wheat. Sifted wheat is still wheat. So what was Jesus saying? It is assumed that he spoke about the counsel of the Holy Ghost, which leaders should be seeking on behalf of the people. To be sifted as wheat is to take away the substance of our faith, which is the hearing of the counsel of the Father and the eternal life Christ came to give to the sons of God – Hebrews 11:1-6. The next comment of Jesus was: "I have prayed for you that your faith fail not." In other words I have prayed for you that you will be guided by the Holy Ghost. This leading of the Spirit was confirmed to Peter in *John 21:15–19*.

It is natural that the devil would seek to corrupt the minds of leaders, because of their influence on the lives of the people. The shepherds of Israel were accused of not feeding the flock and killing them with the sword. In *Revelation 6:3–4*, the devil seeks to take peace from the earth, as the one who comes to kill to steal and to destroy *(John10:10)*. Moses said of Aaron, he made the people naked. Peter warned of immoral and greedy false teachers who will use people as a means of reaching their own selfish goals. The New Testament indicates that deceptive teachers will characterise the Church Age and that their activities will increase in later times *(1 Tim. 4:11; Matt. 24:11–13)*.

"For the people turneth not unto him that smiteth them neither do they seek the LORD of Hosts. Therefore the LORD will cut off from Israel head and tail, branch and rush in one day. The ancient and honourable he is the head, the prophet that teacheth lies he is the tail. For the leaders of this people cause them to err and they that are led of them are destroyed" (Isa. 9:13–15).

The revelation that this doctrine brings to this Church Age is that God will also hold leaders responsible for the souls of the people in the Church Age. *Ezekiel 34: 1–6* places the blame for Israel's sins squarely on the shoulders of her leaders. In the dispensation of the Church Age, it will not be any different.

The Pergamos Church—the Second of the Silver Age Church: AD 500–1500

The Doctrine of Balaam and Nicolaitanes,
The Rider of the Red Horse and the Great Sword to Take Peace From the Earth:
i.e. the Peace of the Kingdom of God.

Matt. 6:24 "No man can serve two masters: for either he will hate the one, and love the other; or else he will hold to the one, and despise the other. Ye cannot serve God and mammon."

The rule of this Church Age began in *AD 500*. Church history reveals that from the time of Pope Leo *(AD 440–461)* to Pope Innocent III *(AD 1198–1216)*, Rome, Antioch, Constantinople, Jerusalem and Alexandra were seats of power over the Church. The book of *Revelation* will confirm that the written judgement is influenced by the prevalence of evil knowledge against good knowledge in human hearts. The peace of God will keep their hearts stayed on God *(Phil. 4:7)*. Evil knowledge causes spiritual death to the soul, and when the truth is not preached, lies will give birth to death as truth gives birth to life *(Eph. 5:14)*.

"Having eyes full of adultery, and that cannot cease from sin, beguiling unstable souls: an heart they have exercised with covetous practices; cursed children. Which have forsaken the right way, and are gone astray, following the way of Balaam the son of Bosor, who loved the wages of unrighteousness" *(2 Pet. 2:12–22).*

Balaam was responsible for Israel's sin *(Num. 25:1–5)*. He was a prophet hired by the King of Moab to curse Israel. His name means 'lord of the people.' Balaam was interested in the reward promised him by the King of Moab, instead of listening to the voice of God. His service could be readily bought, and he taught that immorality and idolatry would work against the people whom no one could curse. This doctrine was introduced into the Church during the time of the reign of Emperor Nero (AD 64); and is associated with wrong worship, that has its roots in the love for money and sexual immorality. To worship God is to have reverence for his truths and obey them. Obedience eventually leads to the worship of God: For example:

"Thou shalt have no other God beside me; thou shalt not make unto thee any graven image of any likeness of anything that is in the earth; thou shalt not bow down thyself to them nor serve them" (Exod. 20:3-4).

"But he answered and said, It is written, man shall not live by bread alone, but by every word that proceedeth out of the mouth of God" (Matt. 4:4).

"And God said unto Balaam, Thou shalt not go with them; thou shalt not curse the people: for they are blessed" (Num. 22:12).

Balaam knew he could not curse the people whom God had blessed so he caused them to commit adultery and fornication for he knew such sins were forbidden of God. Wrong sexual relationship was identified with Sodom and Gomorrah; and will multiply unto whoredom and sodomy. Good knowledge is instruction unto godliness, and when the knowledge of God departs from the hearts of men the peace of God also departs, and man become estranged from God, and will no longer be able to hear the counsel of the Holy Ghost to walk in agape love.

Pergamos was a city mainly connected with the religious system known as Emperor Worship, which had its headquarters in Pergamum in the province of Asia. Emperor worship began in Rome, under Agustus Caesar, and all other religions were tolerated provided they paid homage to Caesar as a god. According to Fleming: *"There were some Christians who taught and practised Nicolaitan teaching, which encouraged Christians to join in idolatrous feasts and to practise immorality."*[5] Donald Guthrey also links the Nicolatanes with those who hold on to the teachings of Balaam and that the false teachings was connected with the meat offered to idols.[6] This view is understandable, because both doctrines will run together; where there is no repentance, there is bound to be continuation and multiplication of evil.

Balaam showed his love for money, when he chose to work for Balak, for the money and position promised him. The message of Christ to the Church is that no man can serve God and mammon; therefore, where there is iniquity there will also be idolatry. In this Church Age, not only was iniquity an issue, but idolatry was also increasing.

The doctrine of Jezebel: Evil Wisdom Which is Witchcraft and Idolatry–Isaiah 5:20–23
The Rider of the Black Horse of the Thyatira Church Age:
Revelation 6:5–6: "A measure of wheat for a penny; and three measures of barley for a penny."
Matt. 6:25: "Therefore I say unto you, Take no thought for your life, what ye shall eat, or what ye shall drink; nor yet for your body, what ye shall put on. Is not the life more than meat, and the body than raiment?"
Matt. 6:33: "But seek ye first the kingdom of God and its righteousness (wisdom); peace (knowledge; joy (counsel) of the Holy Ghost" See Ecclesiastes 2:26.
For sins of rebellion, idolatry and witchcraft. 1 Samuel 15:23
James 3:13-17: "Who is a wise man and endued with knowledge among you? Let him show out of a good conversation his works with meekness of wisdom. But if ye have bitter envying and strife in your hearts glory not and lie not against the truth. This wisdom desendeth not from above, but is earthly, sensual, devilish"

A king rules by counsel, evil queens will also influence the throne through evil wisdom of the world. Counsel is productive and never fails to deliver, because the king will watch over his counsel until it is performed. Jezebel was the wife of King Ahab, and by all account the power behind his throne. "Jezebel imported the worship of Baal (the sun god of the Phoenicians) and Astarte (the moon goddess) into Ahab's kingdom. "Jezebel tried to convince her husband to begin serving the golden calf, under the pretence that such worship would really be of service to Jehovah."[7] Ahab erected in Israel suggestive pillars associated with the pornographic worship of Baal, and soon every form of moral wickedness was practiced in the name of religion. God's prophets were ruthlessly persecuted and murdered.

Jezebel doctrine is a mixture of all three doctrines, one which involves idol worshipping, sexual immorality, false teachings all of which developed because God's people departed from his counsel, choosing rather to listen to the counsel of the devil or other human beings. The Church that departs from the counsel of the Holy Ghost, cannot find approval with God and acceptance with man, because counsel is the missing arrow in the bow of the righteous generation (*Rev. 6:1-2*). It goes to the heart of a matter. Paul sums up the matter of the kingdom eloquently for those who will understand in *Romans 14:17-19*. In the Old Testament when iniquity was great amongst God's people the voice of God was scarce – *1 Samuel 3:1*. Christ's message to the Sardis Church Age is: *remember how ye have received and hold fast and repent."* The letter is from him that hath the seven spirits of the LORD; the same fullness of the Holy Ghost that came on the day of Pentecost.

This is a critical time in the watches of the Church and leaders must prepare the ground for the reform that will restore the 'counsel' to the Church, so that sons of God for whom creation waits will manifest. It does not matter whether the return of Christ is far or nearer than we think, there is a generation that must prepare the foundation, or repair the foundation on which the other will build.

CHAPTER SIXTEEN

THE JUDGMENT IN THE SARDIS CHURCH AGE

Time and time again, according the review of the words of the prophets, the Sardis Church Age proves to be a time when judgement is executed as the iron age of the kingdom of heaven. Through the interpretation of a dream, Daniel saw the spirits of the four generations of human beings struggling for dominion in the earth: the righteous, the ungodly, the wicked, and the evil generations. (See *Daniel 7:2–3*). The righteous generation, symbolised by the lion, was given eagles' wings, meaning great strength. (See *Revelation 12:14*). God, however, gave them into the hands of their enemies and they were mercilessly killed as the two witnesses or the Philadelphia Church. Daniel later saw the Church, the bride of Jesus as one body gathered around the tabernacle of God in heaven as seen in *Revelation 4–5*.

The purpose of these analysis is to give clear and convincing proof that judgement in the Sardis Church Age is inevitable and corporate mourning and repentance are required to restore the righteousness and the power of the kingdom - *Isaiah 9:7 "Of the increase of his government and peace there shall be no end, upon the throne of David, and upon his kingdom, to order it, and to establish it with judgement and with justice from henceforth even forever. The zeal of the LORD of hosts will perform this."*

One revelation of the activities of the Church at the time when she was judged in the Thyatira Church Age is given in *Zechariah 6:1–8 "And I turned and lifted up mine eyes, and looked and, behold, there came four chariots out from between two mountains; and the mountains were of brass. In the first chariot were red horses; and in the second chariot black horses; and in the third chariot white horses; and in the fourth chariot grizzled and bay horses. Then I answered and said unto the angel that talked with me, what are these, my lord? And the angel answered and said unto me, these are the four spirits of the heavens, which go forth from standing before the Lord of all the earth. The black horses which are therein go forth into the north country; and the white go forth after them;' and the grizzled go forth toward the south country. And the bay went forth, and sought to go that they might walk to and fro through the earth: and he said, Get you hence, walk to and fro through the earth. So they walked to and fro through the earth. Then cried he upon me, and spake unto me saying, behold these that go toward the north country have quieted my spirit in the north country."*

The horses came from between two mountains. Mountains are symbolic of national power. Two mountains of brass speak of a time when both spiritual kingdoms are under the influence of the wicked generation and would be judged according to the principle of judgement applied to kingdoms in the past. For example in the day of King Ahaz of Judah the kingdom of David was judged, but judgement was not executed until after the death King Josiah; or according to the prophet Amos who says: *For three transgressions of a kingdom and for four, God will not turn away the judgement thereof"- Amos 1:3,11,13.* (See *Figure 11* below). The black horse is the strength of evil knowledge against the word of God (*the north the place of the word*); the grizzled towards the south *(the place of the Spirit);* the white towards the north speaks of a time of restoration as God's divinely intervenes to save the church from AD 1500 onwards.

God's sovereign rule manifested in time over generations: Dan. 7:1–8; Zec. 6:1–8; Rev. 6:1–8; Zec. 4:1–10

OT Symbols	The generations	The Horses: Zec 6:1-8 Rev 6:1-8; Zec 6:7-8S	The Church: Zec 4:1-10; Rev 2:22-23	
Gold	Righteous	White	Ephesus	Grace
Silver	Ungodly	Red	Smyrna and	
Bronz	Wicked*	Black	Pergamos	Grace
			Thyatira	Judged

*The white riders between two mountains of brass refers to the
The restoration movement of AD 1500 with Martin Luther
and the Reformation.

Iron	Evil	Grey Grizzled towards the south country	Sardis Judgement begins
		Bay: The fullness of Sin results in chaos and famine all over the World.	

Fig. 11. A new and dynamic Church of the Sons of God, as the
Philadelphia Church and a fresh pouring out of the
Holy Ghost as the 'south' implies.

Daniel 7:2 refers to a time when the four winds of the heavens struggle upon the great sea. The four winds of the heavens are the four characteristics of the Holy Ghost: the spirit of wisdom and understanding, and the spirit of knowledge and the fear of the LORD. This is the period when the wicked and evil generations of the world wrestle to gain control of the kingdom of heaven: "as it is written, nation will rise against nation and kingdom against kingdom." The word of God and the Spirit of God must work together in and through the believer, to draw souls to Christ— *John 14:10–14, 23–24*. When the word of God is replaced by human wisdom and ideologies, the work of the Holy Ghost is frustrated and God will divinely intervene to overthrow religion and falsehood. The black horse goes forth into the North Country and the white horse follows. The north is symbolic of the place of the Word of God. The mission of the devil is to take peace (the knowledge of God) from the earth -*Revelation 2:21–22; 6:3–4*. Here we see knowledge of evil fighting against the good knowledge of the words of God. That there are horses going towards the south country shows that the war is spiritual. Nothing comes out or goes towards the east because the presence of God is there: all things stand before him. The strength of evil went forth and sought for permission so that it might go to and fro through the earth: and God permitted this and it will result in the killing of many people- *Zechariah 6:7*.

There will also be famine and starvation in many nations of the world. The reign of evil will spread rapidly in the world and will seriously affect the lives of the people of kingdom of heaven because of the unsoundness of the message preached. Judgement as divine intervention will force the corporate repentance required of the Church which will bring an end to the existence of the Sardis Church Age. It becomes evident that the years of this Church Age is not expected to be as long as others before her because of the rule of evil in the world.

The journey of Elijah: Elijah's ministry may not have lasted more than seven years. In the third year of his ministry, God commanded him to go and show himself to Ahab and he would send rain upon the land. After his victory at Mount Carmel, he began to flee from Jezebel. The summary and comparison of the journeys are as follows:

The journey in the wilderness	**The journey of the Church in the Wilderness: Isa. 41:19**
1 day's journey	1000 years after Pentecost
Elijah slept under the juniper tree	The people of the Pergamos Church Age slept whilst the Enemy worked: *Matt. 13:25*

The juniper tree is a thorny tree. The wood produces long-lasting fire. God told Adam the earth will bring forth to him "thorns" and "thistles." Both represent wickedness and evil. When ungodliness rules wickedness and evil will increase in the world and must continue until God intervenes with judgement.

An angel cooked	The Church Age
Elijah ate and slumbered	AD 1000–1500
The Angel of the LORD cooked *(1 Kings 19:7)*	The Holy Ghost revival to the Thyatira
Elijah went 40 days journey	ChurchAge -from AD 1500–2000
Elijah camped in a cave *(1 Kings 19:9–10)*	"Church fossilised in buildings"
"Elijah was very zealous for the LORD"	She was once zealous for the LORD now she is not affecting the social order

What followed next:

A strong wind	The wind of revival in the Sardis
Earthquake/fire	Church Age—AD 2000
	Fire of judgement that purges to restore and earthquake will root out deadness: *Rev. 3:1–3*

There were left 7000 righteous in Israel in the time of Elijah. They are as the few righteous remnant of Sardis Church who must mourn for a restoration of the counsel: *Isa. 61:3; Matt. 5:4; Rev. 3:1–3; Ps. 14:1–4*

The still small voice of God is heard	The power that will manifest when the counsel of The Holy Ghost is fully restored to the Church Age: *Ps. 14:5–7*. Hence the birth of the Philadelphia Church Age of the two witnesses.

Ezekiel and the Valley of Dry Bones: Ezekiel 37:1-28

The LORD God at the hands of other nations executed judgement upon David's kingdom in its divided stage, with Israel under the Assyrians, and Judah under the four kingdoms from the Babylonian to the Roman Empire. Those nations would have had no power over God's covenant people except God allowed it. From the time of David to whom the promise of a king on his throne forever was made, there was a gradual decline of righteousness within the kingdom that resulted in the judgements on both the northern and southern kingdoms. The prophecy of *Ezekiel 37* spans the time of Judah's return from Babylon to the restoration of Israel in the Church Age even unto the millennial reign of Christ. Ezekiel saw the state of the nation and her restoration as he was carried away in the spirit.

1. **The Valley full of dry bones:** *Eze 37:1* - The dry bones represents the deadness of the Nation Israel and marks an end to God dealing with men in the natural because of the coming into being of the spiritual man in the Church Age.
2. **Prophesy upon bones refers to the coming of Christ the prophet to whom Moses instructed Israel to hearken:** Hear the world of the Lord: *Rev. 13:19; Matt. 17:5; Deut. 18:15; Lk. 9:35*. Christ is the manifestation of the word of God and the true prophet to whom all Israel were instructed to give audience; God also confirming him on the Mount of Transfiguration as the Son to whom Israel should hearken. Ezekiel's prophecy began to be fulfilled in the voice of John the Baptist. Christ also preached repentance for remission of sins.
3. **The New Spirit of Pentecost:** *Eze 37:5–6;* **Joel 2:28** - The beginning of the Church Age and end of Daniel's sixty-ninth week of years for the Jews. **"Covered with skins":** The skins are the garments of salvation, righteousness and praise relating to the righteous. This lasted until the falling away spoken of by Paul as the Church practiced religion, from that time until AD 1500.
4. **Prophecy unto the wind:** This refers to the grace renewal movements from the Reformation of AD 1500 onwards: even to the judgement on the Church Age. "Come from the four winds O breath, breath upon these slain that they may live." **See:** "I will kill her children with death" (*Rev. 2:23; Isa. 66:6*).
    - **(a). The three noises:** The great revival movements from AD 1500; noise from temples; and a noise of God's judgement pronounced upon the Sardis Church Age.
    - **(b). A shaking in the Sardis Church Age:** The decline of righteousness in the kingdom of heaven has reached unacceptable proportions in the eyes of God. He must intervene in the Sardis Church Age to restore righteousness:

        Few in Sardis - *Rev. 3:1–8;*
        Barked fig tree - those who sorrow will mourn for restoration- *Joel 1:7–13*
        The beginning of sorrow - *Matt. 24:8; Rev. 6:7–8*

    - **(c). Bones coming together:** The birth of the Philadelphia Church of Jews and Gentiles - two dead nations coming together to birth a new and vibrant church of the two witnesses: *Zec. 1:17; Isa. 41:8–16, Isa. 51:18–20; Rev. 11:1–13, Eze. 37:15–20*.

5. **Israel possesses the Promised Land forever:** Christ and his kings posses the land forever in the Millennium.

The Seven Feasts of the Old Testament:

To complement this analysis, we shall turn attention to the significance of the seven feasts of Jehovah recorded in *Leviticus 23*, and their relationship to the Church Age from Pentecost to the rapture of the Church of the two witnesses. There were three main annual festivals in Israel: the Passover, the feast of Unleavened Bread, and the Feasts of Tabernacles marking the 'in-gatherings'. The latter was held in the middle of the year. These festivals recalled the nation's history, but they also help to interpret the history of the Church.

The Passover:	Commemorating deliverance from Egypt: Christ was offered as our Passover Lamb to secure man's redemption form sin: *1 Cor. 11:24-25; Lev. 23:4-5*
Unleavened Bread:	The four gospels and teachings of Christ: *2 Thess. 2:13-14; Lev. 23:6-8; Ex. 34:18*
The First-fruits:	Christ's resurrection from the dead, and those who went with him: *1 Cor. 15:20; Lev. 23:9-14; Ex. 34:19-20, 26*
Pentecost:	The decent of the Holy Ghost: *Acts 2:1–4; Lev. 23:15–22*
Trumpets:	The Church Age heralding the Good News: *Matt 28:19-20; Lev. 23:23-25*. This feast herald the good news that the next would followed shortly. The New Testament similitude will be found in the four Church Ages from Ephesus to Sardis: the second Church Age consisting of two churches.
The Atonement:	Atonement' is a plural word in Hebrew that includes deliverance from the penalty of sin, the power of sin; (atonement or redemption of the body and deliverance from the power of sin): *2 Cor. 1:9-10; Phil. 3:21; 1 John 3:2*. This reflects a time in the Sardis Church Age when judgement is determined: *Jer. 1:15*, and mourning is required for restoration of the counsel of the Holy Ghost, or a new outpouring of the Holy Ghost according to the prophet Joel.
Tabernacles:	The newly empowered Philadelphia Church of Sons of God perfected in Christ-likeness and who were seen gathered around the throne in heaven as a great wonder after they were killed and called up to heaven as the two witnesses — *Rev. 11:12*.

When the prophecies are understood from the perspective of the Church Age, and even backed up by ordinances of the Old Testament, the stark reality of the state of the Church confronts us. It does not matter whether our human understanding tells us the Church is doing well – the true position is what Christ has said to the Church Ages: *"ye that hath ear to hear let him hear."*

What is required for restoration in the Sardis Church Age: Historically, God does not judge a people without reproof; before doing so he reveals the action to be taken to avoid judgement. The Ephesus Church had omitted something which is fundamental to the new creation status, which is the guidance of the counsel of the Holy Ghost that gives power to the Christian to be witnesses -*Acts 1:8*. Christ called her to repentance, or else she would have her candlestick removed out of its place; which is that she would be removed out of her ruling position. This is a replay of the very things that happened to Adam and Eve when they disobeyed the counsel of God; they were removed out of the place where the presence of the LORD dwelt. The Book of Joel counsels on the corrective measures that will restore righteousness in the day of the Sardis Church Age, which is also the time of the first trumpet judgement according to this exposition:

"Blow the trumpet in Zion, and sound an alarm in my holy mountain: let the inhabitants of the land tremble: for the day of the LORD cometh, for it is nigh at hand. A day of darkness and of gloominess, a day of clouds and thick darkness, as the morning spread upon the mountains, a great people and a strong; there hath not been ever the like, neither shall be any more after it, even to the years of many generations" (Joel 2:1).

"The morning spread upon the mountains," would be the dawn of the third millennium of the death of Christ from AD 2001 onwards. The mountains are the government of the Church Age and government of nations. The great and strong people will be those of the Philadelphia Church. Before the rise of this great army, there is need to sound the warning of the trumpet; but the problem must first be identified, for if the trumpet gives an uncertain sound, nothing will change -*2 Corinthians 13:12*. The first of the seven trumpet judgements will, therefore, be sounded in this Church Age.

Joel tells us what the problem is: *"The meat offering and the drink offering is cut off from the house of the LORD . . . The field is wasted, the land mourneth; for the corn is wasted: the new wine is dried up, the oil languisheth"*(Joel 1:9-10).

The meat offering in the Old Testament is a type of the "counsel of the Holy Ghost." It was to be eaten only by the High Priest and his sons because it was a "most holy thing." Jesus said to his disciples in *John 4:32*, *"I have meat to eat that ye know not of."* Words are also called "things" and a most holy word must flow from the Spirit of God to the sons of God (*Rom. 8:14*). The Apostle Paul says in *1 Corinthians 12:13*, *"we all drink into one Spirit."* The new wine of the Holy Ghost which came on the day of Pentecost is seemingly dried up in the Church and the power for witnessing, or for signs and wonders, is not manifesting as it was in the early days. The field is the world of mankind, which means that many souls are being lost to sin. The land mourns for the word of God preached is wasted, and the anointing does not bring the desired results because of the state of men's hearts (*Rev. 6:7–8*).

Joel calls leaders to repentance. Leaders lost the counsel for the people: that is why the doctrine of the Nicolaitanes was found in the Ephesus Church. They must first repent and mourn for its return and afterwards call a solemn assembly of the people to equally mourn and repent (*Isa. 61:1–3; Matt. 5:4*). The watchfulness that is required of the Sardis Church is to be prayerful and discerning. However, the kind of prayer that restores righteousness is supplication, as it was also in the day of Daniel and Ezra (*Zech. 12:10–12*). Sin must be acknowledged by a people and repentance sought before restoration (*2 Chron. 7:14*).

"*Blow the trumpet in Zion, sanctify a fast, call a solemn assembly. Gather the people, sanctify the congregation, assemble the elders, gather the children and those that suck the breast: let the bridegroom go out of his chamber, and the bride out of her closet. Let the priests and ministers of the LORD, weep between the porch and the altar and let them say 'spear thy people O LORD' and give not thine heritage to reproach, that the heathen should rule over them. Wherefore should they say amongst the people where is their God.*" (*Joel 2:15-20*). Isaiah 55:3 calls the people to come and listen and take instruction from the Holy Ghost on what he has to say to the Church Age.

Until that time, individuals who read these revelations and understands them, must repent and live holy lives because the judgement that will restore righteousness will come suddenly. The repentance of the Sardis Church Age will give birth to a great and strong people as joy is restored, so that the mandate of Christ given to him and his church in *Isaiah 61: 1–7* can be fulfilled with the birth of the Philadelphia Church Age (*Rev. 3:8, 11:1–13; Ps. 32:8; Eccles. 2:26*).

PART 4
THE UNVEILING OF REVELATION CHAPTERS SIX TO TWENTY-TWO

CHAPTER SEVENTEEN

UNVEILING OF REVELATION CHAPTERS SIX AND SEVEN

In these chapters John saw the travail of the Church as God's governing agent of change in the world from her inception even to the day of the wrath of God. He saw seal after seal being opened to reveal things which would take place within the Church Ages resulting in the decline of righteousness and the judgement that would take place in the rule of the Sardis Church Age, some of which we already understand from previous chapters. Chapter six in this exposition is distributed and assigned to the various periods according to the number of the seals. In Chapter seven the vision concerns the sealing of 144,000 Jews who will form part of the Philadelphia Church Age. Having shown John the victorious Church around the throne after the events of seals one to six and the rapture of the Philadelphia Church, it was now time to show this Jewish statesman the fate of his own people, for he was desperately concerned about them, and as it is with God, to think is to be heard. John was shown in this vision by what means they made it to the presence of the Father.

The Four Angels Holding the Four Winds of the Earth
The Sealing of the 144,000 Jews who Form Part of the Philadelphia Church
The Great Multitude Around the Throne in Heaven

Rev 7:1–2 "And after these things I saw four angels standing on the four corners of the earth, holding the four winds of the earth, that the wind should not blow on the earth, nor on the sea, nor on any tree. And I saw another angel ascending from the east, having the seal of the living God: and he cried with a loud voice to the four angels, to whom it was given to hurt the earth and the sea. Saying hurt not the earth, neither the sea, nor the trees, till we have sealed the servants of our God in their foreheads."

The four angels: Spirits are often referred to as angels. These four angels are characteristics of the Holy Ghost that restrains evil in the world: the spirit of wisdom and understanding, and the spirit of knowledge and the fear of the LORD. They were called forth in the vision of Ezekiel to put life back into dry bones.

"Then said he unto me, Prophesy unto the wind, prophesy, son of man, and say to the wind, thus saith the Lord God; Come from the four winds, O breath, and breathe upon these slain, that they may live. So I prophesied as he commanded me, and the breath came into them, and they lived and stood up upon their feet, an exceeding great army. Then he said unto me, Son of man, these bones are the whole house of Israel: behold, they say, Our bones are dried, and our hope is lost: we are cut off for our parts" (Eze 37:9-11).

The time will come when the restraint will be taken away, but until then, they must continue to work to subdue the power of sin until the Day of the Wrath of God begins on earth.

The four winds of the earth: The four winds of the earth are the four characteristics of sin: rebellion and witchcraft, iniquity, idolatry; and ignorance and the fear of sin. They are the four characteristics of sin as the devil. They control the hearts of the wicked and evil generations of the earth so that they will not believe the truth. They are restrained from blowing upon:

The earth	because the two witnesses will rule in the power of the Holy Ghost;
The Sea	the world of mankind: sin will be subdued so that righteousness will flourish;
Trees	as the righteous generation; because of the power of the Holy Ghost at work in them and through them as the joy is restored – *Isaiah 6:3*.

The four winds of the earth have been operating on earth from creation as stated in: *2 Thessalonians 2:7 "For the mystery of iniquity doth already work: only he who now letteth will let, until he be taken out of the way."* The winds of the earth must relate to the four characteristics of sin that rules in the kingdom of darkness. However in the time of the Philadelphia Church of the two witnesses they will be restrained.

When evil knowledge and the fear of sin rule more abundantly in people's souls, instead of good knowledge and faith, iniquity is great in the earth. See *Ephesians 4:14 "That we henceforth be no more children, tossed to and fro and carried about with every wind of doctrine, by the slight of men, and cunning craftiness, whereby they lie in wait to deceive."*

At creation, God separated the wisdom of heaven from the wisdom of the earth, indicated by the phrase *"let the waters be divided from the waters"*; even though there was a natural separation there was also a spiritual separation, because God speaks to the spiritual as well as the natural in the same breath. For example, when he commanded Adam to be fruitful, multiply, and replenish the earth and subdue it, and to have dominion, he spoke also to the person of Christ; for only in Christ can man have dominion over sin and replenish the earth with the light of the gospel as the true worshippers God sought for amongst mankind. Both the Spirit and the Word work together to accomplish purpose: at creation the Spirit of God moved upon the words that were spoken by God to bring about change. Even so the Spirit in the Church Age will move again upon the word of God to bring change (*Joel 2:29*).

The second Angel from the east: Jesus tells us that it is the Father that sends the Holy Ghost (*John14:16*). To be sealed is to "receive the fullness of the Holy Ghost." This angel must be the Angel of the LORD. He is seen ascending from the east. When it was time to judge the sins of Sodom and Gomorrah: *"And the LORD said, Because the cry of Sodom and Gomorrah is great, and because their sin is very grievous; I will go down now, and see whether they have done altogether according to the cry of it, which is come unto me; and if not, I will know"* (*Gen 18:20–21*). (See *Exodus 3:8*). The Angel of the LORD would have visited earth to determine that it was time to judge the sinfulness of mankind therefore he was seen ascending from the East. He spoke in the plurality of his persons: *"Till we have sealed"* as he did in *Genesis 1:26*. It is the Holy Ghost that seals the believer as one of the persons of the Godhead. He spoke as the LORD God who decides when the time is right to execute judgement. Jesus said, the times are hidden with the Father.

The Sealing of the 144,000 Jews: Revelation 7:1–8; 14:1; Deuteronomy 33:13–17; Daniel 8:3–4

John also saw that the end was determined, but before that time there is a set of people whom God would raise up in the spirit and power of Elijah, but they must first be sealed with the power and authority of the Holy Ghost for the task set before them. The last verse of the quotation of *Matthew 24:29–32* suggests that those who are sealed will go through the great tribulation, or that the great tribulation will not take place until after the servants of God have been sealed. It seems likely that Christ referred to a generation of youths as end time champions of the gospel, according to *Revelation 14:4 and Lamentations 3:27*: *"It is good for a man that he bear the yoke in his youth."* Evidently these people are so young that the end will come in their life time. God certainly demonstrated his calling to young people in the Old Testament, for example, in the lives of Joseph, David, and Daniel; even in the days of the Kings, when children were born at specific times to rule over kingdoms, like King Cyrus or even King Josiah of Judah; or Christ, born King of the Kingdom of David forever. Therefore the sealing of the 144,000 is really the birth of the Philadelphia Church as kings of the kingdom of heaven.

There have been many propositions regarding the identity of these blessed souls. They are so numerous that they will not be mentioned here, because this exposition takes a contrary view to the propositions of men and looks to the Bible to verify and confirm the identity of those whom God will seal with the Holy Ghost at this time. Whatever God does in relation to the Jews will be in line with a pathway he has taken with them in the past. Consistency is God's way of showing mercy to those who must rightly divide the truth of his words.

When God would choose a king for Israel to replace the people's choice he looked for David a youth of his day, born for fulfilment of purpose -*Psalms 139:15*. David could not have been more than seventeen years old when Samuel anointed him king to replace Saul. However, it took many years before he eventually reached the throne.

Again it was the children born of the Israelites in the wilderness who inherited the Promised Land, albeit, they too were matured men and women by the time they crossed the Jordan.

In the case of the Hebrews in Babylon, Daniel and his three friends who stood out amongst the captives were of tender age and at the time, according to Jewish culture, would have been virgins, although because of the position they occupied, probably were made eunuchs. Christ confirmed that there are those who are made eunuchs for the gospel's sake.

The parable of the fig tree also throws some light on the identity of these virgins:

"Immediately after the tribulation of those days shall the sun be darkened, and the moon shall not give her light, and the stars shall fall from heaven, and the powers of the heavens shall be shaken . . . Now learn a parable of the fig tree; When the branch is yet tender, and putteth forth leaves, ye know that summer is nigh; So likewise ye, when ye shall see all these things, know that it is near, even at the doors. Verily I say unto you, This generation shall not pass, till all these things be fulfilled" (*Matt 24:29-32*).

A great deal is said here, but for now we will concentrate on the tender branches and leaves of the fig tree. In several instances, the fig tree is identified as a man, the nation Israel, and even the Church Age. The word generation again rises to explain these branches as a "generation of young people."

This exposition takes the views that from the Day of Pentecost, all who are for Christ were sealed with the Holy Ghost, and the sealing of the twelve tribes is not different: *Ephesians 1:13 "In whom ye also trusted, after that ye heard the word of truth, the gospel of your salvation: in whom also after that ye believed, ye were sealed with the Holy Spirit of promise."*

The selection of the 144,000 Jews is in fulfilment of God's covenant with Abraham; to make his descendants as numerous as stars. This multiplication will find its true fulfilment during the everlasting reign of Jesus. God is a Spirit and his covenant promise will only be established in perfection—*Genesis 17:7 "And I will establish my covenant between me and thee and thy seed after thee in their generations for an everlasting covenant to be a God unto thee and to thy seed after thee."* (See also *Jeremiah 33:25–26*). The Jews throughout the ages have not remained faithful and perfection was not found in many of them; but the words of God abide forever. All Jews in the time of the Gentiles must also accept Christ's atoning blood as the price of their redemption from sin in order to be saved and be part of the new creation. However, in the millennium things will be different for God will multiply them greatly according to his promise to Abraham (*Gen. 22:17–18*).

The triumphant Church: In this chapter, John takes us back to *Revelation Chapter 4* to show us the certainty of the place of security that the saints have with God as children, despite the turbulence of any tribulation period the saints must pass through:

"After this I beheld, and lo, a great multitude, which no man could number, of all nations, and kindred, and people, and tongues stood before the throne, and before the Lamb, clothed with white robes, and palms in their hands . . . And one of the elders answered, saying unto me, What are these which are arrayed in white robes? And whence came they? And I said unto him Sir, thou knowest. And he said to me. These are they which came out of great tribulation and have washed their robes, and made them white in the blood of the Lamb. Therefore are they before the throne of God, and serve him day and night in his temple; and he that sitteth on the throne shall dwell among them" (*Rev. 7:14–15*).

He saw proof that those who believe will be saved. After the sealing, and consistent with the belief that these 144,000 will make up the Philadelphia Church, John saw the saints of the great tribulation before the throne of God (*Rev. 7:13–14*). However, the remnant church on earth must go through the second half of Daniel's seventieth week of years as the Laodiceans Church Age.

CHAPTER EIGHTEEN

THE GREAT TRIBULATION AND THE DAY OF THE WRATH OF GOD

John wrote to servants, brethren, and companions in tribulation, in the kingdom of heaven. He wrote with a definite purpose, which is to warn and comfort those whom he knew must pass through the great tribulation. By the time John wrote these letters he was an elder. He was therefore a mature servant son writing to fellow servants, the righteous generation of the Church of all ages. Many Christians believe that the day we gave our lives to Christ we became mature sons of God. There must be room for growth and conformity as knowledge increases. To an extent, like a baby is born into a family, we are sons of God because of the Spirit, but a child must grow up in stages to adulthood. Many things can happen in the life of a child that will cause the father to disown the child in adulthood. All who are of Christ must accept the truth of God's word with the simplicity and obedience of a child. *"Except ye be converted, and become as little children, ye shall not enter into the kingdom of heaven"* (*Matt. 18:3*). While there is instant adoption into the family of Christ as "our father" there is no instant adoption into God's family; we are servants by calling but God's children by conforming to the image and likeness of God in Christ.

In the parable of the unfaithful servant Christ addressed two types of servants: the wicked servant and the good and faithful servant. Christians are called to conform to the image of Christ and if we do not we cannot be regarded as a good and faithful servants, or an heir. Christ is God's servant son and we are told that we must be like him. Only the good and faithful servants are of the true Church and only they will receive the reward.

Although the Church in general will go through the great tribulation she will be saved from the vial judgements in the day of the wrath of God. *"Woe unto you that desire the day of the LORD! To what end is it for you? The day of the LORD is darkness, and not light"* (*Amos 5:18*).

The words of Moses to "all Israel" proved that her journey to permanent possession of the land would end with the Church Age and in the millennium of Christ, and in the words of Isaiah, there seems to be confirmation that Israel will be joined together with the Church Age as the Philadelphia Church to go through the great tribulation into the glory of Lebanon: *Isa. 1:18-20*.

Since the coming of Christ, God has given himself three periods known as "days" in which to install his everlasting government on earth. The first day began when Christ rose from the dead. It is referred to as this present day or the day of salvation or of grace, then there is the millennial day, and the last day is the eternal day when God will restore all things unto himself under Christ. Both the Father and the Son have three days in which to work. Christ confirmed this in *Luke 13:32–33* when he said:

"Go ye and tell that fox, Behold, I cast out devils, and I do cures today and tomorrow, and the third day I shall be perfected. Nevertheless I must walk today and tomorrow, and the day following: for it cannot be that a prophet perishes out of Jerusalem."

The Son's second day is the Father's first; which means the Son's third day will be the millennial day, when his work will be completed and all enter into the seventh day rest of the Father. Because "John was in the spirit on the LORD's day" it means that his revelation spans events over the three spiritual working days of the LORD, and especially relating to the day of his wrath when he sits in judgement.

The Church and the great tribulation—Matt. 24:8–28: Tribulation refers to severe affliction; or to afflict with the aim of separating good from evil. It can come from the world to the Church or as God's judgement for the purpose of separating the righteous from the other three generations of the earth. Throughout the Church Age men and women have suffered severe persecution which is also referred to as times of tribulation. The period of the great tribulation is distinct from the day of the wrath of God. The Bible makes a definite distinction between the two periods. Tribulation is promised to the Church as God's judgement for purifying the saints for the next stage of the Church Age: *Revelation 2:22 "Behold, I will cast her into a bed, and them that commit adultery with her into great tribulation, except they repent of their deeds."* It is referred to as the great tribulation for two reasons: because it comes to a great people, as the great nation God promised to make of Abraham; and as the final onslaught of the devil against the righteous, it comes to the saints from the world as God's way of separating the just from the unjust and will be quite severe.

The hail and fire referred to as part of the great tribulation in *Revelation 8:7* come to the Sardis Church as a form of judgement and a fire of purging. At the end of this period the Philadelphia Church will emerge a strong church of sons of God manifesting his power on earth in the spirit of Elijah and Moses. This tribulation period will last until the end of Daniel's seventieth week of years, when Christ Jesus will escort the Laodiceans Church to heaven at the sound of the seventh trumpet. See *Revelation 7:14. "These are they who have come out of great tribulation."*

Punishment at its most severe leads to death, whichever way it kills; and men and women have been dying for the sake of the word of God from Old Testament times. The pains of the people who will go through this final phase will not be greater than many who have suffered before, as *Hebrews 11* reveals. The warning of Christ to the saints is that in this world we shall have tribulation, but we must not be troubled, because he has overcome the world for us (*John 16:22*). Christ has subdued all principalities and powers for the Church to have dominion if only we abide in holiness. Tribulation at the end of time will come to the Church Age because of sin but judgement will restore righteousness.

Christ passed through his own tribulation to his glorified position. He told his disciples in *John 16:33*:

"Behold, the hour cometh, yea, is now come, that ye shall be scattered, every man to his own, and shall leave me alone; and yet I am not alone, because the Father is with me. These things I have spoken unto you, that in me ye might have peace. In the world ye shall have tribulation: but be of good cheer; I have overcome the world."

There is a path that is mapped out for the righteous and no one can question why God has made it so. Paul exhorted the disciples in Antioch: *"that we must through much tribulation enter the kingdom of God"* (*Acts 14:22*). This should be an open secret to the Church, for ignorance of what is required leaves room for deception and unpreparedness. However, the Church will be spared from the wrath of the Lamb as the scripture makes clear in *1 Thessalonians 5:9*.

"For God hath not appointed us to wrath, but to obtain salvation by our Lord Jesus Christ". *"And to wait for his Son from heaven, whom he raised from the dead, even Jesus, which delivered us from the wrath to come"* (*Revelation 6:17*). *"For the great day of his wrath is come and who shall be able to stand?"*

At the height of the great tribulation in time of the two witnesses, the beasts of the earth may be soldiers of the countries of the world whom the Antichrist will mobilise to kill the saints. Because his actions will be pleasing to the nations of the world, he will quickly gain world recognition. However the indignation of the LORD will be swift: *"For the indignation of the LORD is upon all nations; and his fury upon all their armies: he hath utterly destroyed them, he hath delivered them to the slaughter"* (*Isa. 34:2*). The bodies of the saints will lie in the streets until they are called up to heaven in full view of the world. This will be the first rapture of the Church. The promise to this church is a place in God's presence, and a new name in the New Jerusalem. This is not a promise for two persons, but for the body of Christ living a complete life of holiness unto the LORD.

The Lord's Day: The Sabbath Day is often referred to as the Lord's Day. The LORD's Day or the day of the LORD is any day on which God proposes to do a thing: whether to show mercy or execute judgement. See *Joel 2:1–11*:

"Blow ye the trumpet in Zion, and sound an alarm in my holy mountain: let the inhabitants of the land tremble; for the day of the LORD cometh, for it is nigh at hand; 2. A day of darkness and of gloominess, a day of clouds and of thick darkness, as the morning spread upon the mountains: a great people and a strong; there hath not been ever the like, neither shall be any more after it, even to the years of many generations . . ." This day of Joel is really the day of the LORD's wrath according to its description.

The day of the wrath of God: *Rev. 6:12–17: "And I beheld and when he had opened the sixth seal, and lo, there was a great earthquake; and the sun became black as sackcloth of hair, and the moon became as blood; and the stars of heaven fell unto the earth . . . For the great day of his wrath is come and who shall be able to stand?"* As already acknowledged in this exposition, the Church will go through the entire period of the great tribulation but will be saved from the day of the wrath of God. (See *Revelation 15:7; 16:19; Romans 1:18; Ephesians 2:3*).

This day will begin after the seventh trumpet is sounded and the evacuation of the saints from earth is complete. By this time the devil and his fallen angels, including Lucifer, would have been thrown out of heaven and the Antichrist revealed (*Dan. 7:8, 21*). Together they will constitute an unholy trinity, to persecute the remnant Jews and terrorise the whole of mankind. At the time of the flood God judged fallen humanity for their sinfulness; but the root of evil was yet to be judged and permanently set aside. God promised by covenant that he would never again destroy the earth by water, but the destruction of the earth by fire is the last and final judgement on the devil and his agents. The prophets have spoken about this day as a day of darkness and gloom. (See *Revelation 16:1–21*).

Amos 5:16–18: "Therefore the LORD, the God of hosts, the Lord saith thus; Wailing shall be in all streets; and they shall say in all the highways, Alas! Alas! And they shall call the husbandman to mourning, and such as are skilful of lamentation to wailing . . . Woe unto you that desire the day of the LORD! To what end is it for you? The day of the LORD is darkness, and not light."

Zephaniah 1:14–18: "The great day of the LORD is near, it is near, and hasteth greatly, even the voice of the day of the LORD: the mighty man shall cry there bitterly. That day is a day of wrath, a day of trouble and distress, a day of wasteness and desolation, a day of darkness and gloominess, a day of cloud and thick darkness. A day of the trumpet and alarm against the fenced cities; and against the high towers. And I will bring distress upon men, that they shall walk like blind men, because they have sinned against the LORD: and their blood shall be poured out as dust, and their flesh as the dung. Neither their silver nor their gold shall be able to deliver them in the day of the LORD's wrath; but the whole land shall be devoured by the fire of his jealousy: for he shall make even a speedy riddance of all them that dwell in the land."

The judgement of the day of the wrath of God is graphically revealed in *Daniel 7:1–14* and interpreted in *Daniel 7:15–28*. During this day God will judge the nations of the world for their treatment of the children of the Church the Elect Lady. *"For Jacob my servant's sake, and Israel mine elect, I have even called thee by thy name; I have surnamed thee, though thou hast not known me. I am the LORD, and there is none else, there is no God beside me: I girded thee, though thou hast not known me. That they may know from the rising of the sun, and from the west, that there is none beside me. I am the LORD, and there is none else"* (*Isa. 45:4–6*).

Part of God's unfolding divine programme was that king Cyrus should be the one who would champion the return of Israel to Jerusalem, but the plan of God was bigger than that because the Elect Lady, spiritual Israel, the Church of all nations, was destined to come out of Judah, and everything he did for Israel was to this end.

What this means for us is that God will judge the nations which have made themselves a stumbling block to his purpose for the Church.

In this day, the false prophet will rule on earth, the likely city being Jerusalem. Lucifer will also rule on earth as the beast because God will give him the desire of his heart after the Laodician Church is taken out of the world at the end of the final three and a half years of Daniel's seventieth week of years. An evil generation of people deserves to have an evil ruler over their heads.

We have seen the prophets' revelation of the day of the LORD's wrath but it is not compulsory for anyone to go through the wrath of this day because God has provided a Saviour: *"The Spirit of the Lord God is upon me; because the LORD has anointed me to preach good tidings unto the meek; he hath sent me to bind up the broken hearted, to proclaim liberty to the captives, and the opening of the prison to them that are bound"* (Isa. 61:1–3).

"Seek ye the LORD all ye meek of the earth, which have wrought his judgement; seek righteousness, seek meekness: it may be ye shall be hid in the day of the LORD's anger" (Zeph. 2:3).

CHAPTER NINTEEN

UNVEILING OF REVELATION CHAPTERS EIGHT AND TEN

John beheld until all the seven seals were opened. Chapter eight reveals the events relating to the seven trumpet judgements as they affect the Church beginning with the Sardis Church. These have already been dealt with in their respective Church Age. After that, he was commissioned to reveal the prophecy to the Churches. Chapter nine deals with the events that took place when the fifth and sixth trumpet sounded.

Revelation Chapter Eight:

The Vision of the Seven Trumpets

"And when he had opened the seventh seal, there was silence in heaven about the space of half an hour. And I saw the seven angels which stood before God; and to them were given seven trumpets. And another angel came and stood at the altar, having a golden censer; and there was given unto him much incense, that he should offer it with the prayers of all saints upon the golden altar which was before the throne. And the smoke of the incense, which came with the prayers of the saints, ascended up before God out of the angel's hands"(Rev. 8:1–3).

The reason for the silence is not clear, but half an hour's silence in heaven can be a long period on earth. The times of the opening of the seals have already been assigned to the Churches and generations of *Revelation 6*.

The seven angels with the seven trumpets: At the end of the vision of the opening of the first six seals, John saw that seven angels were given seven trumpets. Chapter eight reveals the contents of six of the seven trumpet judgements as they relate to the Church Age, beginning at the Sardis Church. It appears that the sounding of the seven trumpets marking the ingathering will be in quick succession. During the journey of Israel in the desert, the trumpet and the alarm were sounded to warn the people to get ready to move out of their location: *"Make thee two trumpets of silver; of a whole piece shalt thou make them: that thou mayest use them for the calling of the assembly, and for the journeying of the camps"* (Num. 10:2).

The angel with the golden Censer - Rev. 8:3: This angel can be no other than Christ our eternal High Priest; he is the only one with the authority to make this kind of intercession for all the saints. When the seventh trumpet is sounded in reality, the saints of the Philadelphia Church of the two witnesses would have already been in heaven. The intercession of Christ is therefore for the saints of the Leodecian Church Age that they may endure, as he prayed for Peter, and the Church before *(John 17:1–3)*.

Revelation Chapter Ten

The Descent of a Mighty Angel From Heaven Clothed With a Cloud
The Voice of the Seven Thunders
The Oath of the End of all Things
The Little Book

The Mighty Angel: Rev. 10:1 *"And I saw another mighty angel come down from heaven, clothed with a cloud: and a rainbow was upon his head, and his face was as it were the sun, and his feet as pillars of fire:"*

The description of the Angel identifies him as the Angel of the LORD for the following reasons:

He was clothed in a cloud	*God wraps himself in a cloud as a garment— Psalms 104:2*
His face shun as the sun	*The sun is a symbol of the Holy Spirit; the glory of God*
His feet as pillars of fire	*His judgement upon sin was determined*
His foot on the sea and the earth	*No place would escape his judgement*
He cried with a loud voice as the roar of a lion	*He is a great king, even as the lion is king* *The lion does not roar from the forest except he has a prey*
He swears by himself	*There is nothing or no one by whom God will swear; he swears by himself*
There is time no longer	*Only God can determine the end.*

"And the LORD shall go forth as a mighty man, he shall stir up jealousy like a man of war: he shall cry, yea, roar: he shall prevail against his enemies. 14. I have long time holden my peace; I have been still, and refrained myself: now will I cry like a travailing woman I will destroy and devour at once. 15. I will make waste mountains and hills, and dry up their herbs; I will make rivers islands, and I will dry up the pools" (Isa. 42:13–14).

God visited the earth in the past in person as a Spirit, as the Angel of the LORD, and as the Captain of the Hosts of Heaven. (See *Joshua 5:14*). In the words of the prophet Isaiah, he will roar at the time of executing judgement. The sign of the rainbow about his head further confirms that he is God, who set the rainbow in the sky as a sign that he would never again destroy the earth by water; neither will he put an end to the entire human race as he did at the flood. Perhaps this is mentioned because there will be a time when the beast will attempt to destroy God's people with a flood.

"And the serpent cast out of his mouth water as a flood after the woman that he might cause her to be carried away of the flood. And the earth helped the woman and swallowed up the flood which the dragon cast out of his mouth" (Rev. 12:15–16).

The voice of the seven thunders: The voice of God is described as the voice of great thunder. John is instructed to seal up his utterance.

The oath of the end of all things: God created the heavens and the earth, the sea and all that are in them; he is the only one who can declare judgement. In the case of Sodom and Gomorrah, he declared the time when his judgement on the people had come. If this is true for two towns, how much more pertinent it is to the destruction of the earth at this time! The entire earth comes up before the LORD of the universe as prey. See *Amos 3:4 "Will a lion roar out of the forest if he has no prey?"* There is nothing perfect on earth by which God can swear; therefore when he does, he swears by himself.

The little book: The little book contains the words of this prophecy. John was made to eat it up so he would remember all he had seen and heard; and so that he could prophesy to the Church concerning all he had witnessed.

CHAPTER TWENTY

UNVEILING OF REVELATION CHAPTER ELEVEN

John is commissioned to reveal the visions to the Jews who were already being heavily persecuted. They would be encouraged to continue the struggle. However, the Church Age was still the time of the Gentiles, and the message would reach the utmost parts of the earth through them until the time when the Jews would be grafted into the work again. This chapter reveals the exploits of the Philadelphia Church and scenes from the seventh trumpet judgement.

Scenes from Seal Six: Revelation 6:12–18; Revelation 11:13–14;

Rev. 11:1–2 "And there was given to me a reed like unto a rod: and the angel stood, saying, Rise, and measure the temple of God, and the altar, and them that worship therein. But the court which is without the temple leave out, and measure it not; for it is given unto the Gentiles: and the holy city shall they tread under foot forty and two months."

The measuring rod: Ps 110:2 *"The LORD shall send the rod of thy strength out of Zion: rule in the midst of thine enemies."* The word of God is the yardstick by which all actions are measured or weighed. Having seen the revelation of things to come, John is now being told what to do about them. He was given a reed that looks like a measuring rod. A reed is a hollow rod, which means he was to sound a warning with great authority, so that those who hear and believe may carry on with the work *(Mk. 4:24)*. He was instructed to measure the temple of God, the altar, and those who worship there. To measure means to carry a message to a people. John was sent to show the dimensions of the message he had received to the people of

God by revealing the information throughout the churches in the seven locations. Only the Church would pay attention to his message and be encouraged because of the revelation encapsulated in his words. The world was already hostile; it was on account of the hostility of the world that John had been exiled on the Isle of Patmos. He was to tell the message to the leaders and true saints of those churches, and all who worshipped in them, the message would give hope to the Church, and to the Jews in particular, who would understand the significance of the gathering around the tabernacle in heaven and know that Christ had not forsaken them. He showed them the point at which they would be regrafted into the Covenant and empowered as God's chosen people. Perhaps he also opened up to them the various prophecies concerning their fate.

The Exploits of the Two Witnesses: Joel 2:1–11; 29–32; Daniel 7:4; Isaiah 57:15–18; Revelation 11:3–4:

"And I will give power unto my two witnesses, and they shall prophesy a thousand two hundred and three score days, clothed in sackcloth; These are the two olive trees, and the two candlesticks standing before the God of the earth." (See: Ezekiel 37:19; Revelation 13:7; Daniel 7:4).

The Angel also revealed to John the fate of the Philadelphia Church as the two witnesses, whom he described as the two olive trees, and the two candlesticks standing before the God of the earth. They would prophesy the first three and a half years of Daniel's seventieth week of years. The prophet Elijah spoke of the God before whom he stood, in the same vein the newly empowered Church stands before God as two nations but one Church: *Rev. 1:20*. He was not to measure the temple courts; in other words, he was not to speak to those outside the church. It was not yet time for the world to hear the whole message. This was a hard message for John to bear; it is also a hard message for anyone belonging to the body of Christ to bear at any stage of the revelation. It is no wonder the identity of the two witnesses has been kept a secret for a long time because of the importance of the message to the end time church.

Paul reminds us in *Romans 5:6–9* that although Christ died for us, it is difficult for one man to volunteer to die for another. Yet the church that must go through the great tribulation needs to know its fate; even as Christ was knowledgeable of the fact that he came as the Lamb slain before the foundation of the world; even the first apostles were subtly informed of their fate when Christ remarked that they *"would indeed drink of the cup and be baptised with the baptism,"* with which he was baptised, even though they might not have understood that they, too, were to be "a first fruit sacrifice." The benefit of knowing the fate of the Church makes the call to holiness an imperative for the person who will endure to the end. There is a need to prepare for the end; and to train up our children so that they know what to expect;

only the well-informed will survive because sin thrives where there is ignorance. For example, Shadrach, Meshach, and Abednego were able to go through their ordeal of fire because they had read the prophecy of Isaiah (*Isa. 43:2*) and they knew their lives were secure with God, whether in life or death.

The Holy City: In the letter of *Revelation 3:7* which pertains to this Church Age, Christ reveals himself as "he that is holy." The Holy City is the Church Age of the two witnesses. A city is symbolic of people gathering in corporate reverence or in defiance of God. This is a holy city; therefore, it means people gathering in corporate reverence of God. The Church is said to be a city on a hill that cannot be hid—*Matt. 5:14*. Christ has already spoken about the saints of his Church; that those who overcome will have written on their foreheads the name of the city of God, which is the New Jerusalem—*Rev. 3:12*. She is also identified as the people who will be trodden under foot for three and a half years—*Rev. 11:2*.

The identity of the two witnesses: Both major and minor prophets have spoken of the two witnesses in different ways. The book of Zechariah confirms them as the two olive trees and the two candlesticks and the Church of the two witnesses: See *Zechariah 4:2–3*.

"And said unto me, 'What seest thou?' And I said, 'I have looked and behold a candlestick all of gold, with a bowl upon the top of it, and his seven lamps thereon, and seven pipes to the seven lamps, which were upon the top thereof: And two olive trees by it, one upon the right side of the bowl, and the other upon the left side thereof.'"

The Word of God and the Holy Ghost are the two witnesses of God sent out to the entire World. However, because the witnesses are within the human heart, the two olive trees can also refer to the combined Church of Jews and Gentiles as the two witnesses in *Revelation 11:1–3*.

Phillips comments that: *"Zechariah saw a vision of two olive trees feeding the golden candelabra with a ceaseless, living supply of oil. The symbolism here points to the day when the nation of Israel will experience a spiritual awakening that will make her a light to all mankind. The revival will come "not by might, nor by power, but by my Spirit, saith the Lord of hosts."*

"The world had a foretaste of Israel's revival on the day of Pentecost, when there was a partial fulfilment of Joel's prophecy (Acts 2:16–21; Joel 2:28–32). After the rapture of the church, there will be another Pentecost that will produce the astonishing revival associated with the ministry of the two witnesses of Revelation 11 and with the preaching of the 144,000 of Revelation 7 during the tribulation. (The language used in the description of the witnesses in Revelation 11 is reminiscent of the description of Zechariah's vision). However, both of these outpourings of the Holy Spirit, one giving birth to the church and the other to the tribulation revival, are only precursors of the universal spiritual awakening—the one described by Zechariah— that will inaugurate the millennium."[1]

The Pentecostal revival referred to by Phillips will take place after the judgement of the Sardis Church according to this exposition. Phillips does not see the 144,000 as forming part of the two witnesses, but bearing in mind the decline of the Church Age, the new pouring out can only come to strengthen her after the corporate repentance is made in the Sardis Church Age and there is a return to the true core values that made her strong in the first instance. However, he agrees that the 144,000 will be part of a great revival movement that will usher in the millennial reign of Christ, although his timing of this event is a little at variance with this exposition.

Throughout the Bible the olive tree is a symbol of humanity. The Gentiles are referred to as a wild olive branch. When Noah sent the dove out of the ark it returned with the branch of an olive tree in its mouth. The dove is symbolic of the Holy Ghost; Christ made reference to the coming of the Holy Ghost as a sign to people. He also said those who look for a sign will see no other than that of the prophet Jonah. The name Jonah means a dove. See the significance to the mystery of the revelations of the sign of Jonah at the back of this book. A person is no more than the Word and the Spirit in him by which he bears witness of the good news:

> *Ps. 52:8 "But I am like a green olive tree in the house of God: I trust in the mercy of God forever and ever."*
>
> *Jer. 11:16–17 "The LORD called thy name, A green olive tree, fair, and of goodly fruit: with the noise of a great tumult he hath kindled fire upon it, and the branches of it are broken. For the LORD of hosts, that planted thee, hath pronounced evil against thee, for the evil of the house of Israel and of the house of Judah, which they have done against themselves to provoke me to anger by offering incense to Baal."*
>
> *Zech. 4:11–14 "Then answered I and said unto him. What are these two olive trees upon the right side of the candlestick and upon the left side thereof? And he answered again and said unto him. What be these two olive branches which through the two golden pipes empty the golden oil out of themselves. And he answered me and said. Knowest thou not what these be? And I said no my lord. Then said he, These are the two anointed ones that stand by the Lord of the whole earth."*

These two anointed ones are the Word of God and the Holy Ghost: See *Zech 4:3*. The candlestick of the Old Covenant is symbolic of the Holy Ghost. The two olive trees on either side are significant of the Jews and Gentiles - *Rom. 11:17*.

Many other places in the Bible confirm the two witnesses as the Church of Jews and Gentiles. For example:

Obediah 17–21	*The house of Jacob and the house of Joseph coming together*
Leviticus 23:17	*The two wave loaves representing the imperfection of man contained leaven.*
Isaiah 41:9–15	*Jacob and Israel*
Ezekiel 37:19	*The stick of Joseph, Ephraim, and the stick of Judah as one*
Zechariah 9:12–17	*I will bend Judah and subdue the bow of Ephraim*

In fulfilment of this prophecy, *Amos 9:13* could read: The word of God will empower the children of God; and God's people shall be full of the Spirit and shall do marvellously and people's hearts will melt. *Isaiah 41:25* could read: The word of God will empower the person with the divine nature of Christ and leaders of God's people will be full of the Spirit and they shall do marvellous things and people's hearts will melt before them—*see Revelation 3:7–13; 11:3–8*.

In this chapter, John reveals the kind of spiritual power and authority by which the militant church of the two witnesses will operate. We are given an insight into the length of time during which they will prophesy. Christ told the Pharisees to search the scriptures for they testify of him.

"It is also written in your law, that the testimony of two men is true. I am one that bears witness of myself, and the Father that sent me beareth witness of me." John 8:17-18. He also said in *John 5:31-36 "If I bear witness of myself, my witness is not true. There is another that beareth witness of me; and I know that the witness which he witnesseth of me is true . . ." But I have greater witness than that of John: for the works which the Father hath given me to finish, the same works that I do, bear witness of me, that the Father hath sent me"*

There are suggestions that the two witnesses are Moses and Elijah. This exposition will disagree with this concept. Moses and Elijah are already in heaven. Any proposition that the two witnesses are the spirits of those already in heaven is difficult to accept for two reasons: the first is the problem of body limitation. Like the angels, any person of spirit or flesh can only be present in one location at any given time, although the spirit can disappear at will. The second is that any child of God now in heaven possesses eternal life, over which death and hell cannot prevail. It is, therefore, reasonable to conclude that the two witnesses are men and women of the two covenants who are indwelt by the Word and the Spirit; they make up the Philadelphia Church empowered for the work at this time. Another source of witness, as we see above, was the work which Christ did: and everything he did was according to the instructions he received from the Father—*John 5:20: "For the Father loveth the Son and sheweth him all things that himself doeth: and he will shew him greater works than these that ye may marvel."* The combination of scriptures confirms that the two witnesses are men and women full of the Word of God the Spirit of God by which they are indwelt—*John 14:24*. Christ's response to the disciples when they sought clarity concerning the coming of Elijah was that he had already come.

*Mal 4:4-5 "Remember ye the law of Moses my servant, which I commanded unto him in Horeb **for all Israel,** with the statutes and judgements. Behold, I will send you Elijah the prophet before the coming of the great and dreadful day of the LORD And he shall turn the heart of the fathers to the children, and the heart of the children to their fathers, lest I come and smite the earth with a curse. Matt 17:3, 10–11 "And behold, there appeared unto them Moses and Elias talking with him. And the disciples asked him, saying, Why then say the scribes that Elias must first come? And Jesus answered and said unto them, Elias truly shall first come, and restore all things. But I say unto you, that Elias is come already, and they knew him not, but have done unto him whatsoever they listed, Likewise shall also the Son of Man suffer of them. Then the disciples understood that he spake unto them of John the Baptist."*

It is true that each time God will intervene in the affairs of men he does so in the spirit of Elijah as he did in the time of John the Baptist. This exposition will draw on the law of double reference that is common to many of the prophecies to explain how they relate to the prophecies of the end time. In *Figure four*, God issued a command at the Mouth of Moses to "all Israel" to depart from Horeb, a journey that would end with Christ's eternal rule after the Church Age. The prophet Malachi made reference to this journey as well as the journey of Elijah and how they will be fulfilled in the Church Age.

God answered Israel's worse king by raising up the greatest and most powerful prophet of the Old Testament in the person of Elijah. Whenever iniquity is great in the world God raises up a man in the spirit and power of Elijah to restore order. The Church Age has reached a time again when death and the evil generation is once again ruling in the world and to preserve the Church, God will again raise up a people in the spirit and power of Elijah who will restore the hidden pathway to dwell in. The end of a thing is greater than the beginning. God began with one man but he will end with the Church as a great nation. This time the warfare is a holy nation against an unholy nation and the kingdom of light against the kingdom of darkness. In this connection, let us consider Elijah's victory at Carmel when he destroyed all the prophets of Baal to the glorious performance of the early Church that will end with the exploits of the Philadelphia Church of Jews and Gentiles.

The prophetic evidence mentioned in this unveiling is overwhelmingly in support of the fact that the two witnesses are the entire Church. The conclusion is that the 144,000 will be chosen from amongst Jewish youths in their teens who have not been defiled by women to qualify for their position with Christ the undefiled. They will be chosen before Daniel's seventieth week of years, which is identified as the time of the Philadelphia Church. If they are chosen at age seventeen at the end of the three and a half years, they would be only twenty years of age to take their position as priests unto the LORD as it was in the Old Testament. By allowing the entire church to be bruised in death and then bring her back to life in the open view of the world, God is also demonstrating to the Laodecians Church Age that will go through the final stage of the great tribulation, that they should hold on to the confession of their faith even in the face of death, because he has power to call them out of death.

Let us continue this unveiling of the truth by linking a few more scriptures together: *Rev. 7:1–8 with Rev. 14:1:*

> *And I looked, and, lo, a Lamb stood on the mount Zion, and with him a hundred and forty and four thousand, having his Father's name written in their foreheads." Deut 33:13–17 "And of Joseph he said, Blessed of the LORD is his land, for the precious things of heaven, for the dew, and for the deep that coucheth beneath . . . For the precious things of the earth and fullness thereof, and for the good will of him that dwelt in the bush: let the blessing come upon the head of Joseph, and upon the top of the head of him that was separated from his brethren. His glory is like the firstling of his bullock, and his horns are like the horns of unicorns: with them he shall push the people together to the ends of the earth: and they are the ten thousands of Ephraim. And they are the thousands of Manasseh."*

> *Dan 8:3–4 "Then I lifted up mine eyes, and saw, and behold, there stood before the river a ram which had two horns: and the two horns were high; but one was higher than the other, and the higher came up last. I saw the ram pushing westward and northward, and southward; so that no beasts might stand before him, neither was there any that could deliver out of his hand; but he did according to his will, and became great."*

Although Christ the king is of the tribe of Judah, yet Jacob the carrier of the blessing transferred that ancient blessing upon the head of Joseph, the Father of Ephraim and Manasseh, the legitimately adopted sons of Jacob. As Jacob crossed his hands in transferring the blessing upon his two grandsons, he declared that Ephraim will be more fruitful than Manasseh. This exposition takes the view that Ephraim, as an elder, is the Father who represents the Gentile race as one of the four beasts called to witness the journey of the Church through time. Manasseh takes the position of Dan, who has been written out of the inheritance of the twelve tribes who were sealed.

The law of first things that has its roots in Genesis will be employed to help solve the mystery of the 144,000. *"And in process of time it came to pass, that Cain brought of the fruit of the ground an offering unto the LORD. And Abel, he also brought of the firstlings of his flock and of the fat thereof. And the LORD had respect unto Abel and to his offering"(Gen.4:3-4). "And Enoch lived sixty and five years, and begat Methuselah: And Enoch walked with God after he begat Methuselah three hundred years, and began sons and daughters. And Enoch walked with God: and was not, for God took him" (Gen 5:21-24).*

Here in Genesis, is the beginning of the first-fruit offerings which are dealt with in Leviticus. The reason for first-fruit redemption originated in eternity, when Lucifer the Son of the Morning rebelled, his name suggesting he was the first angel to be created. His rebellion would have invoked the curse on all first things; therefore, in the time of Israel, when God chose a nation through whom the Messiah would come the first-fruit law with which Cain and Abel were instructed to comply was reinstated in Israel, because death ruled from Adam to Moses. The first fruit principle will not be elaborated on in this exposition except to speak on behalf of the 144,000 and God's perpetual covenant with Abraham.

These chosen people from the Hebrew race will be the first fruits of the New Israel that will be multiplied in the millennium and probably beyond. But the covenant goes back to the time of Noah and his sons: *"And God spake unto Noah, and to his sons with him, saying. And I behold, I establish my covenant with you, and with your seed after you; And with every living creature that is with you, of the fowl, of the cattle, and of every beast of the earth with you; from all that go out of the ark, to every beast of the earth . . . And God said, this is the token of the covenant which I make between me and you and every living creature that is with you, for perpetual generations: I do set my bow in the cloud, and it shall be for a token between me and the earth, that the bow shall be seen in the cloud"* (Gen. 9:8-12).

In remembrance of this covenant in *Revelation 4:3*, the Ancient of Days sat with a rainbow around about his throne. The death of the 144,000 will probably put an end to the first-fruit ordinance, because the millennium will take the Church into eternity when all things will be made new and where the curse on all first originated, because of the fall of Lucifer.

In *Genesis 22:15–18* *"The angel of the LORD called unto Abraham out of heaven the second time, 16. And said, By myself have I sworn, saith the LORD, for because thou hast done this thing, and hast not withheld thy son, thine only son: That in blessing I will bless thee, and in multiplying I will multiply thy seed as the stars of the heaven, and as the sand which is upon the sea shore; and thy seed shall possess the gate of his enemies. And in thy seed shall all the nations of the earth be blessed; because thou hast obeyed my voice."* God recognised Isaac who was redeemed by substitution as Abraham's first-born when he said: *"Take now thy son, thine only son Isaac, whom thou lovest, and get thee up into the land of Moriah; and offer him there for a burnt offering upon one if the mountains which I will tell thee of"* (Gen 22:2).

Through Abraham's obedience a covenant was made between God and Abraham and God promised that he would multiply to him children as stars. This is not a promise that relates to children of the flesh. God has, up until now, multiplied children to Abraham as the sands of the sea and sons as stars, through redemption from sin. The 144,000 as sons of the spirit may fan the flames until the perfect specie of mankind is realised on earth of whom they are first fruits into eternity. Their death and redemption from death will pave the way for God to greatly multiply spiritual children unto Abraham in the millennium in fulfilment of his everlasting covenant with Abraham in *Genesis 17:4–7* *"And I will establish my covenant between me and thee and thy seed after thee in their generations for an everlasting covenant, to be a God unto thee, and thy seed after thee."* It may even be that God will eternally multiply to Abraham earthly sons of stars according to his everlasting covenant and translate them into the spiritual progressively, as he did with Enoch and Elijah.

Why 144,000? Here, too, is another principle at work to determine the number of souls that makes up the first fruit audience. This principle is the law of restitution which has its beginning in Genesis but further developed in Exodus, during the journey of the children of Israel from Egypt.

"If a man shall steal an ox, or a sheep, and kill it, or sell it; he shall restore five oxen for an ox, and four sheep for a sheep. If the thief be found breaking up, and be smitten that he die, there shall no blood be shed for him. If the sun be risen upon him there shall be blood shed for him; for he should make full restitution: if he have nothing, the he shall be sold for his theft. If the theft be certainly found in his hand alive, whether it be ox, or ass, or sheep; he shall restore double"- Ex 22:1–4. (See also 2 Kings 8:5–6; Proverbs 6:31).

Some of these principles are fulfilled in Christ, but this exposition will rely on the final phrase of this quotation and apply the double principle restitution to explain the seven-fold restitution that makes up the 144,000. The sun of righteousness has risen upon all who are of Christ and his blood was shed for the redemption of all. The soul that was stolen became alive because of salvation and the ransomed as a living soul is required to restore double for that which was stolen, because he co-operated with the thief to steal his soul. Plotted on a graph the restitution would look like a "Y." The parable of the talents in *Matthew 25:14–20* explains this further. Servants of God are living souls, saved out of the world. Those who were given five brought five more and one given three brought three more. The one given one brought nothing, and from him even the one he had was taken. Exodus says if the thief is caught and he has nothing to repay he should be sold to make reparation - *Matt 25:29–30*.

For reasons known to God restitution is between one and seven folds. A seven-fold restitution on a "Y" principle over seven generations would be twelve boxes of four sides numbering twelve upwards and across (12 x 12 = 144 souls). But one shall chase a thousand and two ten thousand: 144 x 1,000 = 144,000. On this principle it is possible for one person filled with the word of God and the Holy Ghost (God's two witnesses) to affect at least 144,000 souls with life in a life time if each generation is productive. This then becomes the first fruit of any one person's harvest.

Five and six fold restitution: If a soul committs a trespass against the LORD concerning that which was delivered to him to keep; then it shall be because he has sinned and is guilty, that he shall restore that which was delivered to him to keep, i.e. the principal and add five parts more. This is God's way of protecting himself, so that at no time can any person lay claims on the souls won out of this world. Man is responsible for the keeping of his soul from sin, when he loses his soul he must bring a trespass offering for his soul and five other souls without blemish. Christ our eternal high Priest has made it possible for us to make this restitution, as a trespass offering to God to consolidate our forgiveness. This is not a difficult task if the "Y" principle is followed over six generations of productive restitution, it can be achieved. This puts a commitment upon everyone not only to win souls, but also to make followers of them, through teaching and praying for them to grow into maturity as we would our natural children. Christ prayed for those whom he had won from the world, and not for them only, but for as many as the LORD would give him out of the world. God is able to keep that which is committed unto him against the evil day. The law of restitution commits the Christian to a perfect exemplary walk. This law has not been delved into in detail, but has given sufficient information to help understand how the 144,000 become the first fruit of the Lamb.

During the rule of this Church, the world will see a true demonstration of the power of God coming out of the Church worldwide. These people will be heavily anointed so that the world will not be able to withstand them. Their very presence in a place will put demons to flight. In the time of Christ, whenever he encountered demons they would cry out unless he instructed them to hold their peace. The saints of this Church Age will have power to shut up heaven; they will have power over waters to turn them into blood; and if anyone hurts them the fire of the word in their mouths will devour their enemies.:

"And the house of Jacob shall be a fire, and the house of Joseph a flame, and the house of Esau for stubble, and they shall kindle in them, and devour them; and there shall not be any remaining of the house of Esau; for the LORD hath spoken it"(Obadiah 18). See *Obadiah 2–4* for the house of Edom.

In the end times, the LORD God of Hosts will through his children fight in the midst of the peoples of the earth. However, God will later give them into the hands of the enemy, the devil, who will make war against them and they will be killed. But after three and a half days, they will be raised up from the dead and great fear will fall upon the people of the earth.

"And when they shall have finished their testimony, the beast that ascendeth out of the bottomless pit shall make war against them, and shall overcome them, and kill them. And their dead bodies shall lie in the street of the great city, which spiritually is called Sodom and Egypt, where also our Lord was crucified. 13. And the same hour was there a great earthquake, and the tenth part of the city fell, and in the earthquake were slain of men seven thousand: and the remnant were affrighted, and gave glory to the God of heaven" (Rev. 11:7–13).

They will then hear a voice from heaven saying unto them, "Come up hither." And they will ascend up into heaven in full view of everyone. After the rapture of the two witnesses those Christians who die in the second half of Daniel's seventieth week will not go straight to heaven because the evil ones will police the heavens to resist them as in the time of Daniel. Those who die in this season will rest in the graves waiting to hear the trumpet and receive the escort of Christ and the saints into heaven to attend the marriage supper of the Lamb—*Matt. 24:30–31; John 5:28–29*.

The Spirit of the LORD continues the revelation and puts things into perspective. The Angel tells John that he must go and speak again. Normally when a prophet is commissioned he is sent to a people. John was sent to the demoralised Church of which he was also a part. He was sent to speak to the church and leave the world to the two witnesses of God. God tells him that when the time comes he will empower his messengers to do the work. God will release fresh anointing upon his word by his Spirit to do the work, using the temples of human beings. He will also place a fresh anointing upon his end-time prophets and they will prophesy—*Acts 2:18; Rev. 11:13*. John was to carry the "rod of the strength of God" as the message of Christ to the people as Moses carried the rod of God in his hands to liberate the Israelites from the bondage of slavery in Egypt.

History reveals that John settled in Ephesus after he left the Isle of Patmos. The Church to which John was sent is the same one to which the righteous person belongs even now; and she is still the desired bride of Jesus. He still loves her and is preparing a place for her. It saddens me to write this segment of the revelation because it is obvious that the greater majority of the Church today is not longing for the return of Christ; rather, many are locked in selfish pursuits of prosperity, forgetting that Christ is coming again soon. The counsel of the Holy Ghost from the mouth of the Apostle Peter on good Christian conduct is instructive to the end time Church: *1 Pet 4:7–19:*

"But the end of all things is at hand: be ye therefore sober, and watch unto prayer. And above all things have fervent charity among yourselves: for charity shall cover the multitude of sins . . . If any man suffer as a Christian, let him not be ashamed; but let him glorify God on this behalf. For the time is come that judgement must begin at the house of God: and if it first begin at us, what shall the end be of them that obey not the gospel of God? And if the righteous scarcely be saved, where shall the ungodly and the sinner appear? Wherefore let them that suffer according to the will of God commit the keeping of their souls to him in well doing, as unto a faithful Creator."

The Great City: *"And their dead bodies shall lie in the street of the great city, which spiritually is called Sodom and Egypt, where also our Lord was crucified. And they of the people and kindred and tongues and nations shall see their dead bodies three days and an half, and shall not suffer their dead bodies to be put in graves" (Rev. 11:8–9).*

The great city in which the bodies of the two witnesses will lie is Jerusalem as Sodom. Egypt is also a type of the world, which means other dead bodies will also be in the street of other cities and nations. Conner says Egypt is a symbol of worldliness,[1] but according to the prophecy of Isaiah concerning the end time events, the LORD God has spoken thus:

"And I will punish the world for their evil, and the wicked for their iniquity; and I will cause the arrogance of the proud to cease, and will lay low the haughtiness of the terrible" (Isa. 13:9–11, 11). Other symbols that describe the world united against God are Babylon and Sodom: *"And Babylon the glory of kingdoms, the beauty of the Chaldees' excellency, shall be as when God overthrew Sodom and Gomorrah." (Isa. 13:19).* Although this is a reference to Babylon of the Old Testament, it also has end time application, in view of *Isaiah 14:3–4: "And it shall come to pass in the day when the LORD shall give thee rest from thy sorrow, and from thy fear, and from the hard bondage wherein thou wast made to serve, That thou shalt take up this proverb against the king of Babylon, and say, How hath the oppressor ceased! The golden city ceased!"*

Scenes from Seal Six: The Second woe on earth.

    The Great Thundering, Earthquakes, and Great Hail
    The Tenth Part of the City Fell
    The Remnant Gave Glory to God

The kingdom of darkness is a system of belief communicated or promoted by evil wisdom. Evil will take over people's hearts so that it will seem as though the entire world has become like Sodom and Gomorrah. All the peoples of the world will unite to persecute the children of God and kill the two witnesses. But after they are called up to heaven, many people, especially those from the Jewish race, will turn to Christ. The great city is like Sodom because of the immorality that prevails in the social order; and like Egypt because of the emphasis on wealth and materialism—see *Revelation 3:17*. Those who profess to belong to the kingdom of heaven will be slaughtered for their testimony and many will die. Even the ungodly will be killed because people see only the outward appearance. So those who are wise in these times must be careful to serve God in holiness. All these activities result in the rapture of the Church of the two witnesses. (See also *Zechariah 9:12–17; 10:1–12*.) But woe is determined upon the earth because before long there will be earthquake thundering and lightening and thousands will die. However, the result is that many people will turn to God. This is the end of the second woe, and the third will come very quickly afterwards.

The Vision of the Sounding of the Seventh Trumpet

The Laodiceans Church Age and the Rapture of Those Who are in the Graves: Rev. 11:15–18; John 5:28.
The Declaration—the great voice announces the possession of the kingdoms forever: but judgement must first run its course on earth.
The Great Celebration in Heaven in the Presence of the Entire Church: Revelation 4:5, 10

In this vision John is shown, the travail of the Church up to the time when the seventh trumpet judgement will take place on earth. The sound is heard after the rapture of the two witnesses. But the events leading to the final rapture of the Church will occur during the final three and one half years of Daniel's seventieth week of years. At that time, the Devil and his angels including Lucifer would have been cast out of heaven, and will take up rule on earth with the false prophet as their messenger. And at the sounding of the seventh trumpet those who died in Christ will be raised from the dead, and those alive will be caught

up to meet him in the air. He will not come to earth at this time, until after the seven years gathering of the marriage supper (*Rev. 12:13–17*).

Matt. 24:29 "Immediately after the tribulation of those days shall the sun be darkened, and the moon shall not give her light, and the stars shall fall from heaven, and the powers of the heavens shall be shaken. And then shall appear the sign of the Son of man in heaven, and then shall all the tribes of the earth mourn, and they shall see the Son of man coming in the clouds of heaven with power and great glory. And he shall send his angels with a great sound of a trumpet, and they shall gather his elect from the four winds, from one end of heaven to the other." See also *Isaiah 13:9–10* and *1 Thessalonians 4:16–17*.

John is carried back to the revelation being given to him concerning the sounding of the trumpets and the scene in heaven. At the sounding of the seventh trumpet, the dead in Christ shall rise and those alive will be caught up with them to meet Christ in the air and they will be with him for the seven years of the marriage supper of the Lamb. More will be said on this aspect of the rapture in a later chapter.

CHAPTER TWENTY-ONE

UNVEILING OF REVELATION CHAPTER TWELVE

This chapter takes us back to the vision of the triumphant Church before the throne of God in heaven as seen in Revelation Chapters Four and Five. This scene is after the rapture of the Church of the two witnesses.

Rev. 12:1-5 "And there appeared a great wonder in heaven; a woman clothed with the sun and the moon under her feet and upon her head a crown of twelve stars. And she, being with child cried, travailing in birth, and pained to be delivered. 5. And she brought forth a man child who was to rule all nations with a rod of iron: and her child was caught up unto God, and to his throne."

The travailing woman: The woman so elegantly adorned is the entire Church formed of souls who have passed on including those of the two witnesses and those of the Sardis Church whose souls were seen under the altar at the opening of the fifth seal.

Isa. 66:6–8 "Before she travailed, she brought forth; before her pains came, she was delivered of a man child. "Who hath heard such a thing? Who hath seen such things? Shall the earth be made to bring forth in one day? Or shall a nation be born at once? For as soon as Zion travailed, she brought forth her children. Shall I bring to birth, and not cause to bring forth? saith the LORD: shall I cause to bring forth and shut the womb? saith thy God?"

The voices of *Isaiah 66:6* have already been explained, all of which have resulted in the empowering of the Church of the two witnesses. The woman is still travailing in birth and pained to be delivered. She has been travailing from inception until the time she was caught up to heaven. But despite her being in heaven, some of the children she must bring forth as God's people are not yet fully birthed. This will not happen until all those on earth, belonging to the Laodicean Church, who must attend the marriage supper of the Lamb, have also joined the mass congregation.

It is easy to identify her as the Church because Christ the first born of the new creation is already in heaven, having been caught up to the throne of God before her – *Rev 2:27*. Nevertheless, she is still travailing in birth to produce other desired offspring who must be part of the triumphant church. Before she travailed, she brought forth Christ, who was chosen as the head of the Church from the foundation of the world (*Rev. 12:5*). But as soon as the Church travailed through the great tribulation, she also brought forth another man child. This man child of her travail may be the name of collective humanity, like Adam. At creation both male and female were called Adam; and in the new creation the righteous person in Christ is also called Adam.

The woman clothed with the sun: *"Then shall the righteous shine forth as the sun in the kingdom of their Father" (Matt. 13:43). "For the LORD God is a sun and shield: the LORD will give grace and glory: no good thing will he withhold from them that walk uprightly" (Ps. 84:11).*

The Church is the body of Christ, but the bride of Jesus. The bride is clothed with the sun, demonstrating the completed work of the cross. She reflects the righteousness and the glory of God, which Christ received for the saints *(John 17:5)*. At every stage John sees the victory of the Church and is comforted by what he has seen. This knowledge could not but strengthen his faith to do what must be done when he returns to the saints: preach the message of the gospel with total conviction and without fear.

The moon is under her feet. The moon is a symbol of the word of God. Both the word of God and the Spirit of God works for the perfecting of the saints: there is a perfect work of the Holy Ghost and a perfect work of the word of God in the making of man. *"There is one glory of the sun, and another glory of the moon, another glory of the stars: for one star differeth from another star in glory" (1 Cor. 15:41).* The symbolic reference of the sun, moon and stars as the Holy Ghost, the word of God and sons of God will confirm that the woman has come this far because she has walked through faith and by faith in obedience to the word of God. She has run her race with her bow in her hands as the spiritual authority of the word of God (Rev 6:1–2); and has mounted up with the wings of eagles through the counsel of the Holy Ghost (*Isa 40:31*). The counsel from heaven to her was: "Come up hither," she hears, and is ready to receive her crown. The story of Christ walking on the Sea of Galilee gives us a fair idea what this expressions means. Peter said to Christ, Lord if it is you, bid me come, and Christ said to him "come." Upon this word Peter stepped out onto the raging sea and as long as he kept focused on Christ and the word 'come,' he kept afloat, but when he lost focus on the word he began to sink. The voice from heaven to the two witnesses, "come up hither," is also the word upon which the church was caught up to heaven. **The crown of twelve stars** is a testimony of God's covenant relationship with the Jews. The head of the Church is Christ and he is qualified to have all the stars that are related to the Church.

The second wonder: Rev. 12:3: The devil appears as the great red dragon having seven heads and ten horns, with seven crowns upon his head *(Rev. 17:9–13)*. As the accuser of the brethren, he believes that he still has claim over the lives of God's people, thereby disregarding the work of the cross. The devil is the fallen star called wormwood whom John saw fall from heaven when the sixth seal was opened. He and his fallen angels, including Lucifer are thrown out of heaven, and they will rule on earth, with the false prophet as their messenger.

The war in heaven: Rev. 12:7–17: *"And there was war in heaven the great dragon was cast out, that old serpent, called the Devil, and Satan, which deceiveth the whole world: he was cast out into the earth and his angels were cast out with him . . . And the dragon was wroth with the woman; and went to make war with the remnant of her seed, which keep the commandments of God, and have the testimony of Jesus Christ."* See *Revelation 17:8.*

As Lucifer wrestled with the Archangel Michael for the body of Moses, the devil is still contending with Christ for the Church as his body of true believers. Here again, Michael and his angels fought against the dragon, and the dragon and his angels did not prevail; and there was no more place in heaven for them. The wrestling of the dragon for the bride of Jesus is also reminiscent of Adonijah *(1 Kgs. 2:21)*, when he desired the wife of King David for himself. King Solomon commented that in asking for the wife of David, Adonijah may as well ask for the throne and he was put to death. The dragon will be treated with similar contempt. John the Baptist also told us that he who has the bride is the bridegroom; and he who is the bridegroom is the appointed one who will rule all nations forever. As it was with Adonijah, the devil was not only contending for the bride but for an everlasting kingdom. Whereas Willmington sees the woman as representative of the nation of Israel,[1] it is evident that the woman is in fact the Church of all nations, tribes, and tongues.

The seven heads of the dragon: Rev. 12:3–4; (Rev. 17:9–10, 16–17): The dragon is the devil. His seven heads refer to the seven kingdoms over which he has ruled from the kingdom of David to whom the promise was made of a king on his throne forever. He will rule until the end of the Ages. He has many other names and his names reveal what he does in people's lives. Some of his names are: the prince of the power of the air *(Eph. 2:2)*, satan, and the old serpent. He is the fallen star called Wormwood and the evil spirit sin, that indwells sinners and transmits evil thoughts to his victims through the seven devils by which he opposes the goodness of God in the lives of mankind. The devil has no soul of his own; he therefore needs all these traits so that he can effectively take over the soul of his victims and use them to perpetuate evil against God. *"For the mystery of iniquity doth already work: only he who now letteth will let, until he be taken out of the way"* (*2 Thess. 2:7*). Lucifer, who has acquired the name Satan, is the head of the serpent and a visible spiritual representation of him.

The seven crowns is a statement concerning seven of the eight kingdoms over which he will and has had influence since the kingdom of David: *Rev. 17:11.* He is also identified by the expression *"his tail drew the third part of the stars of heaven, and did cast them to the earth"* (*Rev. 12:4*). It is true that one-third of the angels of heaven sinned and followed the rebellion of Lucifer. His ten horns refer to the ten kings that will serve him after the millennium when he will gather his army to fight against Christ and the Holy City, which is the eighth dynasty.

The woman in the wilderness: The victorious Philadelphia Church is now in heaven, having overcome the devil by the blood of Christ; also by the word of their testimony and love for God. While they are rejoicing the prediction for the sea (the world of people) and the earth is woeful. The wilderness is a place of spiritual scrutiny and trial; it is also symbolic of the world wandering in sinfulness. She is of the woman in heaven; she is the remnant church that has taken up her stand for the LORD since the rapture of the two witnesses. Because the devil is cast down to earth at this time, the Church on earth will experience the greatest persecution in history for a period of forty-two months—the second half of the seven-year period.

"*And when the dragon saw that he was cast unto the earth, he persecuted the woman which brought forth the man child. And to the woman were given two wings of a great eagle, that she might fly into the wilderness, into her place, where she is nourished for a time, and times and half a time, from the face of the serpent*" (*Rev.12:13*). David reminds us of the unfailing steadfast covenant love of God in *Psalm 23:5 "Thou preparest a table before me in the presence of my enemies"*; and sums it up by saying "*surely goodness and mercy shall follow me all the days of my life.*" Throughout the ages we have all tasted of God's goodness: *John 1:16 "And of his fullness we have all received, and grace for grace."* Even at this ninth hour the grace of God is still strong on behalf of the remnant Church in the wilderness.

CHAPTER TWENTY-TWO

UNVEILING OF REVELATION CHAPTERS THIRTEEN AND FOURTEEN

These two chapters refer primarily to the time after the devil and his fallen angels—including Lucifer—have been cast out of heaven. They are about to take up physical rule on earth, with Lucifer claiming to be god over the nations and the man of sin as his prophet - Daniel 7:7–8. However, the Laodiceans Church is still on earth, and the scene relates to the travail of this Church until she is called up to heaven at the sounding of the seventh trumpet.

Revelation Chapter Thirteen:

The Laodiceans Church Age
Scenes From Seal Six—Revelation 6:12
The Beast out of the Sea is Lucifer—Revelation 13:1-8

Rev. 13:1–2 "And I stood upon the sands of the sea, and I saw a beast rise up out of the sea, having seven heads and ten horns, and upon his horns ten crowns, and upon his heads the name of blasphemy. And the beast which I saw was like unto a leopard, and his feet were as the feet of a bear, and his mouth as the mouth of a lion: and the dragon gave him his power and his seat, and great authority. And I saw one of his heads as it were wounded to death; and his deadly wound was healed: and all the world wondered after the beast."

The Beast out of the Sea: (Rev. 12:4). The beast that features here is Lucifer. In the previous chapter we learnt that he and one-third of the angels had been cast out of heaven with the devil. The Sea is the world of people. The devil, Lucifer and the false prophet will rule on earth over a one-world order, during the last three and a half years of Daniel's seventieth week of years; hence he has ten horns. They are ready for all-out war against the remnant Church and the peoples of the earth. *"And the dragon was wroth with the woman and went to make war with the remnant of her seed, which kept the commandments of God, and have the testimony of Jesus Christ" (Rev. 12:17)*. Every god needs a prophet, someone who will publicise or teach his doctrines and promote his cause - *Dan. 7:7–8*. In *Exodus 3:10*, God sent Moses to Egypt as a god to Pharaoh with Aaron as his prophet. Now Lucifer is emulating that pattern. He will not be part of the one world order after the millennium of Christ because both he and the false prophet will be cast into the lake of fire before that time.

The natural kings of the Old Testament have ruled and were dealt with according to the impact they had on the lives of the Jews from the days of Nebuchadnezzar to the time of the Roman Empire. The devil as the dragon is a beast and all who are children of the dragon are regarded as beasts, including the fallen angels, because all are victims of the devil's deceit. However, this beast is definitely Lucifer. This is confirmed by the statement *"the dragon gave him his power, and his seat and great authority."*

Lucifer's seven heads and ten horns, upon which are ten crowns, with the name of blasphemy upon his head is a sign that he will rule over the entire social order. He lives by the seven characteristics of sin therefore he exercises all the power and authority of the dragon. He blasphemes the name of God and all those in heaven. This character knows much about those in heaven because he has been there - *Ezekiel 28:14–15:*

"Thou are the anointed cherub that covereth; and I have set thee so: thou hast walked up and down in the midst of the stones of fire. Thou wast perfect in thy ways from the day that thou wast created, till iniquity was found in thee."

The judgement to wipe out evil must affect its roots. To judge and wipe out the victims of evil without judging the root would make the work unfinished. Christ came to put down rulers and authority and powers; the last enemy to be destroyed will be death. The enemies of God are not really human beings; they are spirits and demons that manifest themselves in the soul that is dead in sin. They become one with those whom they seduce; and unfortunately such individuals without redemption and salvation will also be destroyed with the enemies of God.

One of his heads was wounded to death. At the first coming of Christ he bruised the head of the serpent and took away his power over death - *Gen. 3:15*. The strong character of sin is death; and the keys of death and hell were recovered from Satan as the beast representing the serpent. These keys were returned to him for a little while: hence the deadly wounded was healed. And all that dwell upon the earth whose names are not written in the book of life, shall worship him. It is quite possible that the image that will be erected by the false prophet is of Lucifer as he is described in *Ezekiel 28:13*. The image will be erected in the financial capital of the world known symbolically as Babylon the Great. This city is very likely to be Jerusalem. Nothing more is heard of Lucifer after the beast and the false prophet have been cast alive into the lake of fire; but the devil is still to be dealt with for the last enemy to be destroyed is death.

The warning to the saints: *"He that leadeth into captivity shall go into captivity: he that killeth with the sword must be killed with the sword. Here is the patience of the faith of the saints"* (Rev. 13:10). The sword is the word of God - Rev. 2:6. The saints on earth at this time are being warned of the danger of using the word of God as the sword of the Spirit against their oppressors, as it was in the days of the prophecy of the Philadelphia Church who were given specific authority and power to do extraordinary things -Rev. 11:5–6. This is because the devil and his principalities and powers have been legitimately permitted by God to do many things so that their sins might be full and ripe for the final judgement; and those who use the word of God to kill must equally be judged by the word.

However, the saints on earth will not be totally helpless; their prayers will still be heard in heaven. The parable of the friend at midnight seems to fit into this segment of the unveiling of the truths. *Luke 11:5–7 "Trouble me not: the door is now shut and my children are with me in bed; I cannot rise and give thee."* The watch of the Laodiceans ends at midnight. The children in bed are those of the church of the two witnesses earlier called up to heaven.

The Second Beast—the False Prophet: Daniel 7:8

"And I beheld another beast coming up out of the earth; and he had two horns like a lamb, and he spake as a dragon. And he exerciseth all the power of the first beast before him, and he causeth the earth and them which dwell therein to worship the first beast, whose deadly wound was healed" (Rev 13:11).

The second beast is the false prophet who will impersonate Christ. He comes up out of the earth and is therefore a man. We are told in *Isaiah 33:6* that wisdom and knowledge shall be the stability of our times and the strength of salvation. Here also, evil wisdom and evil knowledge are the horns that destabilise nations.

"Let no man deceive you by any means: for that day shall not come, except there come a falling away first, and that man of sin be revealed the son of perdition. 4. "Who opposeth and exalteth himself above all that is called God, or that is worshipped; so that he as God sitteth in the temple of God, shewing himself that he is God. 5. "Remember ye not, that, when I was yet with you, I told you these things? 6. "And now ye know what withholdeth that he might be revealed in his time. 7. "For the mystery of iniquity doth already work: only he who now letteth will let, until he be taken out of the way. 8. "And then shall that Wicked be revealed, whom the Lord shall consume with the spirit of his mouth, and shall destroy with the brightness of his coming. 9. "Even he whose coming is after the working of Satan with all power and signs and lying wonders. . . . . . ." (2 Thess. 2:3-12).

He will do all kinds of miracles and signs and wonders. People will be deluded into accepting him—just as Christ had said, the wicked generation looks for a sign.

Because they did not accept the sign of the Son of Man, they will be deceived into accepting the false prophet. Unlike Christ, when he is asked for signs to prove his authority, he will perform them for he seeks to deceive.

See *Daniel 8:5–7, 12: 5*. *"And as I was considering, behold a he goat came from the west on the face of the whole earth, and touched not the ground: and the he goat had a notable horn between his eyes. 6. And he came to the ram that had two horns, which I had seen standing before the river, and ran unto him in the fury of his power. 7. And I saw him come close to the ram, and he was moved with choler against him, and smote the ram, and break his two horns: and there was no power in the ram to stand before him, but he cast him down to the ground, and stamped upon him, and there was none that could deliver the ram out of his hands. 12. And a host was given unto him* (the he goat) *against the daily sacrifice by reason of transgression, and it cast down the truth to the ground; and practiced and prospered."*

The Antichrist is the goat and the ram with two horns is the Philadelphia Church of Jews and Gentiles. This supports the view that the Church of the two witnesses will be called up to heaven, in the middle of Daniel's seventieth week of years - *See Daniel 7:4*. None could deliver the ram because God is the one who permits; and this time he will not deliver so that destiny will be fulfilled. There are many schools of thoughts on the identity of the false prophet. It seems likely that he will emerge from the people who profess to belong to God or the kingdom of heaven. The nation of Israel was a special target for the devil, simply because God identified them as his chosen race. And there is a stronger possibility that this false prophet will come out of the very nation of Israel itself, rivalling the birth of Christ for the throne of David. Whatever the case, the nation of Israel will be strongly influenced by him, for they are the people still looking for a Messiah, the rest of the world is not; some have found false gods whom they already worship, others are not concerned about the coming of any person claiming to be Christ. Interestingly, the tribe of Dan was not mentioned in the sealing of the tribes. It is possible that they have been disinherited because of their idolatry; yet it is said that he shall judge his people as one of the tribes. *"Dan shall judge his people, as one of the tribes of Israel. Dan shall be a serpent by the way, an adder in the path that biteth the horse's heels, so that his rider shall fall backward. I have waited for thy salvation Oh LORD" (Gen.49:16-18)*.

There is also much inference to be drawn from the blessings of Jacob upon his children. A little serpent, by the way, can destroy a mighty army; biting the heels of horses, *(Genesis 3:15)*, he can cause many to stumble. Dan was a small tribe amongst the sons of Jacob. The tribe of Dan did not live up to the blessings of a mighty warrior in the past, and seems to have had very little in common with other tribes as time went by — See *Judges 1:34; 5:17*. They did not go to war with Deborah. Dan is from the north; he was stationed on the north side of the tabernacle in the wilderness; he is a firstborn son. Christ is seated at the right hand of God, the position of the north; he is also a firstborn son. Samson was from the tribe of Dan, and a judge who died with the enemy of his people. These are all similitudes of one who qualifies to be a rival to Christ.

It might even be impossible to detect who this person will be because he will not initially show signs of evil; anyone having knowledge of the evil he could perpetuate might be ready to kill him even at birth. However, one may keep an eye on the tribe of Dan to watch for the false prophet.

The false prophet will exercise great power on earth and cause many people to worship the devil. He will also cause everyone, children and adults alike, to receive a mark in their right hand, or in their foreheads. And no one will be able to buy or sell anything unless they have the mark of the beast. The prophet Ezekiel may have something to say about the false prophet: Ezekiel takes up a lamentation for Israel and ends his prophecy by saying: *"This is a lamentation and shall be for a lamentation.'* Although one lamentation is intended, another is envisaged.*"What is thy mother? A lioness: she lay down among lions; she nourished her whelps among young lions. And she brought up one of her whelps: it became a young lion, and it learned to catch the prey; it devoured men. The nations heard of him; he was taken in their pit, and they brought him with chains unto the land of Egypt. Now when she saw that she had waited and her hope was lost, then she took another of her whelps, and made him a young lion. And he went up and down among the lions; he became a young lion and learned to catch the prey, and devoured men. And he knew their desolate palaces, and he laid waste their cities; and the land was desolate, and the fullness thereof, by the noise of his roaring. Then the nations set against him on every side from the provinces, and spread their net over him: he was taken in their pit. And they put him in ward and chains and brought him to the king of Babylon: they brought him into holds, that his voice would no more be heard upon the mountains of Israel"* (Ezek 19:1–14).

Although this prophecy was fulfilled in the days of Jehoiakim when Judah was carried away into Babylon, it also relates to the end time events. According to the prophet Daniel, the false prophet will be totally self-willed and will magnify himself and malign the God of his fathers -*2 Thess 2:3–4*.

"Then the king shall do according to his own will: he shall exalt and magnify himself above every god, shall speak blasphemies against the God of gods, and shall prosper till the wrath has been accomplished; for what has been determined shall be done. He shall regard neither the God of his fathers nor the desire of women, nor regard any god; for he shall magnify himself above them all. But in their place he shall honour a god of fortresses; and a god which his fathers did not know he shall honour with gold and silver, with precious stones and pleasant things" (Dan.11:31-45).

The false prophet will be totally debased, so much so that he will have no desire for women, thus it is possible that he will also be a homosexual. In line with the words of Christ, as it was in the days of Sodom, so shall it be in the end. He will be an evil man, a messenger of Satan, and will exercise great power and authority in the earth and many will be deceived by his miracles. He will prosper for a while because God will permit it. He will even have power to make the image of the beast speak.

The mark of the beast: In biblical numerology, six represents human imperfection. The number is that of a man, and his number is six hundred and three score and six (666). This number represents someone who is totally evil: a quintessential humanist, perfectly evil, with defiled flesh, an evil soul, and an evil spirit; one who speaks evil words. The dragon is a beast, and those who are his children, both angels and humans, must show that they are with him and pledge their allegiance to him, becoming totally evil in thoughts, words and actions.

The mark is spiritual because we are dealing with the age of the spirit. The statement of *Revelation 18:18 "Here is wisdom. Let him that hath understanding count the number of the beast."* has identified the mark as being associated with evil wisdom. However, because Satan will govern the world at this time, the mark will definitely emanate from the kingdom of darkness through the false prophet, signifying a man or a spiritual kingdom which is completely evil. The influence of money will be much in evidence in the kingdom. Persecution of the saints will be very great; therefore, the people of the kingdom of heaven will be greatly subdued.

The following extract is taken from *The Nelson Spirit-Filled Bible*:

"This mark may not be physical but spiritual in that it has to do with the willingness of men to worship the beast or pressure imposed on man through hardship to serve the beast in which case people will do so not from the heart, but as a means to survive. The forehead represents our wills, our volition, whilst the hands speak of activities, so we say of someone who is stubborn willed as head-strong. Through their own willingness or actions the system will get people to worship the beast. The false prophet will himself be self willed and maligned against God."[1]

Paul teaches of the completeness of our sanctification. *"Now may the God of peace himself sanctify you completely; and may your whole spirit, soul, and body be preserved blameless at the coming of our Lord Jesus Christ"* (*1 Thess. 5:23*). The perfect person like Christ lives by seven characteristics of the Word of Life and seven characteristics of the Holy Ghost. The perfect person is one who willingly serves God with heart and hands. The ungodly people serve God with their hands but their hearts are far from him. In *Matthew 15:8–9* Jesus said *"This people draweth nigh unto me with their mouth, and honoureth me with their lips; but their hearts are far from me. But in vain they do worship me, teaching for doctrines the commandments of men."* So it is with the mark of the beast. Those who have the mark on their foreheads are those who willingly serve the beast, and those with the mark on their hands are those who do so out of compromise, or for the love of money. It is quite possible that many have already taken the mark of the beast without realising it, because we are looking for a physical, visible, and forcefully imposed mark. Nevertheless, those who love and worship God with all their heart, soul, and mind, will avoid the mark at any stage in time, whether we know what the mark is or not.

A person's freedom of choice as to how they spend eternity cannot come under compulsion from any human being; even God does not compel anyone to serve him. It must come out of an individual's heart; either because they are deceived or because they willingly elect to follow what is wrong. No one can force another to go to hell, even if the punishment is death, because whoever chooses the way of God cannot die even if the breath is taken away.

The Bible warns that anyone having the mark of the beast will share the terrible fate of the beast—*Rev 14:11 "And the smoke of their torment ascends forever and ever; and they have no rest day or night who worship the beast and his image, and whoever receives the mark of his name."* No one should fear accidentally taking the mark of the beast. To do so involves "worshipping the beast"—*Matt 4:8; Rev 13:15;* and the decision will be clear because it will be a life or death matter. What people really need to do is to guard against evil. *1 John 2:18* tells us that the spirit of Antichrist is already active in the world. If our allegiances are to God we will not serve the Antichrist—now or then.

Lucifer will be demoted to become as a man "earthbound"; whilst those who accept Christ as Saviour will become as angels.

"All they shall speak and say unto thee: Art thou also become weak as we? Art thou become like unto us?... They that see thee shall narrowly look upon thee, and consider thee, saying Is this the man that made the earth to tremble, that did shake kingdoms. That made the world as a wilderness, and destroyed the cities thereof; that opened not the house of the prisoners" (Isa.14:10-11, 16-20).

Revelation Chapter Fourteen

The Lamb and the Guileless 144,000 with him: the Gift of God to the Lamb – Revelation 14:1-7
The Six Angels who Commission the Final Harvesting of Souls

Rev. 14:1–5 "And I looked, and, lo, a Lamb stood on the mount Zion, and with him an hundred and forty-four thousand, having his Father's name written on their foreheads." The 144,000 sealed Jews were given to the Lamb as the first-fruits of God. In other words, God, having reaped a great harvest of souls from the earth through the death of the Lamb, now tithes to the Lamb the first fruits of his increase. Together with the voice of harpers in heaven, they sang a new song unto the LORD before the elders and the four beasts and no one could learn that song except them because they were guileless.

In the Old Testament, kings chose people who were very close to them; and in the days of David followers gathered to him because they were being drawn to him as God, who anointed him king, had touched their hearts. Christ, the newly crowned King of the whole earth, will be given these 144,000 chosen souls, who are of Abraham's seed, to serve him continually.

The voice of the first angel: Rev. 14:6–7. *"And I saw another angel fly in the midst of heaven, having the everlasting gospel to preach unto them that dwell on the earth, and to every nation, and kindred, and tongue, and people. Saying with a loud voice, Fear God and give glory to him; for the hour of his judgement is come: and worship him that made heaven, and earth, and the sea, and the fountains of waters."*

The threat to the Laodiceans Church, made because they were neither hot nor cold and would therefore be rejected by Christ, is now fulfilled. The gospel is preached by angels instead of humans because even the intent of their hearts will be known by the devil, and since the keys of death and hell are once again in his hands, he can slay people even before they open their mouths to speak.

The voice of the second angel: Rev. 14:8: *"And there followed another angel, saying: Babylon is fallen, is fallen, that great city, because she made all nations drink of the wine of the wrath of her fornication."* The Great City Babylon, represents the system of government in the world of sinfulness, which will be totally crushed. She is said to have made all nations to drink of the wine of her fornication. The human problem is sinfulness before God. Only the Word of God and the Spirit of God and the blood of Christ can save people from sin (*1 John 5:8*). Lucifer as the Beast is described as the King of Babylon in *Isaiah 13:19* and *14:4–20*.

The voice of the third angel warns against satanic worship: Rev. 14:9–14. The third angel warns against satanic worship and or the taking of the mark of the beast. There will be much killing at this time; but the assurance for the saints is that they are the blessed of the LORD; and they will have rest from their labours; and those who endure to the end will be rewarded for their faithfulness.

The voice of the fourth angel out of the temple: Rev. 14:15–16. *"And another angel came out of the temple, crying with a loud voice to him that sat on the cloud, Thrust in thy sickle, and reap: for the harvest of the earth is ripe."* This scene seems to be one connected with the earth. John looks and sees a white cloud and the Son of Man sitting on the cloud having on his head a crown and in his hand a sharp sickle. It appears that during the singing of the 144,000, Jesus Christ will be crowned King in the presence of his bride, or the true Church, over whom he will reign as King forever. It is natural for a king to be crowned in the presence of his subjects; even though as time goes by there are those who will be born who would not have witnessed his coronation. The fourth angel comes out of the temple and shouts to Christ with a loud voice to thrust in his sickle and reap the final harvest of the earth; and he does so.

The fifth and sixth angels with the sharp sickle and power over fire—Rev. 14: 17–18: Two angels emerge from the temple of God in heaven, one having a sharp sickle and the other with power over fire. The sixth angel cries with a loud voice to the angel with the sharp sickle, telling him to thrust in his sickle and gather the clusters of the vine of the earth for her grapes are fully ripe. The angel does so and reaps the harvest of the evil inhabitants of the earth to be cast into the winepress of the wrath of God. *Matt. 13: 30*. *"And in the time of harvest I will say to the reapers; gather ye together first the tares and bind them in bundles to burn them, but gather the wheat into my barn."* John saw the vision of the final destruction of the earth as it will be in the future. However, this will not take place until after the seven vial judgements are poured out upon the earth and the angel, with power over fire, casts his fire upon the earth.

CHAPTER TWENTY-THREE
UNVEILING OF REVELATION CHAPTERS FIFTEEN TO EIGHTEEN

God's Final Judgement on Sin

These chapters record the events during the Day of the Wrath of God and the seven vial judgements on earth. The entire Church as the bride of Jesus is safely caught up to heaven for the seven years marriage supper of the Lamb. However, whilst this is in progress, an evil system of government under the devil, his fallen angels, and fallen human beings is still operating on earth. The Day of the LORD's wrath will begin as the seven vial judgements are poured out upon earth.

Revelation Chapter Fifteen

The Seven Angels and the Seven Last Plagues:
In the Day of the Wrath of the LORD

Rev. 15:1–2, 5–7: "*And I saw another sign in heaven, great and marvellous, seven angels having the seven last plagues; for in them is filled up the wrath of God.* "*And I saw as it were a sea of glass mingled with fire: and them that had gotten the victory over the beast, and over his image and over his mark, and over the number of his name, stand on the sea of glass, having the harps of God.* "*And after that I looked, and, behold, the temple of the tabernacle of the testimony in heaven was opened: And the seven angels came out of the temple, having the seven plagues, clothed in pure and white linen, and having their breasts girded with golden girdles. And one of the four beasts gave unto the seven angels seven golden vials full of the wrath of God, who liveth forever and ever."*

A second rapture took take place at the time of the sounding of the seventh trumpet. See *Matthew 24:29–31*. In this vision John saw that those who had been caught up to heaven were now before the throne of God. The time of God's final judgement on sin has now come and it is marvellous in his eyes. One of the four beasts gives the seven angels seven vials full of the wrath of God to be poured on the earth. The clothing of the angels is similar to that worn by the Old Testament priests; it is likely, therefore, that these seven angels are the spirits of the just made perfect. It was given to the human race to have dominion over the earth and to bruise Satan under our feet, and these selected saints have been commissioned to do the honour and give the orders to execute God's final judgement upon the earth. It would also appear that these vials will be poured out in quick succession.

The temple in heaven was filled with smoke from the glory of God, and from his power; and no one was able to enter into the temple until the seven plagues of the seven angels had been fulfilled. God is alone in the temple. The mercy seat becomes inaccessible to everyone, including Christ our mediator. No further petitions or intercessions will be heard by God until the judgement is all over. Fallen humanity had chosen the way of death through their rebellious, iniquitous, and idolatrous behaviour, culminating and demonstrated in their worship of the beast. Old Testament history teaches that the gravest sin is idolatry.

"They sacrificed unto devils, not to God; to gods whom they knew not, to new gods that came newly up, whom your fathers feared not" (Deut 32:17). Millions of souls are condemned to death—*Rom 1:28 "And even as they did not like to retain God in their knowledge, God gave them over to a reprobate mind, to do those things which are not convenient."* The pain of a loving Father who must execute judgement on such a great company of people forever is enormous. Sin must be destroyed; covenants must be fulfilled and judgement must be applied justly. At the death of Christ it is said that God hid his face; but now millions of souls, including children, must be condemned to the lake of everlasting fire because no sin can enter into Christ's eternal kingdom. It is no wonder the Father wants to be alone in the temple at such a time as this.

Revelation Chapter Sixteen

The Seven Vial Judgements

Rev. 16:1–2 "And I heard a great voice out of the temple saying to the seven angels, Go your ways, and pour out the vials of the wrath of God upon the earth. And the first went, and poured out his vial upon the earth; and there was a noisome and grievous sore upon the men which had the mark of the beast, and upon them which worshipped his image". The vials are poured out when there is no more hope of repentance for people, because the remnant church has been caught up and taken out of the world.

The first vial judgement is upon those who have the mark of the beast and upon those who have worshipped his image. This is a worldwide scenario and is not confined to any one religious group of people, as some have suggested, but to all who have worshipped the beast and bowed to his image.

The second vial: *"And the second angel poured out his vial upon the sea"*, and it became blood and every living thing in it died. All ships were destroyed and all the souls in them died (*Rev. 16:3*).

The third vial: *"And the third angel poured out his vial upon the rivers and fountains of waters; and they became blood. And I heard the angel of the waters say, Thou art righteous, O Lord, which art, and wast, and shalt be, because thou hast judged thus: for they have shed the blood of saints and prophets, and thou hast given them blood to drink; for they are worthy. And I heard another out of the altar say, Even so, Lord God Almighty, true and righteous are thy judgements"* (*Rev. 16:4–6*).

The pattern of judgements is similar in places to that which took place in Egypt, when the gods of the rivers, fountains, and bodies of water were judged. The devil who fell from heaven upon the waters spoke. (See also *Revelation 8:10–11*.) In Moses' final warning to Israel against idolatry and disobedience to the commandments of God, he called heaven and earth to bear witness. Here also, the spirit of the waters declares God's judgement as justified and righteous. A voice from heaven also declares God's judgement as true and righteous: so that out of the mouths of two or three witnesses the justice of God is established.

The fourth vial: *"And the fourth angel poured out his vial upon the sun; and power was given unto him to scorch men with fire. And men were scorched with great heat, and blasphemed the name of God, which hath power over these plagues; and they repented not to give him glory"* (*Rev. 16:8–9*).

This plague shows the power of God as superior to the power demonstrated by the beast and the Antichrist (*Rev. 16:14*), who had no power to stop the scorching. As it was with Pharaoh, the king of Egypt, people hardened their hearts many times before God began to harden their hearts so that they could not repent.

The fifth vial: *"And the fifth angel poured out his vial upon the seat of the beast; and his kingdom was full of darkness; and they gnawed their tongues for pain, And blasphemed the God of heaven because of their pains and their sores, and repented not of their deeds"* (*Rev. 16:10–11*).

In every kingdom the rulers are judged for their conduct in leading the people. This plague is isolated to the seat of the beast and seems to be upon the rulers of his kingdom. His kingdom was full of darkness as in the days of Egypt when darkness covered the land; yet there was light in Goshen. The reason for this isolated darkness is not clear, yet it can be identified with the pattern of God's judgement on a sinful kingdom.

The sixth vial: *"And the sixth angel poured out his vial upon the great river Euphrates; and the water thereof was dried up, that the way of the kings of the east* *might be prepared. And I saw three unclean spirits like frogs come out of the mouth of the dragon, and out of the mouth of the beast, and out of the mouth of the false prophet. For they are the spirits of devils, working miracles, which go forth unto the kings of the earth and of the whole world, to gather them to the battle of that great day of God Almighty" (Rev 16:13–14).*

Euphrates dries up: This River typifies sinfulness in human life. Its drying up means sin will not be operative in the world when the devil is bound for a thousand years. The kings of the east are the saints made perfect in Christ. They will return with him to reign for a thousand years and Jacob shall be gathered to the LORD— Isa. 43:5–7

"Fear not: I am with thee: I will bring thy seed from the east, and gather thee from the west; I will say to the north, Give up; and to the south, keep not back: bring my sons from far, and my daughters from the ends of the earth."

Jerusalem shall become the possession of Christ, Abraham's seed, and she will be called Hepsebah and Bullah Land. Moses understood the secret of the LORD by the things God said to him on the mount Pisgah. God said *"Let it suffice thee speak no more to me on this matter."* Moses knew from what God said to him *(Deut. 3:27)* that it was not yet the time for full possession. It will not be until God gathers the nations to himself in Christ; and the kings of the east as the body of Christ, return to take possession *(Deut. 3:25–26)*. God spoke in a similar manner to Abraham after Lot had departed from him.

"And the LORD said unto Abraham, after that Lot was separated from him, Lift up now thine eyes, and look from the place where thou art northward, and southward, and eastward, and westward: For the land which thou seest, to thee will I give it, and to thy seed forever" (Gen 13:14).

Abraham was to look to the time when the word of God became manifest as the son of Abraham, the Holy Ghost is poured out, and the kings of the east return to occupy the land and Jacob is gathered from the world of sinfulness unto God. Perfect understanding of this promise, through application of the symbolic references to the four cardinal points, should confirm that permanent and peaceful occupation of the Promised Land can only be under Christ, for the blessings of God are without repentance and he adds no sorrow. The river Euphrates will physically dry up, as a sign to prepare the way for the final battle when Christ will return to earth with his army of kings—*Rev. 16:16.*

According to Willmington: *"This River has been the dividing line between western and eastern civilization since the dawn of history: it served as the eastern border of the old Roman Empire. Thus the Euphrates serves as both the cradle and grave of man's civilization. Here the first godless city (Enoch, built by Cain went up—Gen 4:16–17); and here the last rebellious City will be constructed as the Babylon built by the Antichrist."*[1] However, the belief that Babylon will be re-built is not unanimous. Charles Ryrie says: *"Whether the city will be rebuilt once again on the Euphrates is a matter of debate."*[2] However, the corporate journey of Israel as a nation and the Church Age ends when the river Euphrates dries up; and symbolically, when sin dries up in the world in the millennium of Christ. (See *Figure 4*).

The three unclean spirit: *Rev. 16:13–14*. Lucifer and the false prophet are united by the same spirit and speak his words with one voice to deceive men by lying wonders. See *Matthew 12:43–45*. Evil has reached its climax as iniquity increases in the world; the unclean spirits that came out of the mouth of the beast and the false prophet are characteristics of the spirit of sin: evil wisdom as rebellion and witchcraft; evil knowledge as ignorance and deceit; the three characteristics of sin that cause people to rebel against God. Through the ignorance of their hearts people will be deluded by the miracles of the beast and the false prophet, as it was in the days of natural Israel. These unclean spirits work together and will gather men to the Armageddon war in the future—*Rev. 16:14,16*.

The seventh vial: Rev. 16:17-19 *"And the seventh angel poured his vial into the air; and there came a great voice out of the temple of heaven, from the throne, saying, It is done. 19. "And the great city was divided into three parts, and the cities of the nations fell: and great Babylon came in remembrance before God, to give unto her the cup of the wine of the fierceness of his wrath"*

A great voice out of the temple in heaven, from the throne says, "It is done." God was alone in the temple; therefore this voice may be his final utterance against sin as the Alpha and Omega. After this the scene on earth was one of chaos: there were voices, thunder, lighting and an unprecedented great earthquake, and Jerusalem and the world of sinfulness came up before God who pronounced judgement on all things.

The Great City: Revelation 16:19
Babylon, the Great City: Revelation 14:8
Babylon the Great: Revelation 18:1–3.

The great city is Jerusalem as the capital city of the one world order from where the beast and the false prophet will rule. She is also called Babylon the Great *(Rev. 14:8)*, or Babylon. In the day of the wrath of LORD she will be divided into three parts and one-third of the Jewish race will be called out of her; they will be preserved in a secret location for they will be those who will re-populate the earth during the millennial reign of Christ.

Great Babylon The reference to great Babylon is both natural and symbolic. *(Rev 16:19)*. Naturally, the name refers to Jerusalem of the end times *(Rev. 18:2)*, or Nebuchadnezzar's Babylon, which was judged in the Old Testament: *Isa. 13:19*. Symbolically, she consists of cities and nations and is therefore representative of the entire world of sinful mankind, of nations and tongues and kindred, with all its religious, idolatrous, commercial and political systems as Egypt; and its immorality as Sodom. She was also judged at the same time as Jerusalem:

Rev. 16:19–21, Rev. 17:15 "And he saith unto me the waters which thou sawest, where the whore sitteth, are peoples, and multitudes, and nations and tongues. Isa. 13:9–11: "And I will punish the world for their evil, and the wicked for their iniquity, and I will cause the arrogance of the proud to cease, and will lay low the haughtiness of the terrible."

Rhodes refer to Great Babylon both as a literal city along the Euphrates River and as a religious commercial system.[3] The history of this city began with Nimrod when the people gathered in corporate rejection of the commandment of God to repopulate the earth.

Revelation Chapter Seventeen

John is carried away in the Spirit into the wilderness, (*See Isa. 41:19*), a symbolic reference to the world of sinfulness where he is shown that the evil wisdom and evil spirit by which people live are responsible for all the atrocities of the world; even in the midst of abundance of wealth.

Rev. 17:1–3 "Then came one of the seven angels which had the seven vials, and talked with me, saying unto me, Come hither, I will shew unto thee the judgement of the great whore that sitteth upon many waters: With whom the kings of the earth have committed fornication and the inhabitants of the earth have been made drunk with the wine of her fornication. So he carried me away in the spirit into the wilderness: and I saw a woman sit upon a scarlet coloured beast, full of names of blasphemy, having seven heads and ten horns."

Rev. 17: 4–6 "And the woman was arrayed with purple and scarlet colour, and decked with gold and precious stones and pearls, having a golden cup in her hand full of abominations and filthiness of her fornication: And upon her forehead was a name written. MYSTERY, BABYLON THE GREAT, THE MOTHER OF HARLOTS AND ABOMINATIONS OF THE EARTH. And I saw the woman drunken with the blood of the saints, and with the blood of the martyrs of Jesus: and when I saw her I wondered with great admiration."

The great whore is evil wisdom of the world; the social order referred to symbolically as Great Babylon (*Rev. 16:19*). The woman upon many waters; she works in conjunction with the seven spirit of the devil. Together they control the minds of the peoples and nations of the world who have not repented of sinfulness. These people are described as "many waters"—*Revelation 17:15:* "*And he saith unto me the waters which thou sawest, where the whore sitteth, are peoples, and multitudes, and nations and tongues. Ezekiel 19:4:* "*The nations also heard of him; he was taken in their pit, and they brought him with chains unto the land of Egypt."* The whore was seen in the wilderness which, spiritually, is the world of sinfulness: *Proverbs 2:10–22; Isaiah 41:17.* The strange woman who flatters with her lips is evil wisdom of the world that leads to death. She was sitting upon a scarlet coloured beast, decked with gold and precious stones and pearls: she controls the economic and social structure of the world. She had a golden cup in her hand full of abominations and filthiness of her fornication, and she was arrayed in purple, which represents royalty.

The woman is not new in the world; she has been around even before the creation of man and she is responsible for the downfall of many people of the world. She is productive and deceptive; and because she is productive, death passes from one generation to the next. She is the evil wisdom as Jezebel by which the world lives and she bewitches people's souls to make them believe the lie of the devil *(Gal. 3:1)*. (See also *1 Samuel 15:23*.) *"For rebellion is as the sin of witchcraft and stubbornness as iniquity and idolatry."* Good wisdom has an effect on the throne of kings; so also evil wisdom has an effect on the kingdoms of the world over which the devil has influence. Those who live by her are a sinful, adulterous, idolatrous generation and are ridden by her *(Rev. 17:15)*. Worldly wisdom is enmity towards God; she is not subject to his laws; she is in rebellion and those who live by her are ridden by her, and live in rebellion or unbelief.

"*Say unto wisdom, thou art my sister, and call understanding thy kinswoman;* "*That they may keep thee from the strange woman which flattereth with her words*" *(Prov. 7:4–5)*.

"*Let not thine heart decline to her ways; go not astray in her paths. For she has cast down many wounded; yea, many strong men have been slain by her*" *(Prov. 7:25)*.

Evil wisdom produces a pathway to follow. She hates the path of righteousness and leads people along the road to condemnation. Evil wisdom creates evil children. The forehead represents the will, and because the devil is a spirit without a soul, he influences the will of angels and human beings; hence, there are angels who have fallen, and human beings who have fallen. Every word of evil wisdom which Lucifer as Satan and other fallen angels and sinful human beings willingly obey is the mother of harlots and all abominations of the earth. The words people speak or live by determine what they become and where they spend eternity. In *Matthew 4:4* Christ responds to the devil: "man shall live by every word that preceedes out of the mouth of God." What John saw was symbolic and he was told this particular symbol is a mystery; therefore the explanation must be sought after. In solving the mystery of the woman, one will say she is evil wisdom that controls the social, economic, immoral and political fabric of society. The cup in her hand is full of the abominations from which the people of the world are enticed to drink as they serve the devil. This cup marks the fullness of sin in the world; hence the judgement of God is set. **She is drunk with the blood of saints:** She is responsible for the persecution and killing of many of the people of God who would *not* be influenced by her, for example those martyred for the sake of the gospel throughout the ages.

Nebuchadnezzar ruled by the wisdom of the world until he acknowledged that God rules in human affairs. His name comes from the root word *"Nabo,"* which is the name of the Babylonian god of wisdom. In the vision of Zechariah, the prophet saw a flying basket covered with a heavy lid, *Zechariah 5:5–11*. When the lid is lifted, he saw a woman seated inside. He was told the woman inside represents sin and wickedness: *Matthew 13:33; Revelation 2:20; 17:1–7*. According to Willmington, the heavy lid may be the restraining power of the Holy Ghost over evil.[4] In the vision Zechariah saw the removal of wickedness from the land, symbolised by a woman trying to escape in a basket (ephah) but forced back into it. The basket is finally removed altogether from the land—*Zechariah 5:11*. Wickedness is consigned to the land of Shinar (Babylon). By the time of this prophecy, Babylon had become the world focus of idolatry and wickedness. Symbolically, then, wickedness was taken from Judah to Babylon.

The scarlet coloured beast: *"The beast that thou sawest was, and is not, and shall ascend out of the bottomless pit, and go into perdition: and they that dwell on the earth shall wonder whose names were not written in the book of life from the foundation of the world when they behold the beast that was, and is not, and yet is."*

John was carried away into the spirit, into the wilderness symbolic of the world of mankind; therefore the things he saw are spiritual. The colour scarlet represents something infectious and sinful. The scarlet coloured beast is the devil, he has many names, he is emulous of the Holy Ghost, and therefore he is blasphemous in all of his names. The great whore is evil wisdom which is carried by the devil as the old dragon. Jesus spoke of evil wisdom as a productive mother of children: *"But wisdom is justified of her children"* (*Matt. 11:19*). He was speaking to the Pharisees and Sadducees whom John described as generations of vipers - (*Matt. 3:7*). The waters upon which the woman sits are wicked and evil generations of the kingdom of darkness; hence they are also ridden by the woman:

The mystery of the seven heads and the seven mountains: *Rev. 17:9–10 "And here is the mind which hath wisdom. The seven heads are seven mountains, on which the woman sitteth. And there are seven kings, five are fallen, and one is, and the other is not yet come; and when he cometh, he must continue a short space. And the beast that was and is not even he is of the eighth, and is of the seven, and goeth into perdition."*

The seven heads are rulers of governments. The woman is seated on seven mountains, which symbolically refer to the seven kingdoms of the seven kings whose throne she has affected and will affect until the devil is cast into the lake of fire; this means that she exercises her spiritual strength and succeeds in holding people bound in the slavery of sin as she manipulates governments, natural and spiritual; the education system of nations, the world entertainment, and the social media to spread deceit and lies.

Beginning at the kingdom of David, to whom the promise of the king on his throne forever was made, through to the Roman Empire, five kingdoms have fallen; the sixth one is the Church Age until the millennium of Christ, which is the kingdom of heaven. The seventh kingdom will be the millennial kingdom of Christ who will reign for a thousand years. At this time the devil will be bound and thrown into the bottomless pit. However, he will be loosed for a season to form the eighth kingdom that make up the seven kingdoms over which he has influence. The devil, is of the seventh kingdom of Christ because there will still be people on earth producing children after the nature of fallen Adam. (See *Figure 2*).

The Mystery of the Ten Horns: Revelation 17:12-18

"And the ten horns which thou sawest are ten kings, which have received no kingdom as yet; but receive power as kings one hour with the beast . . . These have one mind, and shall give their power and strength unto the beast . . . The waters which thou sawest, where the whore sitteth, are peoples and multitudes and nations and tongues. And the ten horns which thou sawest upon the beast, these shall hate the whore, and shall make her desolate and naked, and shall eat her flesh, and burn her with fire. For God hath put in their hearts to fulfil his will, and to agree, and give their kingdom unto the beast, until the words of God be fulfilled. And the woman which thou sawest is that great city, which reigneth over the kings of the earth" (Rev. 17:12, 16-17).

The ten kings: The mystery confirms that evil wisdom as the woman for she has power to unite those of like minds to do her bidding. The ten kings belong to the eighth kingdom that will be united against Christ when the devil is released for a little while after the millennial reign of Christ. This commentary is taken from *The Nelson Spirit-Filled Life Bible*:

*"The ten horns: Some see the governors of the chief provinces of the Roman Empire, who for **one hour** (AD June 68 to AD December 69), were involved in the bloody civil strife that nearly destroyed Rome as an illustration of the spiritual principle that anti-Christian political and military power inevitably destroy the economy and the nation or civilization that they under gird, thus inducing their own retribution and fulfilling the purposes of God"*[4] The Old Roman Empire was divided into ten kingdoms, but we are dealing now with things of the spirit, and sin, which is the root cause of human wickedness.

Jerusalem is also described as the harlot city. "To eat the flesh of the whore" means that the people of the world would have consumed so much evil wisdom that she will manipulate them into burning Jerusalem with fire, for God has put it in their hearts to do so. .

Revelation Chapter Eighteen

God who created the heavens and the earth for his good pleasure is the one who determines the end. He has the final say and exercises his will and dominion over sin and sinfulness by declaring an end to the kingdom of darkness and the atrocities of sin.

The Mystery of the Angel From Heaven
The mystery of Babylon the Great

Rev. 18:1–3 "And after these things I saw another angel come down from heaven having great power; and the earth was lightened with his glory. And he cried with a mighty strong voice, saying, Babylon the great has fallen and is become the habitation of devils and the stronghold of every foul spirit, and a cage of every unclean and hateful bird. For all nations have drunk of the wine of the wrath of her fornication, and the kings of the earth have committed fornication with her, and the merchants of the earth are waxed rich through the abundance of her delicacies."

This angel seems to be the Angel of the LORD because judgement is of God. Before the city of Sodom was destroyed, reports of her atrocities had reached heaven and God came down to pass judgement on her. See *Revelation 18:8 "For strong is the Lord God who judgeth her."*

Babylon the Great: Rev. 18:20-21. *"Rejoice over her, thou heaven, and ye holy apostles and prophets; for God hath avenged you on her. And a mighty angel took up a stone like a great millstone, and cast it into the sea, saying, thus with violence shall that great city Babylon be thrown down, and shall be found no more at all."*

This also is a name for Jerusalem, the capital city from where the beast and the false prophet will rule. God will put it in the hearts of men to burn her with fire. Daniel helps us to understand the allegory about the times of the end. See *Daniel 1:1*

"In the third year of the reign of Jehoiakim king of Judah came Nebuchadnezzar king of Babyon unto Jerusalem, and besieged it. And the Lord gave Jehoiakim king of Judah into his hand with part of the vessels of the house of God; which he carried into the land of Shinar to the house of his god; and he brought the vessels into the treasure house of his god"

Symbols and Types:

Jehiokim the Name Means	God sets up
Nebuchadnezzar Means	Wisdom of the Chaldean or Babylon
King of Babylon	Symbol of evil wisdom ruling in the world
Jerusalem	The City of God or the kingdom of Heaven
Vessels	The people of the kingdom — the ungodly generation
Three Years	In the 3rd millennium of the day of Grace

Using the above symbols and types we may translate the above passage thus: within the third millennium of the setting up of the kingdom of heaven, evil wisdom that rules in the world came against the kingdom of heaven and besieged the hearts of the ungodly, leaving many dead and many about to die (*Rev. 3:1–6*). And the LORD gave the kingdom which he had set up into the hands of evil wisdom and the ungodly, wicked, and evil generations.

What we understand from this transposition is that as the time of Christ draws near modern occult movements are gathering many of their forces into a contemporary revival of the evil system of Babylon with Jerusalem as its capital. And as Judas betrayed Christ, those who will act against him at his second coming are already within his kingdom. Their influence will continue to rise for a final showdown between Christ and Satan.

Fornication means having another god besides the true God or living by the wisdom of the world and not the wisdom of God. This is the human sinfulness from the beginning: Adam rejected the wisdom of God and chose the wisdom of the serpent. When the final showdown comes, the false prophet will be given power over the Church to destroy and kill the witnesses of God. He will overcome them, not because he has power in himself, but because God will permit him. However the time will come when the power will be taken away and those himself and Lucifer once ruled over will turn against them and set about to destroy Lucifer; however, they will be unable to destroy him in person and the image of him that speaks will be burnt instead.

Evidence abounds that the signs of the end times are already being manifested, and there is a wakeup call to the Church to repent and practise righteousness and godly living in order to fulfil the purpose for which God has given eternal life: to become great soul winners. The main targets of the devil in the world of humanity are the rich and learned in society; world leaders and people who are born to be leaders because of their potential. Evil wisdom seeks to develop in them a nature and character that is contrary to the nature and character of Christ and consequently of God.

Another voice from heaven saying: *"Come out of her my people, that ye be not partakers of her sins, and that ye receive not of her plagues. For her sins have reached unto heaven, and God hath remembered her iniquities."* This call may well be to the one-third of the chosen people of the Jewish race, who will be saved. They are being called out of the world and will be taken to a place specially prepared for them. They are those who will repopulate the earth during the reign of Christ and perhaps beyond according to *Genesis 9:12*.

Anything that lives on earth can only survive by the word of God. The Bible tells us that two-thirds of the Jews will perish (*Zech 13:8–9*). Whilst none of those who were exiled in Assyria returned from captivity, a remnant of the Jews from the southern kingdom returned from exile under Zerubbabel, Nehemiah and Ezra: See *Revevlation 12:14; Zechariah 13:1–2*. These scriptures reveal that Israel will recognise Christ as their Messiah and king; that they will be cleansed and settled in the land, and that Jerusalem will once again be filled with people young and old; and from there Christ will rule over the World as the King of the kings of the earth (*Zech 6:12–14; 8:4–8*).

The reaction of the world to the fall of Babylon–Rev.18: 9–20: This chapter also reveals the kind of judgement to befall the Great City as the seat of the beast and the economic capital of the world, which is likely to be Jerusalem.

"And when ye shall see Jerusalem compassed with armies, then know that the desolation thereof is nigh. Then let them which are in Judea flee to the mountains;

and let them which are in the midst of it depart out; and let not them that are in the countries enter thereinto. For these be the days of vengeance, that all things which are written may be fulfilled... And they shall fall by the edge of the sword, and shall be led away captive into all nations; and Jerusalem shall be trodden down of the Gentiles, until the times of the Gentiles be fulfilled. There shall be signs in the sun, and in the moon, and in the stars; and upon the earth distress of nations, with perplexity; the sea and the waves roaring ... And when these things begin to come to pass, then look up, and lift up your heads; for your redemption draweth nigh" (Luke 21:20–28).

The "great millstone cast into the sea" indicates the violence by which Babylon will be thrown down and be found no more—*Rev. 18:21–24 "In her was found the blood of prophets, and of saints, and of all that were slain upon the earth.* There is already a lamentation against her, because Christ has already referred to Jerusalem as having slain all her prophets.

CHAPTER TWENTY-FOUR

UNVEILING OF REVELATION CHAPTERS NINETEEN TO TWENTY-TWO

The great privilege of a true statesman: John is shown scenes pertaining to the marriage supper of the Lamb, the end of all sinfulness and the New Heaven and New Earth. These scenes are shared with the people of God so that we can remain focused, and zealously contend for the kingdom and the crowns that await all believers who are of the called and chosen.

Revelation Chapter Nineteen

The Destruction of the Beast as Lucifer and the False Prophet: Revelation 19:20-21

Rev. 19:1–2 "And after these things I heard a great voice of much people in heaven, saying, Alleluia; Salvation and glory, and honour, and power unto the Lord our God: For true and righteous are his judgements: for he hath judged the great whore, which did corrupt the earth with her fornication, and hath avenged the blood of his servants at her hand."

The reaction of the saints in heaven: John heard the voice of worship from the Church of both covenants now gathered around the throne in heaven headed by the twenty-four elders and the four beasts: these are people made perfect in Christ. They gave thanks to God for having judged evil wisdom in the person of sin, which has really been the downfall of human beings from the beginning.

The Marriage Supper of the Lamb: Revelation 19:8-9:

"And to her was granted that she should be arrayed in fine linen, clean and white: for the fine linen is the righteousness of saints. And he saith unto me, write, blessed are they which are called unto the marriage supper of the Lamb. And he saith unto me, These are the true sayings of God.

The great multitude, which John saw in Chapter 4, is now before the throne of God; arrayed in white linen. This is the time when the Church of both covenants will partake of the marriage supper, while those on earth are going through the seven vial judgements. It seems likely that Christ was crowned king shortly after the Church was called up to heaven (*Rev 11:13*). Until this time he has been a prince in heaven. *"And from Jesus Christ the prince of the kings of the earth"* (*Rev 1:5*). Later in this chapter he rides as 'King of kings and Lord of lords'

The White Horse; his Rider and his Armies: Revelation 19:11-17; Matthew 25:32-46

Rev. 19:11–12 "And I saw heaven opened, and behold a white horse; and he that sat upon him was called Faithful and True, and in righteousness he doth judge and make war. His eyes were as a flame of fire, and on his head were many crowns; and he had a name written, that no man knew, but he himself."

Christ rides the white horse as the Word of God, as the Wisdom of God, and as the one who operates in the power of the word of God. He descends on earth with ten thousand of his saints for the final showdown with the devil and his fallen hosts, headed by the beast Satan and his false prophet. ***Jude 14*** *"And Enoch the seventh from Adam prophesied saying behold the Lord cometh with ten thousand of his saints to execute judgement."*

The End of Lucifer and the False Prophet: *Rev. 19:19–21: "And I saw the beast, and the kings of the earth, and their armies, gathered together to make war against him that sat on the horse, and against his army. And the beast was taken, and with him the false prophet that wrought miracles before him, with which he deceived them that had received the mark of the beast, and them that worshipped his image. These were cast alive into the lake of fire burning with brimstone. And the remnant was slain with the sword of him that sat upon the horse, which sword proceeded out of his mouth: and all the fowls were filled with their flesh."*

John saw a vision of the world gathering against Christ to make war with him and his army of kings. They will be led by Satan and the false prophet. Both Satan and the false prophet will be bound and cast alive into the lake of fire burning with brimstone, where they will remain forever. *"Hell from beneath is moved for thee to meet thee"* (*Isa 14:9–11*). However, the time to dispense with the devil is not yet: but he must be bound for a season.

Revelation Chapter Twenty

The Binding of the Serpent, also called the Devil and Satan
The War to end all Wars
The Great White Throne Judgement

Rev. 20:1–2 "And I saw an angel come down from heaven, having the key of the bottomless pit and a great chain in his hand. And he laid hold on the dragon, that old serpent, which is the devil, and Satan and bound him a thousand years, And cast him into the bottomless pit, and shut him up, and set a seal upon him that he should deceive the nations no more till the thousand years should be fulfilled; and after that he must be loosed a little season."

The binding of the serpent: The old serpent which deceived Eve, and is responsible for all the deceit and lies in the universe, is the devil, the sinful spirit who is also called Satan. The binding of him means that evil will be removed from the earth for a period during the millennial reign of Christ. Evil will be confined to the bottomless pit; where the devil will be shut up and sealed so that he should deceive the nations no more until after the appointed time has passed.

All the saints including those who were killed for the witness of Jesus Christ, who had not worshipped the beast nor taken his mark in their foreheads or hands, will also reign with Christ a thousand years:

"And I saw thrones, and they sat upon them, and judgement was given unto them: and I saw the souls of them that were beheaded for the witness of Jesus, and for the word of God and which had not worshipped the beast neither his image, neither had received his mark upon their foreheads, or in their hands; and they lived and reigned with Christ a thousand years. But the rest of the dead lived not again until the thousand years were finished. This is the first resurrection. Blessed and holy is he that hath part in the first resurrection: on such the second death hath no power, but they shall be priests of God and of Christ, and shall reign with him a thousand years" (Rev 20:4).

There are basically two views regarding the length of time of the millennial reign of Christ. One view is that after Lucifer and the false prophet are cast into the lake of fire, and the devil is bound for a thousand years, Christ will set up an earthly kingdom and will reign with the resurrected saints in peace and righteousness for that period. Some believe this could be an undetermined period of time, while others regard it as a literal period. The view taken by this unveiling is that the period is literal. However, at the end of the period, the devil shall be released from the bottomless pit to go and deceive the nations to gather against Christ and the saints.

"And when the thousand years are expired, Satan shall be loosed out of his prison. And he shall go out to deceive the nations which are in the four quarters of the earth, Gog and Magog, to gather them together to battle: the number of whom is as the sand of the sea... And the devil that deceived them was cast into the lake of fire and brimstone, where the beast and the false prophet are, and shall be tormented day and night forever and ever" (Rev. 20:7–10).

These scriptures clearly separate Satan, as Lucifer the fallen angel, from Satan the spirit that deceives both angels and humanity, because at the end of the age he is cast into the eternal lake of fire where the beast and the false prophet are already serving their eternal sentence.

The war to end all wars and the ten kings who have no kingdom yet: It appears that many who submitted to Christ's rule during the millennium did so because of the strong influence of his rule and not from inner commitment. After this period, the devil will be released from the bottomless pit to practise his art of deception, in what is to be known as the eighth kingdom. He will gather the peoples of the world against Christ and his faithful saints to fight the Armageddon war.

These people are the descendants of the remnant Jews who have been given another chance to accept the lordship of Christ. However, because there are still elements of sinfulness in the world, sin will still divide the generations; and when the devil is released he will work on the sinfulness in human nature and will deceive many to rebel against Christ. He will gather an army from amongst them to fight against Christ in the Holy City and fire will come down from God out of heaven and destroy his army. See *Ezekiel 38:1–23*. This fulfils the words that the devil's kingdom will be the eighth but he will still be part of the seventh kingdom. He will finally be cast into the lake of fire forever; this time there is no binding of him. Death and hell will also be cast into the lake of fire. *Revelation 20:14–15 "And death and hell were cast into the lake of fire. This is the second death. And whosoever was not found written in the book of life was cast into the lake of fire."* Death is of the spirit sin that kills the soul, and Hell or Hades is the temporary place where sinful souls remain in death awaiting the final judgement.

The great white throne judgement: The final judgement on sin. Those who died in sin will be raised from the dead to face judgement at the great white throne; and their souls will be cast into the lake of fire where the devil, the beast, the false prophet and all the angels whom he deceived are already suffering the consequences of their actions.

Jesus Christ is the king sitting on the great white throne. Those who will be judged are those whose names were not found in the book of life. It promises to be the greatest of all judgement because all sinfulness since the commencement of time will be judged and finally put away from the face of God forever (*Rev 21:4*).

Revelation Chapter Twenty-one

A New Heaven and a New Earth
The Holy City, the New Jerusalem

Rev. 21:1–2   *And I saw a new heaven and a new earth: for the first heaven and the first earth were passed away; and there was no more sea."*

John is given a preview of the new world to come. He saw a new heaven and a new earth, one which is doubtless devoid of sin. God has finally succeeded in getting the spiritual children of dust and stars he has desired since the beginning, as cherubim and seraphim- *(Gen. 3:24; Isa. 6:6; Rev. 21:7)*.

The Holy City: In this City, God will dwell amongst his people.

"And I John saw the holy city, a New Jerusalem, coming down from God out of heaven, prepared as a bride adorned for her husband. And I heard a great voice out of heaven saying, Behold the tabernacle of God is with men, and he will dwell with them, and they shall be his people, and God himself shall be with them and be their God" (Rev. 21:2).

John saw God seated on the throne and he makes the following declaration:

"Behold I make all things new. And he said unto me, Write: for these words are true and faithful. And he said unto me, It is done, I am the Alpha and Omega, the beginning and the end. I will give unto him that is athirst of the fountain of the water of life freely. He that overcometh, shall inherit all things; and I will be his God, and he shall be my son. But the fearful, and unbelieving, and the abominable, and murderers, and whoremongers, and sorcerers, and idolaters, and all liars, shall have their part in the lake which burneth with fire and brimstone: which is the second death."

This statement identifies and re-emphasises the fact that evil is the root cause of humanity's downfall. No one nation or person, despite their religious persuasion, will bear the judgement for the downfall of all, but each sinful individual is as guilty as the other, for all have sinned and come short of the glory of God. Therefore, let everyone who looks to religions that have no answer for human sinfulness before God think about their fate and the impending doom awaiting everyone whose names are not found written in the Book of Life because they did not avail themselves of the blood of Jesus Christ as God's solution to sinfulness.

Revelation Chapter Twenty-two

A Pure River of the Water of Life

The pure river of water: John saw a pure river of the water of life, clear as crystal, proceeding out of the throne of God and of the Lamb. This pure river is symbolic of the purity of the Holy Spirit flowing from God and the Lamb to those who are their subjects. Like the one river in Eden, we now see another river coming from the presence of the LORD. He saw also the tree of life which bore twelve kinds of fruits which yielded her fruit every month; and the leaves of the tree were for the healing of the nations. This may be the tree of righteousness and the covenant word of the Lord by which the saints will continue to live; for there will be no more night or day by which to calculate months. The Bible tells us that *"He sent forth his word and healed them" (Ps. 107:20).*

There shall be no more curse, for the devil that deceived has been cast into the eternal lake of fire; therefore sin shall be gone forever and Christ will reign eternally after he has reconciled all things to God. The 144,000 which God gave to him will serve him and they shall see his face; and his name shall be in their foreheads, and they shall willingly obey him.

The Great City Babylon, which is the world of wickedness, has been judged and the wrath of God finally poured out. The Armageddon war that will end all wars is over. We see also the devil finally cast into the lake of fire and the judgement of the great white throne completed.

In this chapter we are given a glimpse of the glorious future of God's chosen people; those who have overcome the deception of the devil; who have remained faithful in tribulation; those who are the called, chosen, and faithful saints of Christ. John shows us the end of the old heaven and the old earth and tells us that all things shall be made new. John in fact saw a new heaven and a new earth descending from God out of heaven; and it is possible that it will be a thousand times more beautiful than the present world we live in.

There is no better way of concluding the unveiling of Revelation than to agree with John: *"And he said unto me; these sayings are faithful and true: and the Lord God of the holy prophets sent his angel to shew unto his servants the things which must shortly be done"* (*Rev. 22:6*). These faithful and true sayings are of God to Jesus who says:

"Behold I come quickly: blessed is he that keepeth the sayings of the prophecy of this book. "And behold I come quickly; and my reward is with me, to give every man according as his work shall be. "I am the Alpha and Omega, the beginning and the end, the first and the last. "I Jesus have sent mine angel to testify unto you these things in the churches. I am the root and the offspring of David, and the bright and morning star." - *Rev. 22:7,12-13,16.*

The Angel reports to John what God tells Jesus to reveal to his servants: The titles of God show that these sayings are in reported speech because of the first person of the noun. This takes us back to the beginning.

Rev. 1:1 "The Revelation of Jesus Christ, which God gave unto him, to shew unto his servants things which must shortly come to pass; and he sent and signified it by his angel unto his servant John."

This comment is taken from *The Nelson Spirit-Filled Life Bible*: *"Jesus calls his people to be fully separated from the world's value system and to be totally committed to him. They are to find the spiritual power source in their lives in Christ, not in occult practices. The believer is to gauge success by the measuring rod of God, rather than by the world's social and financial standard. When the Christian understands God's view from the eternal, the present comes into correct perspective."*

PART 5

OTHER BOOKS OF THE BIBLE SUPPORTING THE MYSTERIES OF REVELATION

CHAPTER TWENTY-FIVE

BOOKS SUPPORTING THE UNVEILING

Jonah Chapters 1 & 2
Symbols:
The name Jonah:　　　　　　*means a dove*
Nineveh:　　　　　　　　　　*the Assyrian nation is a symbol of power and might*
Sodom, Babylon:　　　　　　*the world*
The world:　　　　　　　　　*wilderness; sea*
Jesus:　　　　　　　　　　　*the whale as king of the sea*

Christ tells us that the world will see no other sign than the sign of the prophet Jonah; this means there must be a great deal typified in the story of the life of this prophet.

Jonah's refusal to go to Assyria: Nineveh was especially hated by the Jews because of their exceptional cruelty to the Jewish people. Israel had been terribly harassed by the constant attacks of the Syrians on their northern border. Jonah prophesied of the restoration of Israel's northern border to the position they occupied under King Solomon; this prophecy was fulfilled in the reign of Jeroboam II even though history has not accredited him as a godly ruler (*2 Kgs. 14:23–27*). The north is the symbolic accredited position of *'The Word of God.'* This prophecy means that Christ will restore humanity to the position of being able to commune with God; it also tells us that Christ will bring restoration to the Jews and the world even though the world has no regard for him and hates him and his disciples with cruel hatred.

　　Lessons from Jonah: The message is the same as the one Christ brings to the Churches: that is to say:
　　- there is always a punishment for sinfulness: *Jonah 1:1–2*

- although the wickedness of the people of the world may be very great, yet God loves them and wants to warn them of the impending doom: *Romans 6:23; John 17:3; 2 Corinthians 5:21*.

Nineveh: It took three days for Jonah to reach Nineveh and warn the city. The city is 3 miles long and 1.5 miles wide; there were forty days to the destruction of Nineveh plus the two days of warning, making a total of forty-two days. Compare this with the three and a half years of Christ's teachings on earth; with the travail of the Church in the period of the great tribulation; and the three and a half years of the reign of the beast. Jonah began to warn Nineveh after one day, taking a total of three days to complete his assignment besides the three days in the belly of the whale. Christ will complete his work in the third millennium of his death.

The relevance of the book of Jonah to end time prophecies: The book is important because it contains signs of the end time, and Christ quoted from him. See *Matthew 12:38–41; Luke 11:29–32*. "*As Jonah was three days in the belly of the whale even so shall the Son of God be three days in the earth. They shall see no other sign but the sign of Jonah.*"

> there is a definite day of the wrath of God that will come upon the earth;
>
> those who repent will be saved if they listen to the teachings of Christ as Nineveh also listened to the prophecy of Jonah and were saved: *John 3:36; 5:24; 8:47;*
>
> three days of Jonah in the belly of the whale—three days of Christ in the earth before his resurrection;
>
> Jonah, like Christ, came out of Galilee.
>
> Jonah took three days to accomplish his assignment; even so it seems that within three days the mystery of the Son of Man will be over—if we regard a day as a thousand years.

Throughout the Bible three days are significant of different things:

> the three days it took Abraham to reach the mountain where he would have sacrificed Isaac.
>
> the three days of the sanctification for the Israelites to meet with God: *Exodus 19:14*

the three days the sick man was kept at the inn in the parable of the Good Samaritan;

the three days it took for Jonah to warn Nineveh, including the one day travel

The name Jonah means a "dove": The dove has been used to indicate rest after terrible judgement. Also after the flood the dove was sent out two times; the first time he found no place for his feet. Noah stretched out his hands and took the dove into the Ark. The second time he brought back an olive branch in his mouth. Christ came to bring rest to Israel; the Spirit descended on him as a dove; he finally gives them rest in his millennial reign. The first time Christ came he had no place to rest. *Matthew 8:20 "Foxes have holes, birds have nests but the son of man has no place to rest his head."* God stretched out his hand and took Christ to himself. The second time Christ returns to earth, he will come with his bride as the olive branch to enter into the eternal day of rest.

Although no one knows when the return of Christ will be, one thing that is certain is that his return is imminent. Those who look for signs other than those the Bible gives us in *Matthew 24:30* may be disappointed. Those who are expectant should hold on to their confession of faith, knowing that in due season we will all reap if we faint not.

Ezekiel Chapter 19

Lamentation for Israel
The Parable of the Withered Vine

> *Ezekiel 19:1–8 "Moreover take thou up a lamentation for the princes of Israel. And say, What is thy mother? A lioness; she lay down among lions, she nourished her whelps among young lions. And she brought up one of her whelps: it became a young lion, and it learned to catch the prey; it devoured men. The nations also heard of him; and he was taken in their pit, and they brought him with chains into the land of Egypt. Now when she saw that she had waited, and her hope was lost, then she took another of her whelps, and made him a young lion. And he went up and down among the lions, he became a young lion, and learned to catch the prey, and devoured men. And he knew their desolate places, and he laid waste their cities; and the land was desolate, and the fullness thereof, by the noise of his roaring. Then the nations set against him on every side from the provinces, and spread their net over him: he was taken in their pit."*

This lamentation is for Israel, the nation that produced Christ who was sacrificed for sin; it is also for the spiritual children of the kingdom of heaven. Ezekiel laments over the imminent death of princes. It is noteworthy that Ezekiel laments for princes and not kings. The mother refers to the kingdom of Judah. *"She brought up one of her whelps."* It became a young lion and learned to catch prey; it devoured people. This speaks of the things that happened in Judah before the first coming of Christ in the days of Jehoahaz and Jehoakim, kings of Judah. The nations heard how Jehoahaz trampled on all that was sacred in Judah. He was taken as a beast of prey in their pit. He was carried captive into Egypt and when he did not return they made Jehoakim king in his stead.

Ezekiel's prophecy had its fulfilment then but the pattern will be repeated in in the Church Age. Israel did not whole-heartedly acknowledge Christ as their Messiah and after waiting a long while, they will be deceived into accepting the Antichrist, who is likely to emerge from the tribe of Dan and he will devour people as prey.

Ezek. 19:10–11 "Thy mother is like a vine in thy blood, planted by the waters: she was fruitful and full of branches by reason of many waters. And she had strong rods for the sceptres of them that bare rule, and her stature was exalted among the thick branches, and she appeared in her height with the multitude of her branches. But she was plucked up in fury, she was cast down to the ground, and the east wind dried up her fruit: her strong rods were broken and withered; the fire consumed them . . . And her fire is gone out of a rod of her branches, which hath devoured her fruit, so that she hath no strong rod to be a sceptre to rule. This is a lamentation, and shall be for a lamentation."

Ezekiel laments for the church of the two witnesses who were slain by the false prophet, and also for the remnant church left on earth after the rapture of the church of the two witnesses. She was plucked up in fury – this refers to the severe persecution which the church of the two witnesses will pass through; she was cast down to the ground, and the east wind dried up her fruit; the events of this time will occur because God permits it, not because the devil is victorious; but his cup will become full for judgement. *"Her strong rods were broken"* – this refers to the time of the persecution of the church of the two witnesses, referred to as *"all in the sea that had life died"* – *Rev. 16:3*.

Unveiling of the Book of Daniel Chapter Eight

Daniel 8:1 *"In the third year of the reign of King Belshazzar a vision appeared unto me, even unto me Daniel, after that which appeared unto me at the first."*

The book of Daniel relates to two periods, the natural period during the reign of the four kingdoms from Nebuchadnezzar to the Roman Empire, but it also speaks prophetically about the rule of the four generations of people in the kingdom of heaven which Christ set up during the rule of the Roman Empire, as one that can never be destroyed. Daniel is told at the end of the vision that it shall not find its fulfilment until the time of the end. The vision also relates to Daniel's vision of *Chapter 7* and hence of *Chapter 2*, already explained in the unveiling of the truths of the revelations of John; therefore to understand it one must see it in the context of these two previous visions.

The ram with two horns is representative of the church of the two witnesses, which is the Philadelphia Church of *Revelation* 3. Horns refer to the spiritual authority of this church to which all the prophets have attested. The river before which they stand is representative of the Holy Ghost; God's people are requested to walk before God in the perfection which is in Christ as it was required of Abraham - *Gen. 17:1*. The Jews have been God's chosen race but were set aside for a while until the time of the end, according to *Revelation* 7, when 144,000 of them were sealed by the Holy Ghost for the work at the end. The higher horn came up last because greater is the end of a thing than the beginning; also according to the scriptures the best wine was kept for last. Paul informs us that God has not cast off his people but that their being set aside means the acceptance of the Gentiles.

God will once again gather Jacob's seed according to the blessing: *Genesis 28:3, 14-15 "And God Almighty bless thee, and make thee fruitful, and multiply thee, that thou mayest be a multitude of people. And give the blessing of Abraham, to thee, and to thy seed with thee; that thou mayest inherit the land wherein thou art a stranger, which God gave unto Abraham." 14. "And thy seed shall be as the dust of the earth, and thou shalt spread abroad to the west and to the east and to the north, and to the south: and in thee and in thy seed shall all the families of the earth be blessed. 15. And behold, I am with thee, and will keep thee in all places whither thou goest, and will bring thee again into this land; for I will not leave thee, until I have done that which I have spoken to thee of."*

Much can be inferred from this blessing. In the first instance, what is at stake is the blessing of Abraham, which is both natural as it relates to Jacob, and spiritual as it relates to Israel — *Isaiah 43:1–3*. Also, according to the word of the LORD, Jacob would first spread abroad to the west, which meant that his seed would be scattered throughout the world; but he would be drawn again to the presence of the LORD by the word of God and the Spirit of God at the coming of Christ as the righteous man from the East. This is the fulfilment of the anointing which shall be poured out upon the latter day church. This is borne out by the following two verses: *Isaiah 43:5–6*

"Fear not I am with thee; I will bring thy seed from the east, and gather thee from the west; I will say to the north give up and to the south, Keep not back: bring my sons from far and my daughters from the ends of the earth".

The promise of God to Abraham is that he would give him children of dust and children of stars. The ultimate end for a human being is perfection in Christ; and the church of the two witnesses must come together and work together for the fulfilment of all things to make good the work of Christ who has broken down the wall of partition between Jews and Gentiles, making them one in him. The pushing of the ram westward, northward and southward is the work of the church of the two witnesses.

The second thing one should note from these two verses is that Israel will be gathered again to the land that is promised them. In line with *Daniel 11:30*, the Antichrist, as a seed of Israel shall also return to his homeland and become great.

"The he goat waxed very great": A goat is symbolic of sinful humanity. So is the west. This "he goat" definitely refers to the Antichrist and the one world order that will emerge under his leadership during the day of the wrath of God. The rest of this chapter is in accordance with all that is unveiled in the revelations of John.

The vision confirms that the Antichrist will have a period of three and a half years to complete his assignment from the time of the killing of the church of the two witnesses, an action which will bring him to prominence in the world.

The Allegorical Interpretation of Job Chapters One and Two:

Job the Gentile ruler	An example of God's perfect man
House	Another name for kingdom: eg. the House of David
Job's Children Feasting in Eldest Brother's House	The children of the kingdom feasting in the House of Christ
The Oxen	The righteous generation of the kingdom of heaven
The asses	The ungodly generation of the kingdom of heaven
The Sabeans:	A materialistic people from Chaldea and Sabia, a type of the world
The sword by which the servants were slain	Evil wisdom of the world seducing the souls of man
The slain servants	Leaders of God's people
The one witness in each case:	The people who will stand together for Christ in any season
The fire of God fall from heaven	The judgement of God on sinfulness
Sheep and servants burn:	The church of the two witnesses

The Chaldeans of three bands	The world system: an unholy trinity—the devil; evil souls, evil wisdom
Camels	Beast of burden—sinners heavily laden with sin
The one witness	The people who will stand together for God in this season
A great wind from the wilderness Sons and daughters in house but only sons are killed	A great voice from the world of men—the Antichrist. The time of the Laodiceans Church when the righteous will be killed for their testimony.
Job's wife	A type of evil wisdom
Eliphaz the Temanite - from Northern Edom: *Obadiah 10, 18*	The name means God dispenses. A type of the ungodly person—who will be dispensed with even as the necks of the ass that were not redeemed were broken: the ungodly person who does not appreciate his redemption will be lost forever.
Bildad the Shuite — from Middle Euphrates	The name means son of contention. Euphrates symbolically refers to a world of sinfulness. Sinners are in the river of sin in the world; those who repent receive salvation.

Zophar the Naamanthite From Beirut and Damascus	The name means 'hairy and rough'; Naaman a proud man was from Damascus. Naaman refused the waters of Jordan preferring the rivers of Damascus. Represents the proud people of the world who reject the river of the Holy Ghost for the river of sin. Pride is a characteristic of the evil generation who will be utterly destroyed in the day of the LORD. History records that Samaria sided with Syria against Jerusalem—Isa 10:9. Damascus and Syria together with Ephraim would be destroyed utterly because of their attack upon Judah and Jerusalem—Obad. 10, 18. Similarly the judgement will be against the three other generations in the world for their treatment of the church—God's agent of change in the world—Matt. 28:19–20; Mark 16:15 All the ten tribes of Israel went into captivity, except for a small remnant who turned whole-heartedly to God and away from idolatry. Of all those of the ten tribes taken into captive none returned so also none of the people taken captive by the devil over time will enjoy eternity with God.
Elihu from Ram / The name Ram means height	The name Elihu means God himself; or Son of Bara which means the son of the Father, or the Son of God – Isa. 9:6

By merely reading through the meaning of the names and the symbolic analysis of the events of the first two chapters of the book of Job, having read the unveiling of the book of Revelation, one can quickly see the reflection of those things mentioned in John's revelations in the allegory of Job. Without knowledge of these facts it would be impossible to see the hidden truths contained in these two chapters.

Job was a ruler whom God singled out as a perfect man from amongst the children of men; one who walked in the fear of God and demonstrated the love and compassion evidenced in the life of Christ; and in many respects he is a representation of a perfect man. The allegory begins with *'the day when sons and daughters were drinking wine in the eldest brother's house.'* The first mention of Job's children is a prelude to what happens to them later; but that day began with the drinking of wine. In the same vein, the period which that day typifies begins with the rule of the ungodly generation of the kingdom of heaven, referred to in the unveiling of Revelation as the time of the rule of the churches of Smyrna and Pergamos. It is the time when the sons and daughters of Christ were having a sporting good time in the kingdom of heaven which belongs to Christ as the eldest brother of all who are genuinely born again. By all indications, the events of this day have already taken place *(Rev 6:2–3)*.

This is also a reflection of the children of the kingdom of heaven who seek after the power of the Holy Spirit to glorify themselves as miracle workers, forgetting that God is more interested in the number of souls won for the kingdom rather than in the miracles and signs and wonders performed at anyone's hands; because such works when they are done genuinely, are the work of the Holy Spirit.

The period extends to the time of the days of the Church of Sardis; here the fourth seal shows the falling of hail and fire characterised by bloodshed and death, killing many people including the righteous.

The first scene: The first two chapters of Job as an allegory would fit correctly into the picture beginning with the Church of Smyrna *(Rev 2:8–11)*.

Job 1: 13–14 "And there was a day when his sons and his daughters were eating and drinking wine in their eldest brother's house. And there came a messenger unto Job and said, The oxen were ploughing, and the asses feeding beside them. And the Sabeans fell upon them, and took them away; yea they have slain the servants with the edge of the sword; and I only am escaped alone to tell thee."

The oxen ploughing and the asses feeding beside them speak of the labour of the righteous in the kingdom; the asses are the ungodly generation who walk beside them only to enjoy the blessings of the kingdom, and to have a good time. *(Luke 17:26–29)*.

The Sabeans are a materialistic generation of people of the Chaldean and Sabean regions associated with Babylon. This is a reflection of the kind of materialistic doctrine preached in the church without an emphasis on holiness and godly living; and it is the weapon that the adversary is using to destroy the righteousness of the kingdom. The slain servants are leaders, slain with the sword of evil because their messages are geared to take the peace of God from the earth so that people will kill one another; this killing may not be physical yet since evil causes death to the soul. This is the time of the churches of Smyrna and Pergamos, reflecting much ungodliness in the kingdom of heaven. It is these two churches that give birth to the Church of Thyatira.

It is clear from the allegory that a day will also come when the Church will appear before God as children of God redeemed from all the nations of the world. Satan will be present as well and at that point he will once again accuse the brethren before God and will be finally cast out of heaven. Before the end comes, there are, however, seven stages through which the Church must pass - *(Rev. 2, 3)*.

Job and his three friends are representations of the four generations of people in the world; the friends of Job may not have been ungodly persons, the symbols relate to them only by the places from which they originate. What happened in the case of Job will again happen at the end of the age; the righteous person will be restored and increased by God. Those who are against the righteous will face the wrath of God. Fortunately for Job's friends, they received forgiveness, which in effect shows that as many as call on the name of the Lord in the day of the wrath of God will be saved.

Eliphaz is a Temanite from the same family lineage as Job, even as it is with the righteous and the ungodly who are of the kingdom of heaven. *Bildad* is a Shuite from the region of the Middle Euphrates; but interestingly *Zophar* is a Naamathite from Damascus, the capital of Syria. The name means hairy and rough. Hair is symbolic of subjection; in the case of the Nazarite, he grows his hair to show his subjection to God. From an allegorical point of view, it does not seem that the name has much to do with the present scene. However, the prophet Obadiah prophesied the destruction of Damascus and Syria together with Ephraim because of their attack upon Judah and Jerusalem. Damascus and Syria are of the region allocated to Dan when the kingdoms were divided among the sons of Jacob (*Amos 1:3; 5:27; 2 Kings5:12; 2 Sam. 8:6; Obad. 15; Zech. 9:14*).

After the dialogue between Job and his friends and the intervention of God, Job prayed for his friends to receive God's forgiveness. The important observation made from these references is the spirit behind each individual; they are the same spirits at work in the two spiritual kingdoms on earth. It is the impact these spiritual influences have on generations—as righteousness declines in the professed kingdom of heaven—that will result in the judgement at the end of the ages.

The other person present in the story is Elihu; he spoke last as the youngest of the five men. His name means *"God himself"* or *"Son of Bara"*; the latter means "Son of the Father," from *Ram* meaning "height." Without prejudice, one can certainly liken him unto Christ, who confirmed that the Father spoke through him in *John 14:10–12*.

The hidden truth behind the story of Job, as it relates to the end time, cannot be clearer. As I have already said, the reason for writing this book is to present a wake-up call to the Church that the end of all things is imminent, that those who will destroy the kingdom of heaven are within it, and that it is time for the people of God to awake to righteousness and godly living.

This warning is an extract from the prophetic warning of E. R. Lindsey; taken from January 1972, "Heartbeat" pages 25 and 26, which I came across quite by chance. E. R. Lindsey had served God faithfully even as a child; he once had an out of body experience and was taken to heaven on several occasions where he saw terrible things. He says there will be a time when many volcanoes will erupt. The whole earth will shake. Believing that the United States is helpless to defend herself, the Communist Block will launch their atomic rockets upon the free world. The attack will last for three and one half days. The combination of these terrifying events will annihilate a third of the human race, as well as a third of all that grows. In the aftermath of this calamity, out of Syria will come a man with a plan of peace, which the whole world will accept and total peace will reign for three and one half years, with undreamt of progress being made in the greatest reconstruction program ever undertaken by the human race. A relatively small group of faithful followers of Jesus Christ have come through all these calamities unharmed, for the protecting hand of the Almighty God was upon them. Now they are free to proclaim the message of the Kingdom with great power and anointing with no interference. At the conclusion of these three and one half years, this man of Syria who is really the "Man of Sin," the "Anti-Christ," will impose Martial Law upon all nations. The identification mark, No. 666 will be required of every man before they will be permitted to buy or trade.

Already there are signs that the Church has fallen from the commendable position as the desired bride of Christ symbolic of the Church of Ephesus, because her criticism was that "her love for God was no longer fervent." The next church is the one of Smyrna (*Rev. 2:12–17*). This exists at the time when "power has been given to the rider of the red horse to take peace from the earth and that they will kill one another." Jesus Christ said, "My peace I leave with you; my peace I give unto you." The peace under attack is the word of God. It is so evident that the word of God is not ruling in the hearts of many generations and nations of the world at the moment. The church is still preaching the gospel of peace and safety when we should be preaching the judgement of God. *1 Thessalonians 5:2* warns, "whilst the church is preaching peace and safety, a sudden destruction will come upon the land." The warning to the Church of Smyrna is to "gracefully bear suffering and be faithful until death."

The one servant is the person who will stand up for the truth and righteousness of God in any season. Many will walk in the love of the Spirit through obedience to the words of God and, led by the Spirit, they will walk in the dominion of children of God.

This book unveils the truth from a spiritual perspective, and all who read it may have a better understanding of what is to come. God's truth cannot always be fully understood by any one person, but I believe, along with other narratives, these revelations will play their part. My prayer is that we may all learn to separate the present from the past and strive to embrace the future, so that a life lived today forms a basis for a better tomorrow with Jesus; only then may we partake of the seven blessings promised to the faithful.

> *"Blessed is he that readeth, and they that hear the words of this prophecy, and keep those things which are written therein: for the time is at hand" (Rev. 1:3).*

> *"Blessed are the dead which die in the Lord from henceforth: Yea saith the Spirit, that they may rest from their labours; and their works do follow them" (Rev. 14:13).*

> *"Blessed is he that watcheth and keepeth his garments, lest he walk naked, and they see his shame" (Rev. 16:15).*

"Blessed and holy is he that hath part in the first resurrection: on such the second death hath no power; but they shall be priests of God and of Christ and shall reign with him a thousand years" (Rev. 20:6).

"Blessed is he that keepeth the sayings of the prophecy of this book" (Rev. 22:7).

"Blessed are they that do his commandments that they may have the right to the tree of life, and may enter in through the gates into the city. 15. For without are dogs and sorcerers, and whoremongers, and murderers, and idolaters, and whosoever loveth and maketh a lie" (Rev. 22:14–15).

NOTES

Introduction
1. Robert T. Boyd, World Bible Handbook, Harvest House Publishers (1983), pg. 674
2. Finis Jennings Dake, God's Plan for Man, Dake Bible Sales Inc. (1997), pg. 803
3. Robert T. Boyd, World Bible Handbook, Harvest House Publishers (1983), pg. 266

Chapter one
1. Author Pink, Gleaning in Genesis, The Moody Press (1978), pg. 34.
2. W. E. Vine, Merrill F. Unger, William White, Jr., Vines Complete Expository Dictionary of Old and New Testament Words; Thomas Nelson Publishers, (1985), pg. 98
3. Lawrence O. Richards and Gary J. Bredfeldt, Creative Bible Teaching, Moody Press, (1970), pg. 137

Chapter two
1. Kevin J. Conner, Interpreting the Symbols and Types, City Bible Publishing (1980), pg. 163
2. Spirit-Filled Life Bible, Thomas Nelson Publishers (1995), pg. 1139
3. Author Pink; Gleaning in Genesis, Moody Press, (1978), pg. 11
4. John Phillips, Bible Explorers Guide, Loizeaus Brothers Inc. (1987), pgs. 206, 212, 202
5. Kevin J. Conner, Interpreting the Symbols and Types, City Bible Publishing (1980), pgs. 158, 167, 142
6. Geoffrey W. Bromley, The International Standard Bible Encyclopaedia, Volume Two, William B. Eerdmans Publishing Company, (1982), pg. 634
7. Zondervan Compact Bible Dictionary, Zondervan Publishing House, (2002), pg. 461

8. Geoffrey W. Bromley, The International Standard Bible Encyclopaedia, Volume Two, William B. Eerdmans Publishing Company (1982), pg. 467
9. W. E. Vine, Merrill F. Unger, William White Jr., Vines Complete Expository Dictionary of Old and New Testament Words; Thomas Nelson Publishers (1984), pg. 166

Chapter three
1. John Phillips; Bible Explorers Guide, Loizeaus Brothers Inc. (1987, pg. 211
2. Ibid; pg. 81
3. Kevin J Conner, Interpreting the Symbols and Types, City Bible Publishing (1992), pg. 156
4. John Phillips, Bible Explorers Guide, Loizeaus Brothers Inc. (1987), pg. 204
5. Author W. Pink, Gleaning in Genesis, Moody Press, Chicago (1978), pg. 336

Chapter four
1. Spirit Filled Life Bible Commentary, Thomas Nelson Publishers (1995), pg. 1895

Chapter five
1. Dr. Bill Hamon, Prophets and the Prophetic Movements, Destiny Image Publishers Inc. (2001), pg. 29.

Chapter six
1. Spirit Filled Life Bible, Commentary on the Churches; Thomas Nelson Publishers (1995), pg. 1897

Chapter seven
1. Arthur W. Pink; Gleaning in Genesis, The Moody Press (1978), pg 72
2. Ibid; pg. 72
3. John Phillips; Bible Explorers Guide, Loizeaux Brothers Inc. (1987), pg. 203
4. Ibid; pg. 209
5. Spirit Filled Life Bible Commentary on Ps 119:1-2, (KJV); Thomas Nelson Publishers (1995)
6. W. E. Vine, Merrill F. Unger, William White Jr., Vines Complete Expository Dictionary of Old and New Testament Words; Thomas Nelson Publishers (1984), pg. 382.

Chapter eight
1. A. W. Tozer, The Incredible Christian, Christian Publication, Inc. (1964), pgs. 74-75
2. Dr. H, L. Willmington; Willmington's Guide to the Bible, Tyndale House Publishers Inc. (1984), pg. 542.

Chapter nine
1. Dr. Bill Hamon, Prophets and the Prophetic Movements, Destiny Image Publishers, Inc. (2001), pgs. 24, 25.

Chapter ten
1. Spirit-Filled Life Bible (KJV) Commentary; Thomas Nelson Publishers (1995), pg. 72
2. John Philips, Exploring Revelations, Loizeaus Brothers (1987), pg.116
3. Dr. Bill Hamon, Prophets and the Prophetic Movement, Destiny Image Publishers Inc. (2001), pg. 23
4. Dr. H. L. Willmington, Willmington's Guide to the Bible, Tyndale House Publishers Inc. (1984), pg. 545

Chapter twelve
1. Donald Guthrie, The Relevance of John's Apocalypse; William B. Eerdmans Publishing Co. (1987), pg. 84.

Chapter thirteen
1. Finis Jennings Dake, Dake Study Bible, Dake Bible Sales Inc. (1997, pg. 803

Chapter fourteen
1. Dr. Bill Hamon, Prophetic Scriptures yet to be fulfilled, Destiny Image Publishers Inc. (2010), pg. 193
2. Jim Collins; How are the Mighty Fallen; Random House Business Books (2009), pg. 20
3. Ibid; pg. 103.
4. Spirit Filled Life Bible, Thomas Nelson Publishers, (1995), pg 1897
5. Mike Poddicommbe (Growth + decline cycle-png (901x501)
6. John Hagee, Prophecy Study Bible (1997), pg. 1576
7. Jim Collins; How are the Mighty Fallen; Random House Business Books (2009), pgs. 103, 104.
8. Ibid; pg. 113
9. Ibid; pg. 83

10. Ibid; pg. 107
11. Ibid; pg. 113
12. Ibid; pg 117

Chapter fifteen
1. W. E. Vine, Merrill F. Unger, William White Jr., Vines Complete Expository Dictionary of Old and New Testament Words; Thomas Nelson Publishers (1984), pg. 535
2. John Phillips, Bible Explorers Guide, Loizeaux Brothers (1987), pg. 244
3. Dr. H. W. Willmington, Willmington's Guide to the Bible, Tyndale House Publishers Inc. (1984), pg. 514
4. Spirit Filled Life Bible commentary, Thomas Nelson Publishers (1995)
5. Don Fleming World Bible Dictionary, World Publishing (1990), pg. 333
6. Donald Guthrey, The Relevance of John's Apocalypse; William B. Eerdmans Publishing Co. (1985); pg. 73
7. J. I. Packer & M. C. Tenney, Illustrated Manners and Customs of the Bible, Thomas Nelson Publishers (1980), pg. 645

Chapter sixteen
1. Spirit Filled Life Bible commentary, Thomas Nelson Publishers; (1995), pg. 1722.

Chapter twenty-one
1. Dr. H. Willmington; Willmington's Guide to the Bible, Tyndale House Publishers Inc. (1984), pg. 561

Chapter twenty-two
1. Spirit Filled Life Bible; Thomas Nelson Publishers (1995), pg. 1936

Chapter twenty-three
1. Dr. H. L. Willmington; Willmington's Guide to the Bible, Tyndale House Publishers Inc. (1984), pg. 570
2. Charles Calswell Ryrie; Ryrie Study Bible; Moody Press (1994), pg. 1944
3. Ron Rhodes, Forty Days through Revelations; Harvest House (2011), pg. 210
4. Spirit Filled Life Bible Commentary; Thomas Nelson Publishers (1995), pg. 1921

SYMBOLS AND PHRASES USED IN REVELATION

ass	the ungodly generation of the kingdom of heaven
Babylon	Human rebellion against God; the capital city of the Beast*
balances	to be weighed by God, a time of famine* *(Dan. 5:27)*
beasts	Gentile world power* *(Dan. 4:16)* fallen angels or fallen mankind
bear	powerful destructive foe* *(Dan. 7:5)* cunning and deceptive; symbol of ungodliness
birds	agents of evil; demons, satan, spiritual wickedness* Gentile Nation – *(Isa. 31:5; Matt. 13:4, 19, 32)*
black	mourning, moral evil, famine* *(Jer. 4:28; Rev. 6:5)*
blue	royalty, heavenly character
bow	far reaching conflict, deceit and falsehood; military power* *(Jer. 9:3)* spiritual authority or fighting strength of the word of God *(Hosea 1:5)*
brass/bronze	strength and endurance, judgement, symbol of the wicked generation *(Eze. 22:18)*
candlestick	the Church
cattle	the ungodly generation

cherubim	angels affected by sin *(1 Kings. 7:29; Gen. 3-31; Eze. 28:14)* human sons made perfect or redeemed from sin
city	mankind gathering in corporate defiance of God; or corporate reverence of God; the Church in both its glorified and apostate form
crown	delegated authority; sovereignty, power*
dragon	satan* the devil as the evil spirit Sin
east	the presence of the LORD God
Eden	the glory of the presence of God
eyes	perfection and intelligence
field	the world
fish	the scattered Jewish people in the last days* sinful mankind
fowl	evil spirit, the wicked one, the great ones of the earth instruments of destruction *(Isa. 18:6; Eze. 31:6; Rev. 18:2; Matt. 13:19)*
fox	crafty or cunning person; or people* *(Luke 13:4)*
goats	children of the devil *(Dan. 8:21)*
gold	divinity*
grass	mass of mankind* *(Rev. 8:7)*
hailstone	severe judgement* *(Isa. 28:17)*
harlot	a deprived and corrupt religious system* *(Rev. 17:5; Hos. 3:1-5)*
heads	supreme authority; intelligence and power in man* Leaders of governments
horn	strength and glory* *(Dan. 7:8; Rev. 8:9)* power and authority

Symbols And Phrases Used In Revelation

horses	successful power in war* *(Rev. 6:1-8)*
jasper	display of God's glory* *(Rev. 4:3)*
key	right of exercise divine authority* *(Matt.16:19; Rev. 1:18)*
lamb	gentleness, meekness, tenderness* *(Luke 10:3; Rev. 5:6-7)*
leaven	sin, moral doctrinal evil* *(Gal. 5:9)*
legs	Roman Empire; strength* *(Dan 2:33)*
leopard	swift and powerful conquest* *(Dan 7:6)*
lion	Christ, Majesty and royal power* *(Rev. 5:5)* symbol of strength; the righteous
locusts	fallen angels *(2 Peter 2:4)* numerous foes, total and far reaching destruction* (Joel 1:4)
moon	delegated authority* symbolic of the word of God
mountain	national power, moral stability and greatness especially where those qualities are expressed nationally or spiritually* *(Dan. 2:35)*
olive tree	the nation Israel* people – Jews or Gentiles *(Rom. 12:24)*
ox	servant; strength
oxen	patience, strength and ability to labour for others *(1 Tim. 5:18; Job 1:14)*
Paradise	pleasure garden; the place of His presence *(Luke 23:43)*
purple	royalty, worldly regal power
rainbow	covenant promise
red	bloodshed and judgement; sinfulness of men* *(Rev. 6:4)*
river	spirit indwelling; spiritual authority *(Isa. 8:5-8)*
rod	power and authority; chastisement or judgement* *(Heb. 9:4)*

scarlet	man's sin as seen by God; human pump and glory* *(Num.4:8; Rev. 17;3-4)*
scorpion	evil spirits (demons); evil words *(Eze. 2:6; Rev. 9:5)*
sea	Gentile nation or the world of mankind *(Rev. 8:8)*
serpent	worldly wisdom* *(Rev. 12:9)* the devil and evil people
seven stars	the saints of the seven churches
sheep	lost people who easily go astray* chosen people of God in Christ
smoke	darkness; spirit of deception *(Rev. 9:2)*
stars	angelic hosts* *(Rev 8:10)*
sun	supreme ruling power* *(Rev. 1:16; 8:12)*
thorns	wicked, problematic, troublesome people *(Gen. 3:18)*
thistle	evil *(Gen. 3:18)*
trees	kings or rulers, people of prominence* *(Rev. 7:1, 9:4)* redeemed mankind or generations *(Isa. 37:24)*
trumpet	clarion call, judgement or war, alarm, summons* *(Rev. 8:6)* call to attention or to war;
waters	people, nations *(Rev. 17:15)*
wheels	divine government *(Eze. 1:15)*
whirlwind	God's manifest power, judgement *(Hos. 8:7; Isa. 66:15*; Eze. 1:4)*
white	purity, cleanness* *(Rev. 3:4)*
whore	evil wisdom, the corrupt city *(Isa. 57:3; Rev. 17:1)*
whoredom	religious apostasy, spiritual vileness, idolatry* *(Rev. 17:1; Hos. 5:3)*
wilderness	symbol of the world, or a defeated Christian life* *(Rev. 18:7)*

Symbols And Phrases Used In Revelation

wind	The Holy Spirit; God's unseen but felt presence* *(Acts 2:2)*
wings	spiritual strength, characteristics of the Spirit
wild ox	Gentile nation
woman	Israel, the Church, both true and false* *(Rev. 12:1-5)* symbol of wisdom – can be good or evil
worm	something contemptible, death* *(Psa. 22:6)*
wormwood	bitterness of sin, name of the devil

PHRASES

Babylon the Great	the place of the rule of the Anti-Christ, Jerusalem; *(Rev. 16:19)*; evil wisdom of the world *(Rev 17:5)*
Covering Cherub	Lucifer
Great Babylon	the world of sinfulness
man, with a measuring rod	one with a message to tell
the apple tree	the evil generation
the beast that carries her	The Devil or Lucifer
the birds of the air	the Gentile nation; sinful mankind
the Day of the LORD	the day of his wrath
the day of the wrath	the day of God's judgement upon the world
the Elect Lady	The Church
the faithful city	the church *(Isa. 4:2-6)*
the fig tree	security prosperity and blessing* the righteous generation

197

the four horns	power: good or evil; ruling authorities
the four winds Spirit of God	the four winds of heaven – characteristics of the the four winds of earth characteristics of sin
the fish of the sea	symbol of the souls of men; scattered Jewish people in the last days*
the Great City	financial capital of evil: Jerusalem (Babylon)
the great whore	Jerusalem (Babylon), or evil wisdom
the Holy City	Jerusalem under Christ; or the Church *(Isa. 52:1)*
the kings of the east	souls made perfect in Christ
the Lord's Day	the first day of the week or the day of His Wrath
the Morning Star	Christ the first born of the new creation
the pale horse	power of death and hell
the palm tree	victory; symbolises the righteous * *(Rev. 7:9)*
the pomegranate	the ungodly generation
the river Euphrates	symbol of the evil spirit sin
the river of Eden	symbol of the Holy Spirit
the seven crowns	governments or world powers
the seven horns	complete spiritual authority
the seven mountains	the seven seats of Government
the son of the morning	Lucifer
the strange woman	evil wisdom *(Prov. 23:27-28)*
the ten horns	worldwide rule and power of evil

Symbols And Phrases Used In Revelation

the two witnesses/ the two Olive trees	the Church of Jews and Gentiles
the wild Olive tree	the Gentile nations
the wild olive branch	the ungodly generation of the kingdom of heaven
the word of God	the truth of God's words
the word of the LORD	the counsel of the Holy Ghost

Assembled with the help of Bible Explorers Guide—by John Phillips

*Taken from Bible Explorers Guide

Lightning Source UK Ltd.
Milton Keynes UK
UKHW032235260319
339964UK00004B/154/P